CYBER ESPIONAGE AND INTERNATIONAL LAW

The advent of cyberspace has led to a dramatic increase in state-sponsored political and economic espionage. This monograph argues that these practices represent a threat to the maintenance of international peace and security and assesses the extent to which international law regulates this conduct. The traditional view among international legal scholars is that, in the absence of direct and specific international law on the topic of espionage, cyber espionage constitutes an extra-legal activity that is unconstrained by international law. This monograph challenges that assumption and reveals that there are general principles of international law as well as specialised international legal regimes that indirectly regulate cyber espionage. In terms of general principles of international law, this monograph explores how the rules of territorial sovereignty, non-intervention and the non-use of force apply to cyber espionage. In relation to specialised regimes, this monograph investigates the role of diplomatic and consular law, international human rights law and the law of the World Trade Organization in addressing cyber espionage. This monograph also examines whether developments in customary international law have carved out espionage exceptions to those international legal rules that otherwise prohibit cyber espionage as well as considering whether the doctrines of self-defence and necessity can be invoked to justify cyber espionage. Notwithstanding the applicability of international law, this monograph concludes that policymakers should nevertheless devise an international law of espionage which, as *lex specialis*, contains rules that are specifically designed to confront the growing threat posed by cyber espionage.

Cyber Espionage and International Law

Russell Buchan

•HART•
OXFORD • LONDON • NEW YORK • NEW DELHI • SYDNEY

Hart Publishing

Bloomsbury Publishing Plc

Kemp House, Chawley Park, Cumnor Hill, Oxford, OX2 9PH, UK

1385 Broadway, New York, NY 10018, USA

29 Earlsfort Terrace, Dublin 2, Ireland

HART PUBLISHING, the Hart/Stag logo, BLOOMSBURY and the Diana logo are trademarks of Bloomsbury Publishing Plc

First published in Great Britain 2019

First published in hardback, 2019

Paperback edition, 2021

Reprinted in 2019 (twice)

A catalogue record for this book is available from the British Library.

Library of Congress Cataloging-in-Publication data

Names: Buchan, Russell, 1983- author.

Title: Cyber espionage and international law / Russell Buchan.

Description: Oxford, UK ; Portland, Oregon : Hart, an imprint of Bloomsbury, 2019. | Includes bibliographical references and index.

Identifiers: LCCN 2018034245 | ISBN 9781782257349 (hardback)

Subjects: LCSH: Espionage—Law and legislation. | Internet in espionage.

Classification: LCC KZ4079 .B83 2018 | DDC 341.3—dc23

LC record available at https://lccn.loc.gov/2018034245

ISBN: PB: 978-1-50994-501-6
ePDF: 978-1-78225-735-6
ePub: 978-1-78225-736-3

Typeset by Compuscript Ltd, Shannon

To find out more about our authors and books visit www.hartpublishing.co.uk. Here you will find extracts, author information, details of forthcoming events and the option to sign up for our newsletters.

ACKNOWLEDGEMENTS

This project would not have been completed without the support and assistance of a number of institutions and individuals. I thank the University of Sheffield School of Law for providing me with the necessary resources to produce this monograph. I also extend my gratitude to the NATO Cooperative Cyber Defence Centre of Excellence in Tallinn, Estonia, for hosting me during my sabbatical in late 2016. The Centre provided me with a warm and intellectually rich environment to pursue my research. This monograph has benefited from the many deep and stimulating conversations that I have had with Iñaki Navarrete on the topic of international law and espionage, which I enjoyed immensely. I thank Iñaki for assisting me with the research for chapter 5 of this monograph and I also thank Adam Keenaghan for meticulously editing the final manuscript. I am indebted to Cormac Behan, Patrick Capps, David Hayes, Clair Gammage, Tarcisio Gazzini, Gregory Messenger and Nicholas Tsagourias for reading through various chapters of this monograph and providing useful comments. On a personal level, I am grateful for the love and support of my husband, Shane, and I apologise once again for the many early mornings, late nights and lost weekends that you had to withstand during the course of this project. Finally, this monograph is dedicated to Juanita Patrick: your love, humour and happiness are dearly missed and we think about you every day.

Russell Buchan
June 2018

TABLE OF CONTENTS

TABLE OF CASES

International

Eritrea-Ethiopia Claims Commission

European Commission

European Court of Human Rights

International Court of Justice

International Criminal Tribunal for the Former Yugoslavia

International Tribunal for the Law of the Sea – Seabed Disputes Chamber

Permanent Court of Arbitration

Permanent Court of International Justice

United Nations Human Rights Committee

WTO Panel Reports

WTO Reports of the Appellate Body

WTO – other

National

Australia

Canada

China

The Netherlands

Switzerland

United Kingdom

United States of America

USSR

TABLE OF INSTRUMENTS

Treaties – etc

National Legislation

Australia

Canada

Denmark

Estonia

Italy

Jordan

New Zealand

Spain

United Kingdom

United States of America

Introduction

1. Background

After land, sea, air and outer space, cyberspace has emerged as the 'fifth domain'[1] of human activity. Over the past several decades, this environment has been progressively 'woven into the fabric of daily life'.[2] Most recent figures indicate that, by the end of 2017, 54 per cent of the world's population were users of the Internet, an increase of 1052 per cent since 2000.[3] Indeed, our reliance upon cyberspace will continue to grow with the proliferation of the so-called 'Internet of Things', a phenomenon that describes a network of physical objects – devices, vehicles, buildings and other items – which are embedded with electronics, software, sensors and network connectivity that enables them to collect and exchange data.

Enormous benefits are now associated with cyberspace. Cyberspace is an inclusive, vibrant and dynamic environment that connects people, empowers communities, expands existing markets and forges new ones, and acts as a global information exchange through which knowledge is disseminated and acquired. However, as well as driving progress, cyberspace has emerged as a repository for a number of threats and vulnerabilities[4] and '[can] be used for purposes that are inconsistent with international peace and security'.[5]

Initially, cyber threats were divided into two distinct categories: cyber network attacks and cyber network exploitation.[6] Cyber network attacks (cyber attacks) describe those computer operations that are designed 'to alter, disrupt, deceive, degrade, or destroy computer systems or networks or the information and/or

[1] The Netherlands Ministry of Defence, *The Defence Cyber Strategy* (2012) 4, www.ccdcoe.org/strategies/Defence_Cyber_Strategy_NDL.pdf.

[2] UN Secretary-General, 'Foreword', *Group of Governmental Experts on Developments in the Field of Information and Telecommunications in the Context of International Security*, UN Doc A/68/98, 24 June 2013, 4.

[3] Internet World Stats: Usage and Population Statistics, 21 June 2018, www.internetworldstats.com/stats.htm.

[4] 'Cyberspace touches every aspect of our lives. The benefits are enormous, but these do not come without risk'; UN Secretary-General, 'Foreword', *Group of Governmental Experts on Developments in the Field of Information and Telecommunications in the Context of International Security*, UN Doc A/70/174, 22 July 2015, 4. 'State and non-state actors conduct cyber operations to achieve a variety of political, economic, or military objectives. In conducting their operations, they may strike at a nation's values as well as its interests or purposes'; United States Department of Defense, *The DOD Cyber Strategy* (2015) 1, www.defense.gov/Portals/1/features/2015/0415_cyber-strategy/Final_2015_DoD_CYBER_STRATEGY_for_web.pdf.

[5] Report of the Group of Governmental Experts 2013 (n 2), 6.

[6] National Research Council, *Technology, Policy, Law and Ethics Regarding U.S. Acquisition and Use of Cyberattack Capabilities* (WA Owens, KW Dam and HS Lin, 2009).

programs resident in or transiting these systems or networks'.[7] Cyber network exploitation refers to 'the use of cyber offensive actions … usually for the purpose of obtaining information resident on or transiting through an adversary's computer systems or networks'.[8]

As cyberspace has matured, the threats emanating from this environment have become more sophisticated and multifaceted. The consequence is that the bifurcation of cyber threats into destructive cyber attacks on the one hand and non-destructive yet nevertheless damaging cyber network exploitation on the other[9] is no longer adequate to capture the vast array of threats associated with cyberspace. In recent years, a more complex taxonomy has formed and cyber threats now range from hacktivism, cyber vandalism, cyber-crime, cyber terrorism to cyber war.[10] The threat of cyber espionage has emerged as a particular concern for the international society.[11]

Espionage describes the non-consensual collection of confidential information that is under the control of another actor. States are the most prolific perpetrators of espionage[12] and, broadly speaking, they engage in two types of espionage, each defined by reference to the type of information being collected.[13] Political espionage is designed to enhance national security by accessing political and military information that is under the control of other states and, increasingly, prominent

[7] ibid 1–2.

[8] ibid.

[9] 'The main difference between cyber attack and cyber exploitation is that cyber attack is destructive in nature while cyber exploitation is focused on intelligence gathering and, in order to be covert, purposively does not try to affect the normal processes of the computer or network exploited'; A Wortham, 'Should Cyber Exploitation Ever Constitute a Demonstration of Hostile Intent That May Violate UN Charter Provisions Prohibiting the Threat or Use of Force?' (2012) 64 *Federal Communications Law Journal* 643, 646.

[10] 'Broadly, one can distinguish between cyber war, cyber activism ("hacktivism"), cyber espionage, cyber terrorism, cyberattacks against critical infrastructure, and financially motivated cyber theft'; ZK Goldman and D McCoy, 'Economic Espionage: Deterring Financially Motivated Cybercrime' (2016) 8 *Journal of National Security Law and Policy* 595, 597.

[11] 'More than 100 countries currently have the capacity for digital espionage and their professionalism is growing, as is the threat it poses'; National Coordinator for Security and Counterterrorism: Ministry of Security and Justice, *Cyber Security Assessment Netherlands* (2017) 18, www.ncsc.nl/english/current-topics/Cyber+Security+Assessment+Netherlands/cyber-security-assessment-netherlands-2017.html. 'Some of the most sophisticated threats to the UK in cyberspace come from other states which seek to conduct espionage with the aim of spying on or compromising our government, military, industrial and economic assets, as well as monitoring opponents of their own regimes'; UK Cabinet Office, *The UK Cyber Security Strategy: Protecting and Promoting the UK in a Digital World* (2011) para 2.5, www.gov.uk/government/uploads/system/uploads/attachment_data/file/60961/uk-cyber-security-strategy-final.pdf.

[12] 'Clandestine intelligence activities are usually associated with nation-states'; MS McDougal, HD Lasswell and WM Reisman, 'The Intelligence Function and World Public Order' (1973) 46 *Temple Law Quarterly* 365, 383.

[13] 'The number of state actors in cyberspace that are involved in cyber espionage targeted at computers connected to the Internet as well as closed networks continues to grow, with their aim being to collect information on both national security as well as economic interests'; Estonia, *Cyber Security Strategy 2014–2017* (2014) 5, www.mkm.ee/sites/default/files/cyber_security_strategy_2014-2017_public_version.pdf.

non-state actors such as terrorist organisations and their affiliates. States have also demonstrated a proclivity for economic espionage, which is where they seek to boost their national economy by stealing trade secrets that are under the control of companies located within foreign jurisdictions and then passing this confidential information to domestic companies.[14]

States obtain confidential information from a variety of different sources. Information is generally derived from human sources (known as Human Intelligence (HUMINT)) and electronic sources (known as Signals Intelligence (SIGINT)).

Historically, states performed espionage by sending their agents into the physical territory of their adversaries. This is HUMINT in its classic form and has been romanticised in popular culture by espionage novels written by the likes of Ian Fleming and John le Carré. Developments in technology have enabled states to spy on their enemies by using more sophisticated electronic methods (that is, SIGINT), such as the use of high frequency antennas to capture electronic transmissions emanating from the territory of other states and the use of satellites in outer space that are able to observe and monitor events on Earth.[15]

The dawn of cyberspace has dramatically increased the SIGINT capacity of states.[16] The vast quantity of information that resides in cyberspace, the speed and ease with which cyber operations can be launched, and the anonymity that this environment affords, means that '[t]he internet provides a technological platform and target-rich environment for governments to engage in espionage on a scale, speed, intensity, and depth never before witnessed in spycraft'.[17] It is therefore unsurprising that espionage has 'metastasize[d]'[18] since the emergence of cyberspace and that '[political and economic] cyber espionage projects [are] now prevalent'.[19]

[14] 'Espionage can also include the use of state-controlled assets for the purpose of gaining information from a corporation with the aim to improve the knowledge of a competitor based in one's own country'; S Kirchner, 'Beyond Privacy Rights: Crossborder Cyber-Espionage and International Law' (2014) 31 *John Marshall Journal of Information Technology and Privacy Law* 369, 370.

[15] 'States have often used new technologies for espionage purposes'; I Kilovaty, 'World Wide Web of Exploitations – the Case of Peacetime Cyber Espionage Operations under International Law: Towards a Contextual Approach' (2016) 18 *Columbia Science and Technology Law Review* 42, 62.

[16] 'By its very nature, cyberspace is a medium particularly well suited to espionage in general and commercial and industrial espionage in particular'; S Argaman and G Siboni, 'Commercial and Industrial Cyber Espionage in Israel' (2014) 6 *Military and Strategic Affairs* 43, 44.

[17] DP Fidler, 'Tinker, Tailor, Soldier, Duqu: Why Cyberespionage is More Dangerous Than You Think' (2012) 5 *International Journal of Critical Infrastructure Protection* 28, 29. For Granick, the dawn of cyberspace signals 'a golden age for surveillance'; JS Granick, *American Spies: Modern Surveillance, Why You Should Care, and What To Do About It* (Cambridge, Cambridge University Press, 2017) 53.

[18] DP Fidler, 'Economic Cyber Espionage and International Law: Controversies Involving Government Acquisition of Trade Secrets Through Cyber Technologies', 20 March 2013, *ASIL Insights*, www.asil.org/insights/volume/17/issue/10/economic-cyber-espionage-and-international-law-controversies-involving.

[19] P Warren, 'State-Sponsored Cyber Espionage Projects Now Prevalent, Says Experts', 30 August 2012, *the Guardian*, www.theguardian.com/technology/2012/aug/30/state-sponsored-cyber-espionage-prevalent. 'No single reason can be given for the increase in trade secret theft. However, one reason

Indeed, the scope and frequency of cyber espionage within the contemporary world order was laid bare in June 2013 when Edward Snowden – a former contractor for the United States (US) National Security Agency (NSA) – disclosed a trove of classified documents to the British newspaper *the Guardian*. These documents revealed that a number of states including the US and the United Kingdom (UK) had utilised an 'extraordinary range of spying methods' to obtain confidential information from a variety of different actors located across the globe.[20] A particularly prominent spying method was the use of cyber operations to collect confidential information that was being stored in or transmitted through cyberspace.[21] Targets of cyber espionage comprised state and non-state actors, including officials of international organisations such as the EU, state organs (including heads of state such as German Chancellor Angela Merkel and Israeli Prime Minister Ehud Olmert), religious leaders (the Pope), companies (such as the Brazilian oil company Petrobras), non-governmental organisations (including UNICEF and Médecins du Monde) and individuals suspected of being involved in international terrorism and other criminal enterprises.[22]

2. The Argument

Notwithstanding the fact that 'intelligence activities are now accepted as a common, even inherent, attribute of the modern state',[23] states have failed to devise either treaty law or customary international law that directly regulates espionage committed during peacetime, demonstrating a degree of 'artful ambiguity'[24] and 'creative ambivalence'[25] on their behalf towards the regulation of this practice. In the absence of international law that specifically addresses peacetime espionage, international lawyers determine that international law is 'remarkably oblivious'[26] to espionage and that, as a result, this is an activity that is 'neither legal nor illegal

for the dramatic increase is undoubtedly the world's ever expanding use of the computer'; H Nasheri, *Economic Espionage and Industrial Spying* (Cambridge, Cambridge University Press, 2005) 9.

[20] E MacAskill and J Borger, 'New NSA Leaks Show how US is Bugging its European Allies', 30 June 2013, *the Guardian*, www.theguardian.com/world/2013/jun/30/nsa-leaks-us-bugging-european-allies.

[21] ibid.

[22] J Ball and N Hopkins, 'GCHQ and NSA Targeted Charities, Germans, Israeli PM and EU Chief', 20 December 2013, *the Guardian*, www.theguardian.com/uk-news/2013/dec/20/gchq-targeted-aid-agencies-german-government-eu-commissioner.

[23] GB Demarest, 'Espionage in International Law' (1996) 24 *Denver Journal of International Law and Policy* 321, 321.

[24] C Forcese, 'Spies Without Borders: International Law and Intelligence Collection' (2011) 5 *Journal of National Security Law and Policy* 179, 205.

[25] ibid 210.

[26] RA Falk, 'Foreword' in RJ Stanger (ed), *Essays on Espionage and International Law* (Columbus, Ohio State University Press, 1962) v. Demarest contends that '[i]nternational law … simply ignores the question of peacetime spying'; Demarest (n 23) 339.

under international law'.[27] This assessment is problematic for a number of reasons, however.

First, from a systemic perspective, the claim that espionage is 'unaddressed'[28] by international law sits uncomfortably with the *Lotus* principle, which provides that in the absence of 'prohibitive rules' of international law 'every State remains free to adopt the principles which it regards as best and most suitable'.[29] In other words, the *Lotus* principle precludes the pronouncement of a *non-liquet*, meaning that under international law state conduct is either lawful and permissible or unlawful and prohibited. Although in recent years the *Lotus* principle has come under criticism for reflecting 'an old, tired view of international law',[30] its legal authority has been affirmed many times by the International Court of Justice[31] (ICJ) and most recently in the *Kosovo* advisory opinion.[32] The upshot of the *Lotus* principle is that, if international law does not directly prohibit espionage, this is a practice that must be permissible under international law.

Second, from a doctrinal standpoint, while espionage per se is residually lawful according to the *Lotus* principle, it is overly simplistic to conclude that international law has 'little impact on the practice of intelligence gathering'.[33] On the contrary, international law has a lot to say on the topic of espionage.[34] In particular, there is a 'checkerboard'[35] of general principles of international law as well as

[27] AJ Radsan, 'The Unresolved Equation of Espionage and International Law' (2007) 28 *Michigan Journal of International Law* 595, 596. '[I]nternational law neither endorses nor prohibits espionage'; CD Baker, 'Tolerance of International Espionage: A Functional Approach' (2003) 19 *American University International Law Review* 1091, 1092. The view that there is little interaction between international law and espionage explains why 'scholarship on espionage has not been very extensive'; Radsan (n 27) 596. Similarly, Chesterman notes that '[a]cademic literature typically omits the subject [of espionage] entirely, or includes a paragraph or two defining espionage and describing the unhappy fate of captured spies'; S Chesterman, 'The Spy Who Came in from the Cold War: Intelligence and International Law' (2006) 27 *Michigan Journal of International Law* 1071, 1072.

[28] Demarest (n 23) 330.

[29] *The Case of the S.S. Lotus (France v Turkey)*, Judgment [1927] PCIJ Rep (Ser A) No 10 1, 19.

[30] *Accordance with International Law of the Unilateral Declaration of Independence in Respect of Kosovo* (Advisory Opinion) [2010] ICJ Rep 403, 478 (Declaration of Judge Simma). For further criticism of the *Lotus* principle see H Handeyside, 'The *Lotus* Principle in ICJ Jurisprudence: Was the Ship Ever Afloat?' (2007) 29 *Michigan Journal of International Law* 71.

[31] *Legality of the Threat or Use of Nuclear Weapons* (Advisory Opinion) [1996] ICJ Rep 226; *Military and Paramilitary Activities in and against Nicaragua (Nicaragua v United States of America)*, Judgment (Merits) [1986] ICJ Rep 14.

[32] *Accordance with International Law of the Unilateral Declaration of Independence in Respect of Kosovo* (Advisory Opinion) [2010] ICJ Rep 403.

[33] G Sulmasy and J Yoo, 'Counterintuitive: Intelligence Operations and International Law' (2007) 28 *Michigan Journal of International Law* 625, 625.

[34] Chesterman asks '[w]hat, then – if anything – does international law have to say about the subject [of espionage]? A surprising amount'; Chesterman (n 27) 1072. '[M]any rules of international law may be engaged by spying, depending on the nature of that spying and its geographic location'; Forcese (n 24) 185. 'I believe there is a great deal of interaction between international law and intelligence activities'; JH Smith, 'Keynote Address: State Intelligence Gathering and International Law' (2007) 28 *Michigan Journal of International Law* 543, 544.

[35] Forcese (n 24) 209.

specialised international legal regimes that indirectly regulate espionage insofar as they appertain to the conduct that underlies the espionage operation,[36] with the consequence being that international law 'constrain[s] some practices in some places and in relation to some actors'.[37]

But why do international lawyers maintain the fiction that there is no interaction between international law and espionage?[38] The truth is that international lawyers have been consciously unwilling to apply international law to this practice and, as Chesterman observes, espionage 'is less a lacuna in the legal order than it is the elephant in the room'.[39] The reasons for this agnosticism are clear.

With regard to political espionage, even though international law implements a number of rules that are intended to protect state sovereignty and thus maintain international peace and security, international lawyers nevertheless perceive the world order to be unpredictable and dangerous. In such an environment, they are reluctant to accept that legal rules are able to effectively protect state sovereignty and thereby maintain international peace and security.[40] International lawyers have thus been loath to apply legal rules that curtail the ability of states to undertake espionage, which is regarded as 'necessary for the national security of a nation-state'[41] because it allows states to better understand the intentions and capabilities of other actors operating within the world order.

International lawyers are therefore faced with a dilemma. On the one hand, they cannot deny that international legal rules are applicable to intrusive activities such as espionage because to do so would challenge the authority of international law. On the other hand, they are equally unwilling to renounce espionage as a tool of statecraft because they wish to preserve the national security benefits that this practice affords. Ultimately, their only way out of this impasse is to eschew the question of whether espionage is compatible with international law and proclaim that 'international law is silent on the subject'.[42] Indeed, seemingly

[36] 'It is the underlying act that determines the legality of such cyber operations, not the fact that they are engaged in for the purpose of espionage'; MN Schmitt, 'Cyber Responses "By the Numbers" in International Law', 4 August 2015, EJIL: *Talk!*, www.ejiltalk.org/cyber-responses-by-the-numbers-in-international-law/. 'While the International Group of Experts agreed that there is no prohibition of espionage *per se*, they likewise concurred that cyber espionage may be conducted in a manner that violates international law due to the fact that certain methods employed to conduct cyber espionage are unlawful'; MN Schmitt, *Tallinn Manual 2.0 on the International Law Applicable to Cyber Operations* (Cambridge, Cambridge University Press, 2017) 170.

[37] C Forcese, 'Creative Ambiguity – International Law's Distant Relationship with Peacetime Spying', 14 November 2013, *Just Security*, www.justsecurity.org/3168/guest-post-creative-ambiguity-international-laws-distant-relationship-peacetime-spying/.

[38] As Sulmasy and Yoo note, '[f]ew have questioned whether intelligence collection activities violate international law'; Sulmasy and Yoo (n 33) 629.

[39] Chesterman (n 27) 1072.

[40] 'One of the fundamental tenets of international law is, of course, that one state not intervene in the internal affairs of another state. It may be a fundamental principle, but it is also fairly tattered. States seek to influence each other daily'; Smith (n 34) 545.

[41] Sulmasy and Yoo (n 33) 628.

[42] G Brown, 'Spying and Fighting in Cyberspace: What is Which?' (2016) 8 *Journal of National Law and Policy* 621, 621.

frustrated by the conundrum that espionage presents for international lawyers Radsan urges: 'Accepting that espionage is beyond the law, we should move on to other projects – with grace.'[43]

Radsan's comments were made in 2007, several years before cyber espionage burst onto the international scene. The dramatic increase in political espionage since the advent of cyberspace has meant that walking away from the espionage debate – with or without grace – has not been possible. While at one point in time it may have been acceptable for international lawyers to turn a blind eye to espionage, it is not appropriate to ignore *cyber-enabled* espionage.[44]

In response, there has been a surge in international legal scholarship dedicated to the topic of political cyber espionage.[45] Yet, under the influence of realist theory, scholars remain fixated upon the national security benefits afforded by political cyber espionage and insist that, as with more traditional forms of political espionage, this conduct operates in a 'legal black hole'.[46] For one commentator, '[c]yberspace remains a netherworld for intelligence activities – whatever surveillance or cyber spying a government does outside of its own national borders is, in most instances, an international law free-for-all'.[47] *Plus ça change, plus c'est la même chose.*

[43] Radsan (n 27) 597. Similarly, Brown and Poellet argue that '[espionage] occupies an ill-defined policy space that permits it to occur without violating international law'; G Brown and K Poellet, 'The Customary International Law of Cyberspace' (2012) 6 *Strategic Studies Quarterly* 126, 133.

[44] '[C]yber espionage has stirred the conventional international complacency by bringing the permissibility of foreign intelligence operations into the daily public spotlight'; D Pun, 'Rethinking Espionage in the Modern Era' (2017) 18 *Chicago Journal of International Law* 353, 385. Deeks explains that since the dawn of cyberspace there has been a 'shift from agnosticism' among international lawyers when it comes to the role of international law in regulating espionage; A Deeks, 'An International Legal Framework for Surveillance' (2015) 55 *Virginia Journal of International Law* 291, 315.

[45] See I Navarrete, 'L'Espionnage en Temps de Paix en Droit International Public' (2016) 53 *Canadian Yearbook of International Law* 1; R Buchan, 'The International Legal Regulation of State-Sponsored Cyber Espionage' in A-M Osula and H Rõigas (eds), *International Cyber Norms: Legal, Policy & Industry Perspectives* (CCDCOE, 2016); K Ziolkowski, 'Peacetime Cyber Espionage – New Tendencies in Public International Law' in K Ziolkowski (ed), *Peacetime Regime for State Activities in Cyberspace: International Law, International Relations and Diplomacy* (CCDCOE, 2013); RD Williams, '(Spy) Game Change: Cyber Networks, Intelligence Collection, and Covert Action' (2011) 79 *The George Washington Law Review* 1162; C Khalil, 'Thinking Intelligently about Intelligence: A Model Global Framework Protecting Privacy' (2015) 47 *George Washington International Law Review* 919; PCR Terry, '"Absolute Friends": United States Espionage Against Germany and Public International Law' (2015) 28 *Revue Quebecoise de Droit International* 173; C Forcese, 'Pragmatism and Principle: Intelligence Agencies and International Law' (2016) 102 *Virginia Law Review Online* 67; Brown and Poellet (n 43); Deeks (n 44).

[46] Fidler (n 17) 29. 'Espionage has been considered unregulated under the international legal system – meaning cyber activities that constitute espionage are neither lawful nor unlawful under international law'; Brown (n 42) 622.

[47] WC Banks, 'Cyber Espionage and Electronic Surveillance: Beyond the Media Coverage' (2017) 66 *Emory Law Journal* 513, 518.

Why are international lawyers averse to examining the application of international law to *economic* espionage? This question is particularly intriguing given that economic espionage impinges upon the sovereignty of the state that hosts the company whose trade secrets have been appropriated and also has a deleterious impact upon its national economy. However, unlike political espionage, economic espionage does not confer upon the perpetrating state direct and immediate national security benefits. Although economic espionage does ultimately strengthen the perpetrating state's national security (by boosting its economic security), its immediate benefit is that it helps domestic companies remain competitive vis-a-vis their foreign rivals.

Seemingly, the concern among international lawyers is that if they undertake an inquiry into the role of international law in regulating economic espionage this may open up a Pandora's box, raising questions as to how international law applies to political espionage. Stated succinctly, if political espionage is a 'dirty word'[48] that is off-limits to the regulatory gaze of international lawyers, then so too is economic espionage.

At least historically, economic espionage was not as prevalent within the world order as political espionage and this made it easier for international lawyers to ignore the threats posed by economic espionage in favour of insulating political espionage from international legal appraisal. Given the upsurge in economic espionage since the dawn of cyberspace and in light of the damage that it inflicts upon state sovereignty and national economies, the public and private sectors have increasingly called upon international lawyers to scrutinise whether and to what extent international law can be used to counteract economic cyber espionage.[49] But to date, international lawyers have directed remarkably little attention towards exploring the application of international law to economic cyber espionage. Of those that have, most preserve the myth that international law remains 'a bystander to this entire fabric of stealth, deception, and greed'.[50] Again, it seems that international lawyers are concerned that, if economic cyber espionage is submitted to intensive international legal review, this scrutiny will be extended to political cyber espionage, which may open up the possibility that international law will be used to restrict the availability of politically motivated espionage and thus deny the national security benefits that it affords.

In light of the above, the objective of this monograph – and its original contribution to existing academic literature – is to identify the international legal rules implicated by political and economic cyber espionage and to assess the extent to which they regulate this conduct.

[48] International Peace Academy, *Peacekeeper's Handbook* (1984) 39, 59–62, 120–21.

[49] See JP Farwell and D Arakelian, 'China Cyber Charges: Take Beijing to the WTO Instead', 20 May 2014, *The National Interest*, www.nationalinterest.org/blog/the-buzz/china-cyber-charges-take-beijing-the-wto-instead-10496.

[50] Banks (n 47) 517.

3. Chapter Overview

This monograph adheres to the following structure. Chapter 1 frames the scope of this project by formulating a working definition of the concept of cyber espionage. The chapter drills down into the various features of this definition in order to provide a fuller understanding of the types of activity that cyber espionage describes and, in particular, to outline the types of conduct that will be subject to international law analysis as this monograph progresses.

Chapter 2 examines the impact of political and economic cyber espionage upon international relations. This chapter claims that states inhabit an international society that links the maintenance of international peace and security to the protection of the principles of the sovereign equality of states and human dignity. It argues that political espionage represents a threat to the maintenance of international peace and security because, where this conduct is directed against a state or a non-state actor located within another state, it violates the principle of the sovereign equality of states and, where this conduct is targeted against individuals, it violates the principle of human dignity. Additionally, this chapter maintains that, because political espionage is incompatible with the foundational principles of the international society, it disrupts the potential for close and effective cooperation within the society and thus inhibits its ability to address threats to international peace and security. Moreover, this chapter describes the direct and indirect costs that economic espionage inflicts upon victim companies and the negative impact this has upon their financial stability. Where companies struggle financially, the national economy of the host state is also adversely affected. Given that national security is nowadays contingent upon economic security, economic espionage can be said to endanger national security and by implication international peace and security. That cyberspace enhances the capacity of states to perpetrate political and economic espionage means that the threat that these practices represent to international peace and security is magnified in the cyber setting. Appreciating the severity of this threat, this chapter concludes that the international society must possess international legal rules that unambiguously prohibit political and economic cyber espionage.

Chapter 3 analyses the application of the rules of territorial sovereignty, non-intervention and the non-use of force to cyber espionage. This chapter argues that cyber operations that penetrate computer networks and systems supported by cyber infrastructure located within the territory of another state trigger a violation of the territorial sovereignty rule, regardless of whether that cyber infrastructure is operated by state organs or private actors. The rule of territorial sovereignty therefore provides an important and powerful source of legal protection against political and economic cyber espionage. Yet, this chapter concludes that cyber espionage is unlikely to transgress the rule of non-intervention given that such conduct lacks the requisite coercive element. Similarly, the prohibition on the use of force is inapplicable to cyber espionage on the basis that this activity does not produce physical damage within the territory of the victim state.

Chapter 4 investigates the role of diplomatic and consular law in regulating political cyber espionage. This chapter argues that diplomatic and consular law confers inviolability upon the premises, documents and official correspondence of diplomatic missions and consular posts. Where a state interferes with diplomatic missions and consular posts by launching acts of cyber espionage against them, or otherwise fails to protect these missions and posts from acts of cyber espionage perpetrated by other actors, this conduct (or lack thereof) undoubtedly violates these rules. This chapter also maintains that diplomatic and consular law prohibits the diplomatic missions and consular posts of sending states from engaging in acts of cyber espionage while operating within the receiving state.

Chapter 5 assesses the application of international human rights law to acts of cyber espionage targeted against individuals, with particular reference to the International Covenant on Civil and Political Rights (ICCPR) 1966 and the European Convention on Human Rights (ECHR) 1950. An important preliminary question relates to the territorial scope of the obligations contained within these human rights treaties. It is well-accepted that states owe these human rights obligations in cyberspace to individuals located within their territory. But what about the situation where a state's online activities impinge upon the human rights of individuals located within *foreign* territory, which is often the case with cyber espionage? As this chapter reveals, the human rights bodies that oversee the implementation of the ICCPR have consistently determined that states are subject to a negative obligation to respect human rights where they exercise their authority and control against individuals located abroad, including where this authority and control is exercised within (or through) cyberspace. The European Court of Human Rights (ECtHR) has failed to articulate a clear and consistent approach as to when a state's human rights obligations under the ECHR apply extraterritorially, although its more recent jurisprudence tentatively endorses the model adopted under the ICCPR. With regard to substantive human rights, this chapter argues that cyber espionage is most likely to run into conflict with the right to privacy (as contained in Article 17 ICCPR and Article 8 ECHR), which protects a person's information and communications from interference. At the same time, this chapter acknowledges that privacy is not an absolute right and explores the circumstances in which it can be permissibly restricted in the context of online surveillance.

Chapter 6 evaluates whether the trade agreements that fall under the authority of the World Trade Organization (WTO) apply to economic cyber espionage. Specifically, Article 10*bis* of the Paris Convention 1967 requires that members assure to nationals (including legal persons, that is, companies) of other members effective protection against acts of unfair competition. This chapter maintains that economic cyber espionage constitutes an act of unfair competition within the meaning of Article 10*bis*. Article 10*bis* therefore prohibits members from engaging in acts of economic cyber espionage against Paris Union nationals located within their territory and, in light of the wording of Article 10*bis*, against Paris Union nationals located abroad, which is important given the transboundary nature of economic cyber espionage. Article 39.2 of the Agreement on Trade-Related Aspects of Intellectual Property Rights (TRIPS) 1994 imposes an obligation upon members to establish causes of action under national law so that nationals (including legal persons) of TRIPS members can protect their undisclosed information from unauthorised acquisition, disclosure or use. While this provision does not directly prohibit members from engaging in economic cyber espionage against nationals of TRIPS members, nevertheless it makes an important contribution to the suppression of this activity insofar as it requires all members to implement minimum legal standards relating to the protection of confidential information.

International legal scholars accept that acts of political cyber espionage may violate certain primary rules of international law, such as the rule of territorial sovereignty and the inviolability provisions of diplomatic and consular law. Yet, by and large, these scholars assert that developments in customary international law have carved out permissive espionage exceptions to these otherwise prohibitive rules. Chapter 7 rejects this contention. This chapter argues that these types of customary exceptions have not come into existence because they are not supported by state practice or *opinio juris*, the essential ingredients of customary international law. With regard to state practice, espionage is usually committed in secret. However, secret state conduct does not qualify as state practice for the purpose of customary international law formation. Moreover, while instances of espionage are widely and credibly reported, states almost always fail to acknowledge responsibility for their espionage operations and unacknowledged state conduct does not count as state practice for the purpose of customary international law development. Even if we accept *arguendo* that sufficient state practice of these types of espionage exists, the policy of silence that states have adopted towards their espionage activities prevents the formation of *opinio juris*, the absence of which precludes the crystallisation of espionage exceptions under customary international law.

Chapter 8 considers the application of the doctrines of self-defence and necessity to acts of political and economic cyber espionage. This chapter argues that states can only invoke self-defence to justify acts of cyber espionage where they are the victim of an actual or imminent threat of an armed attack. Moreover, cyber espionage undertaken in self-defence must not exceed what is necessary and proportionate in the circumstances to halt and repel an armed attack or to prevent further reasonably foreseeable attacks. Additionally, this chapter argues that the defence of necessity can exculpate state responsibility for unlawful acts of cyber espionage where they are necessary to safeguard an essential state interest from a grave and imminent peril and providing they do not seriously impair an essential interest of the victim state(s) or of the international community as a whole. This chapter concludes that the restrictions to which self-defence and necessity are subject are so stringent that, in practice, these defences will be rarely available to justify acts of political and economic cyber espionage.

Contrary to the mainstream view, cyber espionage does not exist in an international law vacuum. However, notwithstanding the applicability of international law, this monograph concludes by arguing that states should devise and implement a *lex specialis* framework that contains bespoke international legal rules that directly and specifically regulate cyber espionage.

1

Defining Cyber Espionage

1. Introduction

The objective of this monograph is to identify the international legal rules applicable to cyber espionage and to assess the extent to which they prohibit or constrain this activity. In order to guide our analysis of these rules, it is first necessary to develop a working definition of the concept of cyber espionage.

To date, states have failed to agree a definition of espionage let alone cyber espionage within international law. However, with the permeation of cyberspace into nearly all aspects of modern life, states have increasingly adopted cyber security policies that are designed to tackle the threats that emanate from this environment. In formulating these policies, states have offered definitions of key concepts and terms associated with cyberspace. Given the prevalence of cyber espionage within contemporary international relations, it is unsurprising that cyber espionage features prominently in many of these policies and most provide a definition of this concept.[1]

While national definitions exhibit diversity, definitional patterns appear and key features of cyber espionage can be extracted.[2] In short, definitions of cyber espionage comprise four constitutive elements: the (i) non-consensual (ii) copying (iii) of confidential information (iv) that is resident in or transiting through cyberspace.

Identifying these elements provides a useful starting point when formulating a definition of cyber espionage. Yet, in order to pin down exactly what type of

[1] NATO's Cooperative Cyber Defence Centre of Excellence provides a repository of national cyber security strategies: www.ccdcoe.org/cyber-security-strategy-documents.html. The US, for example, defines cyber espionage as '[o]perations and related programs or activities conducted … in or through cyberspace, for the primary purpose of collecting intelligence … from computers, information or communications systems, or networks with the intent to remain undetected'; United States Presidential Policy Directive/PPD-20, *U.S. Cyber Operations Policy* (October 2012) www.archive.org/stream/2012USPresidentialDirectiveForeignComputerNetworkTargets/presidential-policy-directive_djvu.txt. The UK defines cyber espionage as 'the use of a computer network to infiltrate a target computer network and gather intelligence'; UK, *National Cyber Security Strategy 2016-2021* (2016) 74, www.gov.uk/government/uploads/system/uploads/attachment_data/file/567242/national_cyber_security_strategy_2016.pdf.

[2] 'Although a working definition of intelligence remains elusive, there are generally recognized practices relating to intelligence collection that can be agreed to by most, if not all, states'; G Sulmasy and J Yoo, 'Counterintuitive: Intelligence Operations and International Law' (2007) 28 *Michigan Journal of International Law* 625, 630.

activity cyber espionage describes and thus the type of conduct that will be subject to international legal analysis throughout this monograph, it is necessary to drill down further into these features and unpack their content.

2. The Intelligence Community

Maintaining national security is one of the most important objectives of the state and it is for this reason that states dedicate huge amounts of resources to collecting information concerning the activities of foreign actors. Indeed, 'virtually every state has an intelligence service that seeks to collect information on potential adversaries',[3] whether it be 'through a consolidated service or a separate foreign service'.[4]

The 'intelligence cycle' is the name given by the Intelligence Community (IC) to describe the process of intelligence production. In its entirety, the intelligence cycle consists of five distinct stages; (i) planning and direction; (ii) collection; (iii) analysis and processing; (iv) production; and (v) dissemination. In short, '[i]ntelligence can be divided into two basic categories: collection and analysis'.[5] These two broad stages distinguish information from intelligence – information that has been collected only becomes intelligence once it has been analysed.[6]

This monograph examines the application of international law to the collection (as opposed to the analysis) of information. The IC collects information from a variety of different sources[7] and intelligence officers prefer to produce intelligence on the back of information that is collected from all available sources (referred to as 'all source intelligence').[8] For heuristic purposes, a dichotomy can be drawn between information that is collected from human sources and information that is obtained through the interception of electronic signals. Moreover, these sources can be designated as open or closed.

[3] JH Smith, 'Keynote Address: State Intelligence Gathering and International Law' (2007) 28 *Michigan Journal of International Law* 543, 544.

[4] AJ Radsan, 'The Unresolved Equation of Espionage and International Law' (2007) 28 *Michigan Journal of International Law* 595, 613.

[5] ibid 599.

[6] Intelligence is '[t]he product resulting from the collection, processing, integration, evaluation, analysis, and interpretation of available information concerning foreign nations, hostile or potentially hostile forces or elements, or areas of actual or potential operations'; Joint Chiefs of Staff, Joint Publication 1-02, *Department of Defense Dictionary of Military and Associated Terms* (8 November 2010, as amended through 15 February 2016) 114, www.fas.org/irp/doddir/dod/jp1_02.pdf.

[7] '[States] use a variety of methods, many of which remain unknown, to gather intelligence on individuals throughout the world'; C Khalil, 'Thinking Intelligently About Intelligence: A Model Global Framework Protecting Privacy' (2015) 47 *George Washington International Law Review* 919, 924.

[8] RL Russell, 'Achieving All-Source Fusion in the Intelligence Community' in LK Johnson (ed), *Handbook of Intelligence Studies* (London, Routledge, 2007) 189–99.

2.1. Sources of Information Collection

Information collected from human sources is known as human intelligence and this concept is usually abbreviated to HUMINT. HUMINT is defined as:

> [T]he collection of information by a trained HUMINT collector … from people and their associated documents and media sources to identify elements, intentions, composition, strength, dispositions, tactics, equipment, personnel and capabilities. It uses human sources as a tool and a variety of collection methods, both passively and actively, to gather information.[9]

For many years HUMINT represented the 'primary source of intelligence'.[10] Yet, as states dedicated more resources to protecting their confidential information and as their counter-espionage capabilities improved, obtaining access to human sources proved increasingly difficult. Additionally, HUMINT had the potential to produce unreliable information because human informants could act as double agents and deliberately feed their handlers false information or, instead, they could simply misunderstand events and relay inaccurate information.

In light of the problems associated with HUMINT and as the technological revolution gathered momentum, signals intelligence – usually acronymised to SIGINT – emerged as a particularly prominent method for collecting information, either as a stand-alone source or being used to verify or supplement HUMINT. The major advantage of SIGINT is that it allows direct access to information and thus minimises the potential for information to be deliberately or inadvertently misrepresented.

SIGINT derives from the interception of signals and is divided into two subfields: communications intelligence (COMMINT) and electronic intelligence (ELINT). COMMINT describes the acquisition of 'foreign communications passed by radio, wire, or other electromagnetic means'[11] which, put simply, means the collection of electronic signals that include speech or text. ELINT involves the collection of 'foreign, non-communications, electromagnetic radiations emanating from other than atomic detonation sources'[12] which, in essence, involves the collection of electronic signals that do not relate to personal communications.

New subcategories of SIGINT continue to be developed by the IC, usually in response to technological innovations. For example, imagery intelligence (IMINT) is the product of information that is collected through the use of visual photography, infrared, lasers, multispectral sensors and radar.

[9] US Department of the Army, *Human Intelligence Collector Operations FM 2-22.3* (2006) 1–4, www.fas.org/irp/doddir/army/fm2-22-3.pdf.

[10] Interagency OPSEC Support Staff, *Operations Security: Intelligence Threat Handbook* (1996) 4.

[11] *National Security Council Intelligence Directive No 6*, 17 February 1972, www.fas.org/irp/offdocs/nscid-6.pdf.

[12] *National Security Council Intelligence Directive No 17*, 16 May 1955, www.history.state.gov/historicaldocuments/frus1950-55Intel/d259.

Cyberspace describes a 'global domain within the information environment consisting of the interdependent network of information technology infrastructures and resident data, including the Internet, telecommunications networks, computer systems, and embedded processors and controllers'.[13] Cyberspace is used to store huge quantities of information and it also acts as an essential communicative device. Unsurprisingly, the IC now regularly conducts operations in cyberspace to acquire information and cyber intelligence (CYINT) has therefore emerged as an important subcategory of SIGINT.

2.2. Open and Closed Sources

Information can be acquired from open and closed sources. 'Open source' describes information that is publicly available and this typically includes information that is contained in speeches, official documents, newspaper reports, technical and professional journals, company websites and online databases.[14]

Open source information is abundant in liberal democracies given that they are political systems predicated upon the principles of freedom of information and freedom of expression. Obviously, even in liberal democracies, state and non-state actors keep certain types of information secret. Indeed, in most liberal democracies freedom of information regimes exempt the state from providing public access to confidential information where necessary to meet a legitimate aim. In the UK, for example, the state can refuse to disclose secret information that relates to its military activities or where it involves communications with foreign governments.[15] Moreover, liberal democracies invariably implement legal rules restricting the right to freedom of expression where necessary to suppress criminal or dangerous activities. In order to avoid the sanctions incurred upon breach of these rules, malicious non-state actors such as terrorists and criminals go to great lengths to conceal their activities and communications.

Consequently, states seek information from foreign actors that is not publicly available, namely, information from closed sources.[16] This form of information collection is referred to as espionage or, colloquially, spying, and with those engaging in this practice being known as spies. Thus, 'espionage is one aspect of a nation's intelligence work, encompassing the government's efforts to acquire classified or

[13] Joint Publication 1-02 (n 6) 58.

[14] Unlike closed source information, 'intelligence analysis that relies on open source information is legally unproblematic' because its public nature invites others to freely view it; S Chesterman, 'The Spy Who Came in from the Cold War: Intelligence and International Law' (2006) 27 *Michigan Journal of International Law* 1071, 1073. 'The gathering of open source information is a separate activity, one that is not subject to any legal concerns'; D Pun, 'Rethinking Espionage in the Modern Era' (2017) 18 *Chicago Journal of International Law* 353, 358 (citations omitted).

[15] Part II, Freedom of Information Act 2000.

[16] 'Espionage is a means of acquiring information that would otherwise be unavailable'; GP Hastedt, *Espionage: A Reference Handbook* (Santa Barbara, California, ABC-CLIO, 2003) 60.

other protected information'.[17] 'Most governments rely on a range of information being gathered to guide their actions. This is not the same as espionage. Espionage is the process of obtaining information that is not normally publicly available.'[18]

Over the years, much has been written as to when information can be regarded as publicly available, and with the emergence of the Internet this debate has become much more intense. This point was presciently recognised by McDougal, Lasswell and Reisman in 1973:

> A further difficultly lies in the fact that the line between lawful intelligence gathering and espionage is thin, and may, in fact, ultimately be irreparably perforated by technological innovations.[19]

Although this is not the place to enter into the complex debate as to when information can be regarded as publicly available in the Internet Age, it is generally accepted that information is not publicly available (that is, it is private and confidential) in those circumstances where the actor that exercises control over the information 'reasonably expects privacy'.[20] In the cyber context, shielding electronic information behind a password-protected firewall is a strong indicator that the actor in control of that information regards it as confidential, as would the encryption of data. As this monograph progresses, we will see that reasonable expectations of privacy extend to metadata as well as content data, where metadata refers to 'all other information about a communication other than the content; the where, when, who, how long, and how'.[21]

3. Cyber Espionage: The Copying of Confidential Data

Cyber espionage describes the use of cyber operations to copy[22] confidential data that is resident in or transiting through cyberspace, even if it is not read or analysed.[23] By focusing upon the copying of data, this definition emphasises that

[17] C Lotrionte, 'Countering State-Sponsored Cyber Economic Espionage Under International Law' (2015) 40 *North Carolina Journal of International Law and Commercial Regulation* 443, 460. '[E]spionage is just a specific method of obtaining information'; C Schaller, 'Spies' (2015) *Max Planck Encyclopaedia of Public International Law*, para 1.

[18] MI5: Security Service, 'Espionage', www.mi5.gov.uk/espionage.

[19] MS McDougal, HD Lasswell and WM Reisman, 'The Intelligence Function and World Public Order' (1973) 46 *Temple Law Quarterly* 365, 395.

[20] C Forcese, 'Spies Without Borders: International Law and Intelligence Collection' (2011) 5 *Journal of National Security Law and Policy* 179, 183.

[21] Big Brother Watch, 'Briefing Note: Why Communications Data (Metadata) Matter?', 16 May 2014, www.bigbrotherwatch.org.uk/wp-content/uploads/2014/07/Communications-Data-Briefing.pdf.

[22] I use the terms copy, collect, obtain, acquire, appropriate and gather interchangeably.

[23] Kilovaty defines cyber espionage as the 'capturing' of confidential information, 'meaning interception or observation of the data'; I Kilovaty, 'World Wide Web of Exploitations – the Case of Peacetime Cyber Espionage Operations under International Law: Towards a Contextual Approach' (2016) 18 *Columbia Science and Technology Law Review* 42, 48.

cyber espionage does not affect the availability or integrity of data or the networks and systems upon which that data resides. If a cyber operation results in data being lost or damaged, or otherwise affects the functionality of computer networks and systems, such an operation is properly classified as a *cyber attack*.[24] As cyber attacks produce destructive effects they engage different international legal rules than acts of cyber espionage, which are exploitative in nature.[25]

Moreover, by defining cyber espionage as the copying of confidential data, this means that other operations and activities that are adjunct to cyber espionage fall outside the scope of this monograph and will not be the focus of international legal analysis. For example, this monograph is not concerned with the role of international law in regulating *how* information is used once it has been copied, such as where copied information is used to exert influence over the victim state or where stolen trade secrets are passed to domestic companies in order to confer upon them a competitive advantage.

4. Close and Remote Access Cyber Espionage

Cyber espionage can be conducted through close or remote access. Close access cyber espionage 'takes place through the local installation of hardware or software functionality by friendly parties (e.g., covert agents, vendors) in close proximity to the computer or network of interest'.[26] An example would be where a spy physically accesses an office and downloads information from a computer network or system onto a flash drive.

Remote access cyber espionage describes those operations that are 'launched at some distance from the adversary computer or network of interest', usually using an 'access path provided by the Internet'.[27] Examples of remote access cyber espionage include: (i) the direct hacking of computer networks and systems; (ii) the use of phishing tools to manipulate an individual into divulging confidential information (such as a password), which is then used by a malicious actor to acquire unauthorised access to computer networks and systems; and (iii) the dissemination of malware such as worms and Trojan horses (through compromised emails, for example) that exploit software vulnerabilities so as to allow back door access to computer networks and systems.[28]

[24] Cyber attacks are defined as operations designed to 'disrupt, deny, degrade, or destroy information resident in computers and computer networks or the computers and networks themselves'; Joint Chiefs of Staff, *Joint Pub 3–13, Joint Doctrine for Information Operations* (9 October 1998) I-9, www.c4i.org/jp3_13.pdf.

[25] OA Hathaway, R Crootof, P Levitz, H Nix, A Nowlan, W Perdue and J Spiegel, 'The Law of Cyber-Attack' (2012) 100 *California Law Review* 817, 829–30.

[26] HS Lin, 'Offensive Cyber Operations and the Use of Force' (2010) 4 *Journal of National Security Law and Policy* 63, 66.

[27] ibid.

[28] For a discussion of the vast array of malware available to cyber hackers to acquire remote access to computer networks and systems see I Ashok, 'FBI Hacked Into Over 8, 000 Computers in 120 Countries

Primarily, this monograph is concerned with examining the compatibility of remote access cyber espionage[29] with international law and this type of espionage is prioritised for international legal analysis for two reasons: first, given that it is easier, cheaper and relatively risk-free to conduct cyber espionage remotely, remote access cyber espionage has emerged as a prominent method for collecting electronic data in the contemporary world order; and second, given that international law is a system of governance that is territorially based and which is designed to regulate activities that occur within physical spaces, the exploitation of a virtual domain such as cyberspace to conduct espionage from afar raises a number of unique and difficult international law questions.

5. Secrecy and Cyber Espionage

Traditional definitions maintain that espionage is a clandestine activity.[30] It is correct that spies usually operate in secret and there are several reasons for this: (i) access to confidential information is facilitated where the owner of the information is unaware that this activity is occurring; (ii) spies are more likely to return home safely and in possession of confidential information when they operate undetected; (iii) espionage performed under the cover of secrecy prevents other actors from observing and learning the spying techniques being used;[31] (iv) secrets are far more valuable when their owner is unaware that they have been appropriated; and (v) spying in secret avoids the national and international embarrassment as well as the political and legal ramifications usually associated with allegations that a state has engaged in espionage.

With Just One Warrant, Court Documents Reveal', 23 November 2016, *International Business Times*, www.ibtimes.co.uk/fbi-hacked-into-over-8000-computers-120-countries-just-one-warrant-court-documents-reveal-1592953.

[29] I appreciate that not all types of cyber espionage can be neatly categorised as close or remote access. Consider, for instance, probes that are physically attached to Internet cables and which capture transiting data. While probes are installed locally by a human being, the appropriated information is usually transmitted back to the operator via the Internet. It was this type of cyber espionage that was used by the UK to undertake its Tempora programme: see O Khazan, 'The Creepy, Long-Standing Practice of Undersea Cable Tapping', 16 July 2013, *The Atlantic*, www.theatlantic.com/international/archive/2013/07/the-creepy-long-standing-practice-of-undersea-cable-tapping/277855/.

[30] Oppenheim defines spies as 'secret agents of a State sent abroad for the purpose of obtaining clandestinely information in regard to military or political secrets'; L Oppenheim (RF Roxburgh, ed), *International Law: A Treatise* (London, New York, Longmans, Green & Co, 1920) para 455. The *Tallinn Manual 2.0* defines cyber espionage as 'any act undertaken clandestinely or under false pretenses that uses cyber capabilities to gather, or attempt to gather, information'; MN Schmitt, *Tallinn Manual 2.0 on the International Law Applicable to Cyber Operations* (Cambridge, Cambridge University Press, 2017) 168.

[31] 'Discussing or showcasing a [cyber] weapon effectively sacrifices it forever'; C Neuman and M Poznansky, 'Swaggering in Cyberspace: Busting the Conventional Wisdom on Cyber Coercion', 28 June 2016, *War on the Rocks*, www.warontherocks.com/2016/06/swaggering-in-cyberspace-busting-the-conventional-wisdom-on-cyber-coercion/. 'States are very hesitant to reveal their [spying] toolkits publicly, for fear of losing an advantage over other states'; A Deeks, 'An International Legal Framework for Surveillance' (2015) 55 *Virginia Journal of International Law* 291, 315.

Yet, from a definitional perspective, secrecy is not a *sine qua non* for espionage.[32] In fact, espionage can be committed overtly as well as covertly. As the UK government explains:

> [Spies] may operate openly, declaring themselves as representatives of foreign intelligence services to their host nation, or covertly under the cover of other official positions such as diplomatic staff or trade delegates.
>
> Some intelligence officers may operate under non-official cover to conceal the fact that they work for an intelligence service – posing as a business person, student or journalist for example. In some cases they may operate in 'deep cover' under false names and nationalities.[33]

6. Non-Consensual Information Gathering

Crucial to the definition of espionage is that confidential information is obtained without the consent of the actor that controls that information. Consent can be provided in a variety of different ways.

Consent can be ad hoc, informal and temporary. Consent can be also embedded within formal legal agreements, which can grant one-off or continuing access to certain types of information when certain conditions are satisfied. For example, companies and individuals often enter into contracts with service providers that permit (in the sense that they grant legal authority to) other actors (including government agencies) to access their information. States also conclude treaties that permit states parties to monitor each other and access information in order to verify whether they are complying with their treaty obligations.[34] As an illustration, Article XII of the (now defunct) Anti-Ballistic Missile Treaty 1972[35] explained that for the 'purpose of providing assurance or compliance with the provisions of this Treaty, each party shall use national technical means of verification at its disposal in a manner consistent with generally recognized principles of international law'.[36] Similarly, the Open Skies Treaty 1992 establishes a regime that permits signatory states to conduct unarmed aerial observation flights over the entire territory of other parties in order to analyse rail, port, industrial and military facilities and to

[32] When defining espionage Halleck explains that 'secrecy has nothing to do with it'; HW Halleck, 'Military Espionage' (1911) 5 *AJIL* 590, 598. '[T]he essence of spying is not false pretense, but simply unauthorized disclosure'; LS Edmondson, 'Espionage in Transnational Law' (1972) 5 *Vanderbilt Journal of Transnational Law* 434, 435.

[33] MI5: Security Service, 'How Spies Operate', www.mi5.gov.uk/how-spies-operate.

[34] See generally KW Abbott, '"Trust But Verify": The Production of Information in Arms Control Treaties and other International Agreements' (1993) 26 *Cornell International Law Journal* 1.

[35] Treaty of the Limitation of Anti-Ballistic Missile Systems, US–USSR, 26 May 1972.

[36] For an overview of the inclusion of 'national means of verification' within arms control treaties see DA Koplow, 'An Inference About Interference: A Surprising Application of Existing International Law to Inhibit Anti-Satellite Weapons' (2014) 35 *University of Pennsylvania Journal of International Law* 737.

identify military equipment by type and capability. The significance of these types of treaties is that they 'effectively establish a right to collect intelligence, at least with respect to assessing compliance with the arms control obligations'.[37]

Treaty-based consent for the collection of confidential information can also derive from the United Nations (UN) Charter and especially the mandatory powers of the UN Security Council. As an example, the United Nations Special Commission (UNSCOM) was a weapons inspection mission that operated in Iraq during the 1990s, which was designed to collect information relating to Iraqi weapons and in particular whether Iraq was in possession of weapons of mass destruction.[38] The activities of this Commission and the fact that they were mandated by the Security Council illustrates that 'the compulsive powers of the United Nations Security Council, operative upon finding a threat to the peace, could be applied to the gathering of critical intelligence and could, moreover, be delegated to another international organ or to a state for the same purpose'.[39]

To summarise, where an actor obtains confidential information but does so with the consent of the actor who controls that information, such conduct cannot be classified as espionage. Whether and to what extent international law applies to this type of information collection falls outside of the research scope of this monograph.

7. Political and Economic Cyber Espionage and the Role of State and Non-State Actors

Since the Treaty of Westphalia 1648, states have been the principal actors within the world order and espionage has thus been an activity typically associated with states.[40] Generally, states seek information that enables them to protect their national security from external threats and this usually means collecting information relating to the political and military affairs of rival states:[41] '[this] include[s] confidential information on political and security affairs, negotiating positions, sensitive economic information and details of policy developments … [as well as] technical information about weapons, details of where troops are located,

[37] Chesterman (n 14) 1091.

[38] SC Res 687 (3 April 1991).

[39] McDougal, Lasswell and Reisman (n 19) 418.

[40] 'Some of the most sophisticated threats to the UK in cyberspace come from other states which seek to conduct espionage with the aim of spying on or compromising our government, military, [and] industrial and economic assets'; UK Cabinet Office, *The UK Cyber Security Strategy: Protecting and Promoting the UK in a Digital World* (2011) para 2.5, www.gov.uk/government/uploads/system/uploads/attachment_data/file/60961/uk-cyber-security-strategy-final.pdf.

[41] 'In the past, espionage activity was typically directed towards obtaining political and military intelligence'; M Herman, *Intelligence Power in Peace and War* (Cambridge, Cambridge University Press, 1996) 9.

information on defences and so on'.[42] This type of information collection is often referred to as traditional espionage, national security espionage or – and the nomenclature preferred by this monograph – political espionage.[43] Where a state conducts political espionage through the medium of cyberspace, I refer to this activity as political cyber espionage.

Traditionally, political espionage is directed against information held by states. However, private actors can also be the targets of political espionage where they operate on behalf of the state and are thus in possession of information that pertains to state activities. For example, in 2007 it was reported that China had hacked into the computer networks and systems of Lockheed Martin (a private company) and obtained sensitive data relating to the design of the F-35 fighter jet, which Lockheed Martin was developing under contract for the US military.[44]

Information held by non-state actors can be the target of political espionage regardless of whether it relates to the performance of state functions. Globalisation has diffused power throughout the international system and non-state actors have become increasingly prominent, including international organisations, non-governmental organisations, terrorist groups, criminal gangs, corporate entities and individuals. Nowadays, non-state actors are capable of engaging in activities that threaten the national security of states. In particular, the emergence of well-organised and heavily armed terrorist groups since the end of the Cold War has profoundly impacted upon the activities of the IC. As President Barack Obama explained in 2014:

> If the fall of the Soviet Union left America without a competing superpower, emerging threats from terrorist groups and the proliferation of weapons of mass destruction place new and, in some ways, more complicated demands on our intelligence agencies.[45]

In short, as the types of actors that can threaten national security have diversified and expanded, so too has the scope and intensity of political (cyber) espionage operations.[46]

[42] MI5: Security Service, 'Targets of Espionage', www.mi5.gov.uk/targets-of-espionage?adhoc_referrer=011719001181.

[43] Mandiant, *APT1: Exposing One of China's Cyber Espionage Units* (2013), www.fireeye.com/content/dam/fireeye-www/services/pdfs/mandiant-apt1-report.pdf.

[44] E Nakashima, 'Confidential Report Lists U.S. Weapons System Designs Compromised by Chinese Cyberspies', 27 May 2013, *Washington Post*, www.washingtonpost.com/world/national-security/confidential-report-lists-us-weapons-system-designs-compromised-by-chinese-cyber-spies/2013/05/27/a42c3e1c-c2dd-11e2-8c3b-0b5e9247e8ca_story.html?utm_term=.e553dc256ecd.

[45] President Barack Obama, *Remarks by the President on Review of Signals Intelligence*, 17 January 2014, www.obamawhitehouse.archives.gov/the-press-office/2014/01/17/remarks-president-review-signals-intelligence.

[46] 'Among the foreign intelligence categories are non-state targets … International terrorist movements and their overseas contacts, merging into state support, have become major non-state targets over the last twenty-five years'; Herman (n 41) 52. 'Given the prevalence of terrorism by non-state actors today, another key function of intelligence collection is to obtain advance notice of planned terrorist attacks originating overseas, whether against a state's embassies or its homeland'; Deeks (n 31) 313. 'The end of the Cold War resulted in a refocusing of national intelligence collection

States also engage in espionage in order to acquire economic information. Since the end of the Cold War, states have increasingly regarded the maintenance of their national security as being contingent upon a prosperous national economy.[47] With a view to promoting economic growth and thus strengthening their national security, states steal trade secrets belonging to companies located within foreign jurisdictions.[48] Once obtained, states pass this information to domestic companies, thereby providing them with an advantage over their foreign competitors.

The state-sponsored theft of trade secrets from companies located within foreign jurisdictions is a practice known as economic espionage.[49] Economic espionage has a long history in international relations[50] and can be traced back 1500 years to a Chinese princess who smuggled silk worms out of China and passed them to an Indian national and by doing so revealed the secrets of silk-making.[51] Yet, 'until recently such experiences have largely remained insignificant with regard to the number of incidents reported and the harm caused over states' economies'.[52] But with the increased emphasis that states now place upon a strong national economy in combination with the widespread use of cyberspace to store confidential business information, instances of economic espionage have risen dramatically.[53] Where economic espionage is committed through cyberspace, I refer to this activity as economic cyber espionage.

As the presence of non-state actors on the international stage has grown, they are not just the targets of espionage but have also become the perpetrators of

priorities away from exclusively state based national defence threats towards non-state threat actors or "global outlaws". The events of 9/11 provided a further catalyst for security intelligence collection capabilities being not just directed at state based threats, but also transnational and sub-state threats such as terrorism, arms, drugs trafficking and the broader human security agenda'; PF Walsh and S Miller, 'Rethinking "Five Eyes" Security Intelligence Collection Policies and Practice Post Snowden' (2016) 31 *Intelligence and National Security* 345, 357.

[47] As Buzan explains, since the end of the Cold War states have equated their national security 'with the economic conditions necessary for [their] survival'; B Buzan, *People, States and Fear: An Agenda for International Security Studies in the Post-Cold War Era* (Colchester, ECPR Press, 2007) 197.

[48] 'Many countries have long considered economic espionage important to national security and economic development'; DP Fidler, 'Economic Cyber Espionage and International Law: Controversies Involving Government Acquisition of Trade Secrets through Cyber Technologies', 20 March 2013, *ASIL Insights*, www.asil.org/insights/volume/17/issue/10/economic-cyber-espionage-and-international-law-controversies-involving.

[49] Mandiant Report (n 43).

[50] 'As long as there have been trade secrets, there have been efforts to steal them in order to gain competitive advantage'; J Strawbridge, 'The Big Bluff: Obama, Cyber Economic Espionage, and the Threat of WTO Litigation' (2016) 47 *Georgetown Journal of International Law* 833, 834.

[51] See K Ziolkowski, 'Peacetime Cyber Espionage – New Tendencies in Public International Law' in K Ziolkowski (ed), *Peacetime Regime for State Activities in Cyberspace: International Law, International Relations and Diplomacy* (CCDCOE, 2013) 425. 'Although the end of the Cold War seemingly brought a surge of economic espionage activity, stealing the ideas of a business competitor is not a new game in the world market. Indeed, economic espionage is a practice that has existed for thousands of years'; H Nasheri, *Economic Espionage and Industrial Spying* (Cambridge, Cambridge University Press, 2005) 18.

[52] I Erdoğan, 'Economic Espionage as a New Form of War in the Post-Cold War Period' (2009) 2 *USAK Yearbook of International Politics and Law* 265, 268.

[53] Although Johnson notes that, 'when it comes to the security agenda of most intelligence services, commerce continues to take a back seat to direct threats to national survival'; LK Johnson, 'Think Again: Spies', 19 November 2009, Foreign Policy, www.foreignpolicy.com/2009/11/19/think-again-spies/.

espionage.[54] Given the speed and ease with which sensitive information can be acquired and under the pressure of a fiercely competitive global market, companies now commit espionage against foreign companies without state support in order to acquire access to the trade secrets of their rivals.[55] Thus, 'governments are not the only participants in the cyber-sleuthing'.[56] The practice of companies engaging in espionage in order to steal trade secrets is known as industrial espionage and, where committed through cyberspace, it is referred to as industrial cyber espionage.[57]

Under customary international law, states are subject to a due diligence obligation to suppress the conduct of non-state actors located within their jurisdiction that causes harm to the legal rights of other states.[58] Under treaty law, those states that are party to the Convention on Cybercrime 2001 have an obligation to enact national laws that criminalise access to computer systems without authorisation and the technical interception without authorisation of non-public transmissions of data within a computer system.[59]

Developing a better understanding of how and to what extent these customary and conventional international legal rules require states to prevent non-state actors within their jurisdiction from engaging in industrial cyber espionage is important given the increase in this type of espionage in the contemporary world order.[60] However, time and space limitations prevent this monograph from engaging in such an inquiry. Instead, this project focuses upon how international law applies to political and economic cyber espionage and this type of espionage is prioritised for legal analysis because the '[t]he greatest threat of electronic attack continues to be posed by State actors'.[61]

[54] 'In the twenty-first century it seems that everyone is eavesdropping on everyone else – government and companies, militaries, law enforcement and intelligence agencies, hackers, criminals, and terrorists'; WC Banks, 'Cyber Espionage and Electronic Surveillance: Beyond the Media Coverage' (2017) 66 *Emory Law Journal* 513, 513.

[55] As Walsh and Miller argue, 'it would be simplistic to portray that only public sector intelligence agencies are involved in economic espionage'; Walsh and Miller (n 46) 360.

[56] Banks (n 54) 516.

[57] Industrial espionage 'describes a company's illegal acquisition of another company's trade secrets with no government involvement'; Fidler (n 48). On the distinction between economic espionage and industrial espionage see K Michal, 'Business Counterintelligence and the Role of the US Intelligence Community' (1994) 7 *International Journal of Intelligence and Counterintelligence* 417.

[58] *Corfu Channel (United Kingdom of Great Britain and Northern Ireland v Albania)*, Judgment (Merits) [1949] ICJ Rep 4.

[59] Articles 2–3 Council of Europe Convention on Cybercrime 2001.

[60] On the application of the due diligence principle to malicious cyber operations conducted by non-state actors see R Buchan, 'Cyberspace, Non-State Actors and the Obligation to Prevent Transboundary Harm' (2016) 21 *Journal of Conflict and Security Law* 429. On the application of the Budapest Convention to malicious cyber operations see P Kastner and F Mégret, 'International Legal Dimensions of Cybercrime' in N Tsagourias and R Buchan (eds), *Research Handbook on International Law and Cyberspace* (Cheltenham, Edward Elgar, 2015) chapter 9.

[61] *Update on the Nature of the Threat Posed by Electronic Attack*, Briefing Provided by GCHQ to the Intelligence and Security Committee (September 2010) www.publications.parliament.uk/pa/cm201213/cmselect/cmdfence/106/10604.htm.

8. Cyber Espionage and International Law

Users of cyberspace implement various defences to protect their computer networks and systems (and the information they hold) from cyber espionage. While technological defences such as anti-spying software provide a certain degree of protection, '[t]echnology alone cannot prevent this larceny';[62] '[i]nternet security is hard … All systems have undiscovered holes in them, and it's only a question of how fast the bad guys can discover the holes compared with how fast the good guys can patch them up'.[63] In light of this, other methods for protecting computer security and data confidentiality become important, such as legal regulation.

States invariably adopt national laws to protect confidential information from political espionage. Overwhelmingly, states classify political espionage as a criminal offence and those convicted of this crime usually receive severe punishments.

States also deploy criminal law frameworks to deter and suppress economic espionage. For instance, the US criminalises economic espionage under the Economic Espionage Act 1996 and this legislation was invoked in May 2014 when a Grand Jury indicted five Chinese military officers for allegedly engaging in cyber espionage in order to steal trade secrets from US companies.[64]

Individuals can also be the victim of espionage. Many states (and certainly liberal democracies) construct legal frameworks that protect the right of their citizens to maintain confidentiality over their personal information and private communications and these frameworks can be utilised to protect against espionage. In the UK, for instance, the Human Rights Act 1998 (which incorporates the European Convention on Human Rights into national law) recognises that individuals possess a fundamental human right to have their private and family life respected (in essence, a right to privacy), a right that can only be restricted where necessary to meet a pressing social need.[65]

It is not the objective of this monograph to engage in a comparative analysis of the domestic legal frameworks adopted by states and to examine the extent to which they apply to cyber espionage. From a practical standpoint, even if national law applies to remote access cyber espionage, it is unlikely that it will be effective in

[62] J Brenner, 'The New Industrial Espionage', 10 December 2014, *American Interest*, www.the-american-interest.com/2014/12/10/the-new-industrial-espionage/.

[63] Tim Berners-Lee, quoted in E Pilkington, 'Tim Berners-Lee: Spies' Cracking of Encryption Undermines the Web', 3 December 2013, *the Guardian*, www.theguardian.com/technology/2013/dec/03/tim-berners-lee-spies-cracking-encryption-web-snowden.

[64] Department of Justice Office of Public Affairs, *U.S. Charges Five Chinese Military Hackers for Cyber Espionage Against U.S. Companies and a Labour Organization for Commercial Advantage*, 19 May 2014, www.justice.gov/opa/pr/us-charges-five-chinese-military-hackers-cyber-espionage-against-us-corporations-and-labor.

[65] Article 8 European Convention on Human Rights.

regulating this practice given the difficulties that states face when trying to exercise their jurisdiction over individuals located abroad. For example, while in May 2014 the US indicted five Chinese officials under the Economic Espionage Act 1996, '[t]he U.S. government knows the likelihood of successfully prosecuting these individuals for violating U.S. criminal law is virtually nil because the cooperation of the Chinese government would be necessary for the U.S. to gain custody and conduct a criminal trial in the U.S.'.[66]

This monograph focuses upon the application of *international law* to cyber espionage. Like national law, international law also suffers from enforcement difficulties. However, unlike domestic law, the advantage of establishing that cyber espionage violates international law is that it provides states with self-help mechanisms (namely, countermeasures) that can be used to induce states into compliance with their international legal obligations. More generally, establishing that cyber espionage contravenes international law rather than national law is beneficial because 'international law serves an expressive function … An assertion that a state has violated international law conveys a different and more potent message than a claim that a particular foreign official violated another state's domestic law.'[67]

9. Peacetime Cyber Espionage

International law is bifurcated into the law of peace and the law of armed conflict and cyber espionage can be committed during times of peace or times of armed conflict. Unlike espionage committed during peacetime, international humanitarian law directly and specifically regulates wartime espionage.

The rules applicable to espionage during armed conflict are contained within the Hague Regulations 1907, the Geneva Conventions 1949, the Additional Protocols to the Geneva Conventions 1977 as well as customary international law. Whether these provisions apply to cyber-enabled espionage raises a number of interesting and difficult interpretative questions.[68] However, due to time and space constraints, this monograph focuses upon the legality of peacetime cyber espionage, which is far more prevalent within the contemporary world order than wartime cyber espionage.

[66] DP Fidler, 'Indictments Show U.S. 'Going on the Offensive'', 19 May 2014, www.info.law.indiana.edu/releases/iu/2014/05/china-cyber-spying.shtml.

[67] AS Deeks, 'Confronting and Adapting: Intelligence Agencies and International Law' (2016) 102 *Virginia Law Review* 599, 614.

[68] On the application of international humanitarian law to cyber espionage see M Longobardo, '(New) Cyber Exploitation and (Old) International Humanitarian Law' (2017) 77 *Zeitschrift für Ausländisches öffentliches Recht und Völkerrecht* 809.

10. Conclusion

This chapter has provided a definition of cyber espionage in order to establish the research scope of this project and to enable us to identify the international legal issues that arise within it. This monograph defines cyber espionage as the non-consensual use of cyber operations to penetrate computer networks and systems with the objective of copying confidential data that is under the control of another actor. In particular, this monograph examines the legality of cyber espionage committed by states for political and economic purposes under international law during times of peace.

2

Cyber Espionage and International Peace and Security

1. Introduction

This chapter situates cyber espionage within its broader theoretical context. As the Edward Snowden revelations demonstrate, states possess an extraordinary technological capacity to acquire access to confidential electronic information. This does not mean, however, that the exercise of this capacity is a desirable feature of international relations.[1] With this in mind, the objective of this chapter is to evaluate the impact that political and economic cyber espionage has upon the maintenance of international peace and security. More specifically, this chapter determines whether political and economic cyber espionage should be prohibited by international law.

2. Political Cyber Espionage

2.1. Realism

Political espionage is typically justified on the basis of realist theory.[2] The argument runs that states exist in a Hobbesian state of nature (that is, anarchy) because the world order does not possess an overarching government that is capable of guaranteeing their survival in the system. In the absence of protection from a centralised authority, states bear the responsibility for maintaining their own security. In such an environment, states must acquire sufficient material power – or,

[1] As President Obama recognised in the context of signals intelligence, 'America's capabilities are unique, and the power of new technologies means that there are fewer and fewer technical constraints on what we can do. That places a special obligation on us to ask tough questions about what we should do'; President Barack Obama, *Remarks by the President on Review of Signals Intelligence*, 17 January 2014, www.obamawhitehouse.archives.gov/the-press-office/2014/01/17/remarks-president-review-signals-intelligence.

[2] M Herman, *Intelligence Power in Peace and War* (Cambridge, Cambridge University Press, 1996). For classic texts on realist theory see HJ Morgenthau, *Politics Among Nations: The Struggle for Power and Peace* (New York, McGraw-Hill, 1985) and KN Waltz, *Theory of International Politics* (London, McGraw-Hill, 1979).

at a minimum, ally with more powerful states – in order to deter potential aggressors and, if necessary, to repel them. All in all, national security is maintained and international peace and security is achieved where there is a balance of power between states.[3]

A balance of power can only be attained where states are aware of the strengths and weaknesses of other states in the system.[4] In the realist world order, the benefit of espionage is that it enables states to access sensitive information relating to their (actual or potential) enemies and, ultimately, to better understand their intentions and capabilities.[5] In particular, espionage allows states to identify threats to their national security before they materialise.[6] Once a state is aware of a threat, it is provided with a window of opportunity to negotiate with the aggressor and attempt to resolve the dispute peacefully. If an amicable solution cannot be reached, the threatened state will be at least aware of the threat's existence and will be able to take steps to counter it during its incipient stage or, if it cannot be thwarted, to put in place measures to mitigate the harm that it produces. In the words of Parks:

> Nations collect intelligence to deter or minimize the likelihood of surprise attack; to facilitate diplomatic, economic, and military action, in defense of a nation in the event of hostilities; and in times of 'neither peace nor war,' to deter or defend against actions by individuals, groups, or a nation that would constitute a threat to international peace and security (such as acts of terrorism).[7]

[3] '[W]ars usually begin when two nations disagree on their relative strength, and wars usually cease when the fighting nations agree on their relative strength'; G Blainey, *The Causes of War* (New York, Free Press, 1988) 293.

[4] 'In an anarchical order, understanding the intentions and capabilities of other actors has always been an important part of statecraft'; S Chesterman, 'The Spy Who Came in from the Cold War: Intelligence and International Law' (2006) 27 *Michigan Journal of International Law* 1071, 1076.

[5] 'Responsible leaders in every nation seek knowledge – and, ideally foreknowledge – of the world around them. For with a better understanding of global affairs, they are apt to protect and advance more effectively the vital interests of their citizens'; LK Johnson, *Secret Agencies: US Intelligence in a Hostile World* (New York, Yale University Press, 1996) 1. As Sun Tzu declared many centuries ago, '[w]hat enables the wise sovereign and the good general to strike and conquer, and achieve things beyond the reach of ordinary men, is foreknowledge'; S Tzu (J Clavell ed), *The Art of War* (New York, Dell, 1983) 77.

[6] 'Espionage is regarded by States as a necessary tool for pursuing their foreign policy and security interests, and for maintaining the balance of power at the inter-State level'; C Schaller, 'Spies' (2009) *Max Planck Encyclopaedia of Public International Law*, para 2. Parks argues that states regard espionage 'as a vital necessity in the national security process'; WH Parks, 'The International Law of Intelligence Collection' in JN Moore and RF Turner (eds), *National Security Law* (Durham, North Carolina, Carolina Academic Press, 1999) 433.

[7] Parks (n 6) 433–34. 'Intelligence gathering has been, and continues to be, a means of looking to the future for answers. It provides knowledge concerning the activities of enemies before they constitute an immediate threat. Having access to early information on potential threats allows states to take precautionary measures to prevent war. Armed with a more complete information picture, a state can communicate its concerns to rivals, engage in negotiation and diplomatic overtures, and potentially settle differences in a peaceful manner'; G Sulmasy and J Yoo, 'Counterintuitive: Intelligence Operations and International Law' (2007) 28 *Michigan Journal of International Law* 625, 633. '[S]pying may serve the common-interest function of warning the spying state of the other's preparations for surprise attack'; J Stone, 'Legal Problems of Espionage in Conditions of Modern Conflict' in

During the Cold War, the US projected this realist view of the world order to justify its espionage operations.[8] For example, on 1 May 1960 the Soviet Union shot down a US spy plane that was within Soviet airspace. President Eisenhower defended the US's use of aerial reconnaissance on the grounds that '[n]o one wants another Pearl Harbour. This means that we must have knowledge of military forces and preparations around the world, especially those capable of massive surprise attacks'.[9]

Espionage is also justified on the basis that states are frequently confronted with threats to their national security that are exaggerated or even unfounded and, where espionage reveals that a threat is not as grave or as pressing as initially thought, an otherwise combustible situation is diffused. For example, after its spy plane was shot down in May 1960, the US announced that it would terminate its use of aerial reconnaissance within Soviet airspace. However, the US continued to spy on the Soviet Union with satellites operating in outer space. Spy satellites were considered to be a far more effective method for capturing confidential information than reconnaissance aircraft and, in the words of one US official, they allowed an 'enormous floodlight' to be shone into a 'darkened warehouse'.[10] According to US President Lyndon B Johnson:

> We've spent $35 or $40 billion on the space program … And if nothing else had come out of it except the knowledge we gained from space photography, it would be worth 10 times what the whole program has cost. Because tonight we know how many missiles the enemy had and, it turned out, our guesses were way off. We were doing things we didn't need to do. We were building things we didn't need to build. We were harboring fears we didn't need to harbor.[11]

Similarly, commentators invoke realist theory to justify the use of espionage against non-state actors that threaten national security, such as terrorists. Commentators claim that the use of espionage against terrorists is necessary because it allows states to better understand the nature of the threat that they represent.[12]

RJ Stanger (ed), *Essays on Espionage and International Law* (Ohio, Ohio State University Press, 1962) 42. '[S]urveillance tends to amplify the raw power of states to survive and – depending on how sophisticated their surveillance techniques are – to accrue power through political and military advantage'; A Deeks, 'An International Legal Framework for Surveillance' (2015) 55 *Virginia Journal of International Law* 291, 323.

[8] For an overview of this incident see T Wicker, 'Powers is Freed by Soviet in an Exchange for Abel, U-2 Pilot on Way to U.S.', 10 February 1962, *New York Times*, www.archive.nytimes.com/www.nytimes.com/learning/general/onthisday/big/0210.html?action=click&contentCollection=meter-links-click&contentId=&mediaId=&module=meter-Links&pgtype=article&priority=true&referrer=&version=meter+at+null.

[9] Statement of President Eisenhower, 42 *Department of State Bulletin* 1091, 11 May 1960, 851–52.

[10] Albert D Wheelon, quoted in WJ Broad, 'Spy Satellites' Early Role as "Floodlight" Coming Clear', 12 September 1995, *New York Times*, www.nytimes.com/1995/09/12/science/spy-satellites-early-role-as-floodlight-coming-clear.html.

[11] Quoted in JT Richelson, *America's Secret Eyes in Space: The U.S. Keyhole Spy Satellite Program* (New York, Harper & Row, 1975) 93.

[12] In response to the Snowden revelations Congressman Mike J Rogers, former Chairman of the House Intelligence Committee, justified the NSA's surveillance activities on the basis that they were

In particular, their argument is that espionage enables states to identify which individuals are involved in terrorist organisations and to pinpoint with greater specificity when and where terrorist attacks will occur. With this information in hand, states can position themselves more effectively, putting in place defensive measures that can eliminate the threat or at least diminish its severity. As President Obama explained, '[intelligence operations] have prevented multiple [terrorist] attacks and saved innocent lives – not just here in the United States, but around the globe'.[13]

To summarise, under the influence of realist theory, commentators assert that political espionage is a necessary and desirable feature of international relations because it can 'actually *promote* the potential for peace and reduce international tension'.[14] As a result, scholars maintain that any attempt by international law to prevent or constrain politically motivated espionage 'will likely prove counter-productive to the goal of promoting international peace and stability'.[15] Indeed, these authors go so far as to say that the 'international regulation of intelligence operations could have the perverse effect of making international conflict more, rather than less, likely … Simply stated, it is not in the interests of nation-states or the international system to permit regulation of their intelligence-gathering activities.'[16]

2.2. The International Society

If the dynamics of international relations can be explained by realist theory, the defence of espionage outlined above is convincing and it points to the conclusion that international law should not prohibit political espionage. Yet, while realism has been '[t]he dominant approach in international relations theory for virtually the past two millennia',[17] realism does not accurately capture the nature or structure of the *contemporary* world order.

When faced with the devastation wrought by the Second World War, states came to the realisation that realist theory provided a far too precarious basis upon which to build a peaceful world order. In short, history demonstrated that it is

necessary to confront the threat posed by the terrorist organisation known as ISIS; R Carroll, 'NSA Surveillance Needed to Prevent ISIS Attack, Claims Former Intelligence Chair', 22 April 2015, *the Guardian*, www.theguardian.com/us-news/2015/apr/22/mass-surveillance-needed-isis-attack-mike-rogers.

[13] President Barack Obama, *Remarks by the President on Review of Signals Intelligence*, 17 January 2014, www.obamawhitehouse.archives.gov/the-press-office/2014/01/17/remarks-president-review-signals-intelligence.

[14] Sulmasy and Yoo (n 7) 634.

[15] ibid 625.

[16] ibid 626. In the context of threats posed by terrorist actors, Sulmasy and Yoo note that '[i]f international law prevents a nation-state from engaging in intelligence gathering, some of the immediate beneficiaries would be international terrorists'; ibid 636. See generally H Scoville, 'Is Espionage Necessary for our Security?' (1976) 54 *Foreign Affairs* 482.

[17] A-M Slaughter, 'International Law in a World of Liberal States' (1995) 6 *EJIL* 503, 507.

incredibly difficult if not impossible for states to effectively balance their material power, not least because alliances can shift quickly and capriciously and because states often fail to accurately identify each other's capabilities and intentions. In light of this, states sought to devise a more effective system for maintaining international peace and security.

Significantly, states recognised that, notwithstanding their various differences (political, legal, cultural etc), they nevertheless embraced a number of common interests and values. More importantly, states recognised that they could protect these interests and values by establishing principles and rules that delineated the standards of acceptable behaviour within international relations.[18]

Most notably, with the massive inter-state violence of the Second World War still fresh in their minds, states recognised that they shared a common interest in protecting their territorial integrity and political independence from external intervention. In response, states created an international society – whose association was later institutionalised by the United Nations (UN)[19] – that was predicated upon the principle of the sovereign equality of states. At the heart of this principle is the belief that, 'whatever inequality may exist between states as regards their size, power, degree of civilization, wealth and other qualities, they are nevertheless equals as international persons'.[20] Thus, within the international society all states *qua* states are sovereign equals and, as such, they are entitled to organise their internal affairs free from external intervention.[21] In a nutshell, sovereignty means 'leave us alone'.[22] By requiring states to abstain from interfering in each other's sovereign affairs, the objective of the international society is to maintain national security and, by implication, international peace and security.

Given these normative and institutional developments, the international society has succeeded in supplanting the Hobbesian state of nature. States no longer inhabit a world order that is unpredictable and dangerous but instead an international society that is principled and ordered.[23] In such an environment, the realist

[18] H Bull, *The Anarchical Society: A Study of Order in World Politics* (Basingstoke, Palgrave, 2002).

[19] '[T]he UN has been called upon to play the role of implementation mechanism … the UN ultimately acts in the interest and on behalf of the whole world community, of which it is the legitimate representative'; A Cassese, *International Law in a Divided World* (Oxford, Clarendon Press, 1986) 159.

[20] L Oppenheim, *International Law: A Treatise, Volume I* (London, Longmans Green & Co, 1920–21) 15.

[21] As Bull observes, 'from the perspective of any particular state what it chiefly hopes to gain from participation in the society of states is recognition of its independence of outside authority, and in particular of its supreme jurisdiction over its subjects and territory. The chief price it has to pay for this is recognition of like rights to independence and sovereignty on the part of other states'; Bull (n 18) 16–17. In a similar vein, Wight explains that 'it would be impossible to have a society of sovereign states unless each state, while claiming sovereignty for itself, recognised that every other state had the right to claim and enjoy its own sovereignty as well'; M Wight (H Bull ed), *Systems of States* (Leicester, Leicester University Press, 1977) 135.

[22] L Henkin, 'That "S" Word: Sovereignty, and Globalization, and Human Rights, Et Cetera' (1999) 68 *Fordham Law Review* 1, 5.

[23] In the celebrated words of McDougal and Feliciano, by situating the principle of the sovereign equality of states as its foundational norm, the objective of the international society is to achieve a 'minimum world public order'; MS McDougal and FP Feliciano, *Law and Minimum World Public Order* (New Haven, Yale University Press, 1961).

justification for political espionage dissipates.[24] In fact, within the confines of the international society, stealing confidential information belonging to another state (or indeed any actor located within another state) is reprehensible because it interferes with that state's right to determine its internal affairs without external intervention. In this sense, political espionage impinges upon state sovereignty, undermines national security and thus represents a threat to the maintenance of international peace and security. However, there are limited circumstances in which political espionage is acceptable within the international society. For example, acts of political espionage that violate state sovereignty are excusable where they are undertaken by a state in order to counteract a grave and imminent threat to one of its essential interests.

With the construction of the international society in 1945, the sovereign equality of states became a key organising principle of international relations. Yet, in order to maintain international peace and security, the international society determined that other common values and interests must be pursued and secured. For example, the UN Charter makes a number of references to the importance of protecting 'the dignity and worth of the human person'.[25] Indeed, as early as 1948, the (non-binding) Universal Declaration of Human Rights (UDHR) was adopted under the auspices of the UN, which also emphasises the importance of protecting human dignity. Note that the international society's commitment to promoting respect for human dignity is not antithetical to or irreconcilable with the international society's commitment to protecting the sovereign equality of states. The international society continues to regard all states as sovereign equals but their sovereignty is fettered to the extent that they have agreed not to act in a manner that is incompatible with the protection of human dignity.[26] Thus, the international society is able to protect the principle of sovereign equality between states and, at the same time and without any normative conflict arising, to promote respect for human dignity within sovereign states.

[24] Radsan, however, continues to view the world order through a realist lens and it is for this reason that he continues to perceive the benefits accrued by political espionage: '[t]he world is simply too dangerous for national leaders to turn a blind eye to external threats. The need for intelligence about one's neighbours and their political, military, and economic development is paramount. In a faster and more integrated world, states can lose their competitive edge very quickly. As one country achieves a breakthrough in technology, another country closes the technological gap through state-sponsored theft. In a dog-eat-dog competition, even friends and allies spy on each other. Loyalty, if there is any, is to national interests, not to the international interest. Until the system of nation-states is replaced, until regional and international integration really take hold, intelligence services will be around to do their states' bidding'; AJ Radsan, 'The Unresolved Equation of Espionage and International Law' (2007) 28 *Michigan Journal of International Law* 595, 613.

[25] Preamble UN Charter. See also Articles 1(3) and 55(c) UN Charter. 'The inclusion of the human rights language in the Charter of the United Nations was a critical juncture that channeled the history of postwar global governance in the direction of setting international norms and law about the international promotion of human rights'; K Sikkink, 'Latin American Countries as Norm Protagonists of the Idea of International Human Rights' (2014) 20 *Global Governance* 389, 395.

[26] In fact, the international society has always fettered state sovereignty because the principle of the sovereign equality of states requires states to abstain from exercising their sovereignty in a manner that intervenes in the internal affairs of other states.

The onset of the Cold War at the start of the 1950s raised the possibility of a third world war and in particular a world war that may involve nuclear conflict. Determined to prevent this, the protection of state sovereignty rapidly emerged as the international society's overriding (and even sole) objective, consuming much of its time, energy and resources and thus preventing it from pursuing its other interests and objectives.[27]

The end of the Cold War represented a seminal moment in the history of the international society because it substantially reduced the possibility of a third world war and also signalled the 'triumph' of liberal democracy as the only legitimate form of political governance within the international society.[28] The end of the Cold War therefore ushered in a 'new world order'[29] that engendered an international political environment that permitted the international society to finally champion its other values and objectives, such as the promotion of human dignity.[30] Since 1990, the international society – acting largely but not exclusively through the UN – has regularly expressed its commitment to promoting human dignity within member states and has determined that where individuals are deprived of their human dignity the maintenance of international peace and security is threatened.[31] Maintaining state sovereignty of course remains a key objective of the international society: but the point being made is that since the end of the Cold War the international society has become far more ambitious and, with the objective of maintaining international peace and security, is equally concerned with the promotion of human dignity.

Fundamentally, human dignity is protected where individuals are free to determine their own destinies.[32] In essence, human dignity necessitates individual autonomy.[33] A core feature of individual autonomy is that human beings possess

[27] B Frederking, *The United States and the Security Council: Collective Security Since the Cold War* (London, Routledge, 2007) 13 (explaining that during the Cold War 'the traditional notion of state sovereignty trumped human rights … How states treated their own citizens was considered a domestic matter').

[28] C Brown, '"Really Existing Liberalism", Peaceful Democracies and International Order' in R Fawn and J Larkins (eds), *International Society after the Cold War: Anarchy and Order Reconsidered* (Basingstoke, Palgrave Macmillan, 1996) 30 ('it does make some sense to talk of the triumph of Western Liberalism').

[29] President George HW Bush, *Address Before a Joint Session of the Congress on the State of the Union*, 29 January 1991, www.presidency.ucsb.edu/ws/?pid=19253.

[30] G Simpson, 'Two Liberalisms' (2001) 12 *EJIL* 537, 556–60.

[31] 'The absence of war and military conflicts amongst States does not in itself ensure international peace and security. The non-military sources of instability in the economic, social, humanitarian and ecological fields have become threats to peace and security. The United Nations membership as a whole, working through the appropriate bodies, needs to give the highest priority to the solution of these matters'; Note by the President of the Security Council, UN Doc S/23500, 31 January 1992, 3. For a review of UN practice linking the maintenance of international peace and security with the protection of human rights see R Buchan, *International Law and the Construction of the Liberal Peace* (Oxford, Hart Publishing, 2013) chapter 4.

[32] D Beyleveld and R Brownsword, *Human Dignity in Bioethics and Biolaw* (Oxford, Oxford University Press, 2001) 52.

[33] J Griffin, *On Human Rights* (Oxford, Oxford University Press, 2008) chapter 8.

the right to maintain confidentiality over their personal information and private communications. Privacy is crucial to the enjoyment of individual autonomy because it allows human beings to exercise their intellect and rationality and make up their own minds as to what aspects of their private lives are exposed to public scrutiny. Moreover, privacy allows human beings to be critical of the political, economic and social issues that impact upon their lives and to share and develop their ideas with other members of their community, that is, to pursue autonomous development.[34]

Where a state engages in political espionage and obtains confidential information belonging to an individual, this conduct constitutes a violation of that individual's privacy, individual autonomy and human dignity. If nowadays the international society insists that the maintenance of international peace and security is contingent upon the protection of human dignity, it follows that acts of political espionage against individuals constitutes a threat to the maintenance of international peace and security, even if the severity of this threat differs depending upon the intensity and frequency of the espionage. There are, however, narrow circumstances in which it is acceptable for states to engage in political espionage against individuals even though it violates the principle of human dignity. For instance, states are justified in undertaking acts of political espionage against individuals (such as terrorists) where they are engaged in conduct that poses a grave and imminent threat to one of their essential interests.

The dawn of cyberspace has 'escalated'[35] the threat that political espionage represents to the maintenance of international peace and security. The reason for this lies in the features of cyberspace and the fact that they enable espionage to be perpetrated on an 'unprecedented scale' within the contemporary international society.[36] First, cyberspace is used as a storage and communicative device, granting cyber spies 'access to databases that contain tremendous amounts of data and metadata'.[37] Second, data stored in cyberspace can be accessed remotely and at speed, meaning that cyber espionage circumvents many of the practical problems usually associated with acquiring physical access to confidential information.[38] Third, because of the potential for identity spoofing, it is very difficult to attribute

[34] NM Richards, 'The Dangers of Surveillance' (2013) 126 *Harvard Law Review* 1934, 1945–52.

[35] K Ziolkowski, 'Peacetime Cyber Espionage – New Tendencies in Public International Law' in K Ziolkowski (ed), *Peacetime Regime for State Activities in Cyberspace: International Law, International Relations and Diplomacy* (CCDCOE, 2013) 463.

[36] European Parliament Committee on Civil Liberties, Justice and Home Affairs, *Draft Report on the US NSA Surveillance Programme, Surveillance Bodies in Various Member States and their Impact on EU Citizens' Fundamental Rights and on Transatlantic Cooperation in Justice and Home Affairs*, 23 December 2013, EP Doc 2013/2188(INI) 16.

[37] I Kilovaty, 'World Wide Web of Exploitations – The Case of Peacetime Cyber Espionage Operations under International Law: Towards a Contextual Approach' (2016) 18 *Columbia Science and Technology Review* 42, 66.

[38] '[Cyberspace is] an unbounded virtual operational venue characterised by speed and an immediacy of results'; H Snyder and A Crescenzi, 'Intellectual Capital and Economic Espionage: New Crimes and New Protections' (2009) 16 *Journal of Financial Crime* 245, 247.

cyber operations to their authors,[39] making cyber espionage a relatively risk-free enterprise.[40] Consequently, and as one commentator puts it, cyberspace has created an environment that is 'God's gift to spies'.[41]

All in all, if the overriding objective of the international society is to maintain international peace and security by protecting the principles of the sovereign equality of states and human dignity, these broad, declarative political principles must be backed up and enforced by binding international legal rules. Hence, it is imperative that the international society implements rules of international law that unambiguously prohibit political espionage and, given its perniciousness, cyber-enabled political espionage in particular. This being said, these legal rules must nevertheless recognise that states are permitted to undertake political (cyber) espionage where it is necessary to address grave and imminent threats to their essential interests.

2.3. Espionage and International Cooperation

Since the end of the Cold War the international society has identified various threats to the maintenance of international peace and security, such as environmental degradation, drug and people trafficking, economic instability, poverty and disease (pandemic influenza, HIV/AIDS, Ebola etc).[42] It is axiomatic that the international society can only resolve these threats to international peace and security where its member states enjoy close and effective cooperation.

Baker argues that espionage is a desirable feature of international relations that must be permitted (or rather tolerated) by international law because it plays a key role in fostering trust and cooperation between states.[43] The gist of his argument is that spying allows states to verify whether other states are complying with their international commitments. Baker contends that where states insist that

[39] The National Counterintelligence Executive explains that in cyberspace state and non-state actors can now 'quickly steal and transfer massive quantities of data while remaining anonymous and hard to detect'; Office of the National Counterintelligence Executive, *Foreign Spies Stealing US Economic Secrets in Cyberspace: Report to Congress on Foreign Economic Collection and Industrial Espionage, 2009–2011* (2011) i. Brenner describes the Internet as 'one big masquerade ball' where actors 'can hide behind aliases … [and] can surreptitiously enslave other computers'; J Brenner, *America the Vulnerable: Inside the New Threat Matrix of Digital Espionage, Crime, and Warfare* (Penguin Press, 2011) 32.

[40] '[Foreign actors] remain undeterred from conducting reconnaissance, espionage, and even attacks in cyberspace because of the relatively low costs of entry, the perceived payoff, and the lack of significant consequences'; JR Clapper, Director of National Intelligence, *Statement for the Records to the Senate Armed Services Committee, Worldwide Threat Assessment of the U.S. Intelligence Community*, 9 February 2016, 3.

[41] James Lewis, Senior Vice President at the Centre for Strategic and International Studies, quoted in DP Fidler, 'Tinker, Tailor, Soldier, Duqu: Why Cyberespionage is More Dangerous than You Think' (2012) 5 *International Journal of Critical Infrastructure Protection* 28, 29.

[42] For a discussion see ME Footer, J Schmidt, ND White and L Davies-Bright (eds), *Security in International Law* (Oxford, Hart Publishing, 2016).

[43] CD Baker, 'Tolerance of International Espionage: A Functional Approach' (2003) 19 *American University International Law Review* 1091.

they are complying with their international obligations and, through espionage, this is revealed to be true, a sense of trust will emerge within the international society.[44] As a result, states will be more willing to cooperate across functional lines and this will lead to the conclusion of additional agreements. These agreements, Baker suggests, will enable common problems to be resolved and, consequentially, this will have a positive impact upon international peace and security. As Baker puts it:

> Mutual trust between treaty parties increases when espionage affirms that the assurances provided are accurate. States will be more willing to cooperate with other states in the future if their espionage confirms that the assurances provided by these parties are truthful.[45]

From a theoretical perspective, Baker's functional defence of espionage is unconvincing for two reasons. First, a central claim of this chapter is that the collection of confidential information belonging to another state (or an actor located within another state) violates the victim state's right to organise its internal affairs free from external intervention. If this is the case, while the spying state may benefit from acquiring confidential information belonging to another state (which, and as Baker rightly claims, may encourage the spying state to cooperate with the state that it has spied upon), the fact of the matter is that such conduct violates the sovereignty of the victim state. Indeed, given that the sovereign equality of states represents a constitutional principle of the international society,[46] acts of espionage undermine the authority and integrity of the international society more generally. Intuitively, it seems unlikely that the members of the international society would trust a state and be prepared to cooperate with a state that flagrantly violates a fundamental norm of the society within which it operates. Said differently, espionage breeds mistrust and hostility. Thus, contrary to Baker's claim, my argument is that espionage represents a barrier to close and effective cooperation, thereby preventing states from addressing matters that threaten international peace and security. As Fidler explains, espionage is '[far from] harmless. It can create significant costs, disrupt national security strategies, and destabilize relations between nations'.[47]

Second, even if we accept Baker's claim that espionage promotes cooperation between states, this defence does not justify state-sponsored espionage that is

[44] 'When armed with such tools as spying and eavesdropping, states enjoy greater certainty that they will be able to validate international compliance, or at least detect when other participants are failing to comply with the treaty'; ibid 1104.

[45] ibid 1105 (citations omitted).

[46] 'The sovereignty and equality of states represent the basic constitutional doctrine of the law of nations'; I Brownlie, *Principles of Public International Law* (Oxford, Oxford University Press, 2008) 289.

[47] DP Fidler, 'Wither the Web?: International Law, Cybersecurity, and Critical Infrastructure Protection' (Fall 2015) *Georgetown Journal of International Affairs* 8, 12. 'Cyber espionage contributes to tension escalation across the world'; N Jupillat, 'From the Cuckoo's Egg to Global Surveillance: Cyber Espionage that Becomes Prohibited Intervention' (2017) 42 *North Carolina Journal of International Law and Commercial Regulation* 933, 935.

directed against individuals, a prevalent practice within the international society. How does stealing confidential information belonging to individuals unconnected to a foreign government facilitate international cooperation? My view is that this type of espionage interferes with the sovereignty of the state that hosts the targeted individual as well as violating that individual's human dignity. As we saw previously, state sovereignty and human dignity are two of the fundamental principles underpinning the international society. Thus, political espionage against individuals also engenders distrust and acrimony within the international society, thereby impeding its endeavours to resolve threats to the maintenance of international peace and security.

Perhaps most importantly, Baker's functional defence of espionage is not supported by state practice. Rather, state practice supports my theory that espionage has a chilling effect upon cooperation within the international society. Consider, for example, the Soviet Union's shooting down of a US spy plane in May 1960. This incident prompted a marked deterioration in relations between the US and the Soviet Union which, in turn, had a negative impact upon the maintenance of international peace and security. Notably, the Four Powers Peace Summit was held in Paris in mid-May 1960 (just days after the US's spy plane was shot down) and was intended to provide the US, the UK, France and the Soviet Union with the opportunity to discuss many of the world's most pressing problems (and which was billed by the UK as a conference 'on which the nations of the world had built so much hope').[48] The Summit effectively collapsed at the end of the first day, with the Soviet Union President Nikita Khrushchev making it clear that he laid the blame for this collapse with the US's involvement in espionage.[49] The deleterious impact that the US's espionage had upon international cooperation was well captured by Tunisia in the immediate aftermath of the Summit's collapse. Before the Security Council, Tunisia explained:

> The entire world placed great hopes on the Summit Conference of 15 May which was so unfortunately interrupted. It regarded that Conference as a means of ensuring the relaxation of international tension, of removing the danger of a terrible world war, and of seeking a formula for truly peaceful coexistence between different nations on the basis of freedom, law and justice. We had hoped that understanding which might have been reached at the Summit Conference would help to facilitate the peaceful solution of certain problems, vital for us and for the whole world, which the persistence of the cold war had made it impossible to solve in the spirit of the lofty principles of the Charter. That indicates how deeply we were disappointed by the failure of the Conference.[50]

Poland also criticised the US's involvement in espionage and emphasised its detrimental impact upon international cooperation. Poland explained that this activity

[48] 858th Meeting of the Security Council, UN Doc S/PV.858, 24 May 1960, para 37 (British Ambassador).

[49] '1960: East–West Summit in Tatters after Spy Plane Row', 17 May 1960, *BBC News*, www.news.bbc.co.uk/onthisday/hi/dates/stories/may/17/newsid_2512000/2512335.stm.

[50] 859th Meeting of the Security Council, UN Doc S/PV.859, 25 May 1960, para 19 (Tunisian Ambassador).

represented an attempt by the US to replace the principled nature of the international society with the 'law of the jungle'[51] and went on to note that such conduct 'would lead us straight into chaos and lawlessness'.[52]

The negative impact that *cyber* espionage has upon the potential for close and effective international cooperation is illustrated by the fallout from the 2013 Edward Snowden disclosures. In particular, Brazilian President Dilma Rousseff was scheduled to travel to Washington DC on a state visit to meet representatives from the Obama administration to discuss issues affecting regional and international stability.[53] Upon hearing the Snowden revelations, President Rousseff cancelled this visit and instead chose to travel to New York to formally denounce the US's activities before the UN General Assembly. When doing so, President Rousseff explained that cyber espionage violates state sovereignty and hinders effective international cooperation:

> Friendly governments and societies that seek to build a true strategic partnership, as in our case, cannot allow recurring illegal actions to take place as if they were normal. They are unacceptable.[54]

Similar concerns were echoed within the Security Council when the Ecuadorian Ambassador identified the 'global mistrust generated by massive espionage'[55] and, repeating comments made by Bolivia to MERCOSUR (a South American trading bloc) in July 2013, 'warn[ed] the international community about the seriousness of these actions [US cyber espionage], which imply a threat to the security and peaceful coexistence among our States'.[56] The Pro-Tempore President of MERCOSUR also submitted a Note Verbale to the UN Secretary-General explaining that US cyber espionage was 'detrimental to the normal conduct of relations among nations'.[57]

After it was revealed that the NSA had spied on German Chancellor Angela Merkel, the Chancellor's spokesperson Steffen Seibert explained that Merkel was 'livid' and had telephoned US President Barack Obama to inform him that the NSA's actions represented a 'serious breach of confidence'.[58] In fact, the German

[51] 858th Meeting of the Security Council (n 48) para 95 (Polish Ambassador).

[52] ibid para 98.

[53] S Romero, 'Brazil's Leader Postpones State Visit to Washington Over Spying', 17 September 2013, *New York Times*, www.nytimes.com/2013/09/18/world/americas/brazils-leader-postpones-state-visit-to-us.html.

[54] J Borger, 'Brazilian President: US Surveillance a 'Breach of International Law'', 24 September 2013, *the Guardian*, www.theguardian.com/world/2013/sep/24/brazil-president-un-speech-nsa-surveillance.

[55] 7015th Meeting of the Security Council, UN Doc S/PV.7015 (Resumption 1), 6 August 2013, 13, www.un.org/en/ga/search/view_doc.asp?symbol=S/PV.7015(Resumption1).

[56] ibid 12.

[57] Note Verbale dated 22 July 2013 from the Permanent Mission of the Bolivarian Republic of Venezuela to the United Nations Addressed to the Secretary-General, UN Doc A/67/946, 29 July 2013, 2, www.repository.un.org/bitstream/handle/11176/303964/A_67_946-EN.pdf?sequence=3&isAllowed=y.

[58] I Traynor, P Oltermann and P Lewis, 'Angela Merkel's Call to Obama: Are You Bugging My Phone?', 24 October 2013, *the Guardian*, www.theguardian.com/world/2013/oct/23/us-monitored-angela-merkel-german.

Chancellor publicly stated that 'we need to have trust in our allies and partners, and this must now be established once again. I repeat that spying among friends is not at all acceptable against anyone, and that goes for every citizen in Germany.'[59] It is clear from the language used by Chancellor Merkel that the US's cyber espionage against Germany had seriously diminished the 'trust' and 'confidence' between these states, presumably threatening their ability to collaborate effectively. Indeed, it is telling that in response to the allegations of US espionage, Germany cancelled a long-standing agreement with the US that allowed the US to request surveillance data from Germany's intelligence services when it related to the safety of American troops stationed in Germany. Germany's Minister of Foreign Affairs, Guido Westerwelle, explained that the decision to suspend the 1968 agreement was 'a necessary and correct consequence' to the US's spying activities.[60]

That cyber espionage has a debilitating effect upon international cooperation was also the view of the Parliamentary Assembly for the Council of Europe which, when reflecting upon the diplomatic fallout caused by the Snowden leaks, explained:

> The Assembly also recognises the need for transatlantic co-operation in the fight against terrorism and other forms of organised crime. It considers that such co-operation must be based on mutual trust founded on international agreements, respect for human rights and the rule of law. This trust has been *severely damaged* by the mass surveillance practices revealed in the Snowden files.[61]

Even US President Barack Obama recognised that political cyber espionage can disrupt cooperation within the international society. In response to the Snowden revelations the US President adopted Presidential Policy Directive 28, which places limits upon the ability of US intelligence agencies to collect signals intelligence. Notably, this Directive acknowledges that 'signals intelligence activities … pose multiple risks. These include risks to … our relationships with other nations, including the cooperation we receive from other nations on law enforcement, counterterrorism, and other issues'.[62]

The disruptive effect that political cyber espionage has upon international cooperation and the efforts of the international society to address threats to international peace and security provides an additional justification for why

[59] J Ball, 'NSA Monitored Calls of 35 World Leaders After US Official Handed Over Contacts', 25 October 2013, *the Guardian*, www.theguardian.com/world/2013/oct/24/nsa-surveillance-world-leaders-calls.

[60] L Smith-Spark and S Simons, 'Germany Ends Information Sharing Pact with Britain, Unites States', 3 August 2013, *CNN* www.edition.cnn.com/2013/08/03/world/europe/germany-uk-privacy/index.html.

[61] Parliamentary Assembly of the Council of Europe, *Mass Surveillance*, Resolution 2045 (2015) para 12 (emphasis added).

[62] *Presidential Policy Directive – Signals Intelligence Activities*, Policy Directive/PPD-28, 17 January 2014, www.obamawhitehouse.archives.gov/the-press-office/2014/01/17/presidential-policy-directive-signals-intelligence-activities.

international law must clearly prohibit such conduct. In the words of Fleck, the use of international law to restrict this type of activity can 'advocate for self-restraint in the interest of confidence-building and stable peace'.[63]

3. Economic Cyber Espionage

The demise of the Soviet Union at the end of the Cold War is largely attributed to its 'failed internal economy'[64] and '[t]he fate of the Soviet Union [thus] provide[s] a stark reminder that national security rests on a strong economic foundation, not mere military strength'.[65] Since the end of the Cold War, then, '[n]ations around the world recognize that economic superiority is increasingly as important as military superiority'[66] and that 'the strength of national economies can ultimately be linked to national security'.[67] Crucial to a state's economic prosperity is that companies within its jurisdiction are successful, thereby generating jobs, paying taxes and making the company (and thus the state) attractive for domestic and foreign investors.

Due to various technological innovations – for example, the emergence of commercial aviation and the dawn of cyberspace – the marketplace is nowadays global in scope and this means that companies operate in an incredibly competitive environment. It goes without saying that in order to be successful in this environment, companies must be aware of the strengths and weaknesses of their competitors and they must be able to predict and pre-empt their activities within the market.

[63] D Fleck, 'Individual and State Responsibility for Intelligence Gathering' (2007) 28 *Michigan Journal of International Law* 687, 693.

[64] C Lotrionte, 'Countering State-Sponsored Cyber Economic Espionage Under International Law' (2015) 40 *North Carolina Journal of International Law and Commercial Regulation* 443, 444.

[65] Lotrionte (n 64) 444.

[66] H Nasheri, *Economic Espionage and Industrial Spying* (Cambridge, Cambridge University Press, 2005) 19 (quoting the legislative history that accompanies the US's Economic Espionage Act 1996). Witkow goes further and argues that 'economic power is far more important in determining world leadership than sheer military strength. With the end of the cold war and a commensurate decrease in military spending, nations are refocusing domestic and foreign policies and programs to increase economic standards of living for their citizens'; BJ Witkow, 'A New "Spook" Immunity: How the CIA and American Business Are Shielded from Liability for the Misappropriation of Trade Secrets' (2000) 14 *Emory International Law Review* 451, 451 (citations omitted).

[67] K Michal, 'Business Counterintelligence and the Role of the U.S. Intelligence Community' (1994) 7 *International Journal of Intelligence and Counterintelligence* 413, 413. 'National security is a broad concept. It includes not just military forces, but also political stability – and the strength of the economy'; G Brown, 'Spying and Fighting in Cyberspace: What is Which?' (2016) 8 *Journal of National Security Law and Policy* 621, 624. 'A nation's economic status makes up a large part of its national security. This economic status is dependent on a nation's ability to compete effectively in the world market'; Nasheri (n 66) 53 (citations omitted).

States have dedicated significant amounts of resources to acquiring trade secrets held by foreign companies.[68] Once appropriated, these secrets are handed to domestic companies, enabling them to react to their competitors' strategies and products. The objective of economic espionage is to ensure that domestic companies remain globally competitive and thus financially successful. Where this is achieved, the national economy is strengthened and, ultimately, national security is maintained. In this sense, '[m]any states view economic espionage as an essential tool in achieving national security',[69] and it is for this reason that they consider this practice to be 'a fair tactic and part of the economic game'.[70]

There is no doubt that economic espionage enables states to enhance their national economy and strengthen their national security. However, the point that needs to be recognised is that '[e]conomic espionage erodes the value of a target state's assets'.[71] This is because '[c]ompanies build their business and stake their success on secrets',[72] including confidential information relating to 'strategy, planning, technological innovation, product development processes, manufacturing and marketing processes, advertising campaigns, financial status, legal issues, key personnel, salary information, tenders and bids data, and more'.[73] More specifically, economic espionage inflicts upon companies two different types of costs.[74]

First, direct costs, which describe the lost revenue that a company would expect to generate from placing an innovative product or service on the market. Where a company steals another company's trade secrets and is able to make similar products or services available to customers, the exclusivity of the victim company's product or service is compromised. Simply put, economic espionage undermines the victim company's competitive edge and thus its profitability. The startup industry – which comprises newly created companies that are involved in the research and design of innovative technologies – is likely to incur considerable costs from economic espionage because their most important asset is their

[68] 'Whereas states previously engaged in espionage primarily for military and foreign policy purposes, today, intelligence operations concentrate more intensely on conducting, or guarding against, economic espionage'; Lotrionte, (n 64) 444. '[S]ince the end of the Cold War, espionage activities have changed from politico-military to economic foci'; Ziolkowski (n 35) 447.

[69] *Office of the National Counterintelligence Executive* (n 39) 4.

[70] Michal (n 67) 416. 'When economic objectives begin to play a more dominant role in defining national security, the interest in economic espionage expands'; Nasheri (66) 53.

[71] MEA Danielson, 'Economic Espionage: A Framework for a Workable Solution' (2009) 10 *Minnesota Journal of Law, Science and Technology* 503, 507.

[72] J Strawbridge, 'The Big Bluff: Obama, Cyber Economic Espionage, and the Threat of WTO Litigation' (2016) 47 *Georgetown Journal of International Law* 833, 834.

[73] S Argaman and G Siboni, 'Commercial and Industrial Cyber Espionage in Israel' (2014) 6 *Military and Strategic Affairs* 43, 46.

[74] R Anderson, C Barton, R Böhme, R Clayton, MJG van Eeten, M Levi, T Moore and S Savage, 'Measuring the Cost of Cybercrime' in R Böhme (ed), *The Economics of Information Security* and Privacy (Berlin and Heidelberg, Springer, 2013).

research.[75] Where this research is lost, the financial implications for these types of companies are colossal, perhaps even placing their continued survival in jeopardy.[76] For example, in 2011 a Dutch startup company called DigiNotar went bankrupt after it was the victim of economic cyber espionage and critical information was stolen.[77]

Moreover, companies are only prepared to invest time and capital in developing new research and design where they are confident that it will produce original products and services that will be lucrative once placed on the open market. It goes without saying that companies will be reluctant to pour effort and resources into innovation if they believe that their competitors will duplicate their products and services quickly and cheaply through espionage.[78] The spectre of espionage therefore discourages research and innovation, making companies less ambitious and ultimately less profitable.

Second, indirect costs, which involve the loss of customer trust and confidence in a company (or one of its products or services) after it is revealed that its computer systems were breached and confidential data was stolen. As an example, in 2015 TalkTalk, a company which provides pay television, telecommunications, Internet access and mobile network services to businesses and individuals in the UK, fell victim to cyber espionage and the confidential data of nearly 157, 000 customers was stolen.[79] By February 2016, TalkTalk reported that it had lost over 100,000 customers due to the data breach, resulting in approximately £15 million in lost revenue.[80]

In addition, indirect costs include monies spent on purchasing, installing and operating security systems that are necessary to protect trade secrets from non-consensual acquisition. Moreover, companies that fall victim to espionage will be seen as vulnerable and susceptible to further exploitation and will face higher insurance premiums.

[75] The threat of economic cyber espionage 'is particularly dire for startups notable for their groundbreaking intellectual property and tremendous economic potential, and, at the same time, for their limited budgets that keep them from effectively defending their valuable intellectual property'; G Siboni and D Israel, 'Cyberspace Espionage and its Effect on Commercial Considerations' (2015) 7 *Military and Strategic Affairs* 39, 54.

[76] 'In the business world, industrial espionage is usually considered one of the biggest threats to an organization's ability to survive in a competitive market'; ibid 39.

[77] For an overview of this incident see G Siboni and S Kronenfield, 'Iran and Cyberspace Warfare' (2012) 4 *Military and Strategic Affairs* 77.

[78] 'Private firms in the United States thrive on making large initial investments of time and capital to develop information, formulas, designs, and products that enable them to subsequently recover the outlays in the marketplace. Firms will only be willing to take the risks associated with developing such proprietary information if they know that none of their competitors will be able to easily duplicate their efforts with a few strokes of the key'; G O'Hara, 'Cyber-Espionage: A Growing Threat to the American Economy' (2010) 19 *CommLaw Conspectus* 241, 273 (citations omitted).

[79] S Farrell, 'Nearly 157, 000 had Data Breached in TalkTalk Cyber-Attack', 6 November 2015, *the Guardian*, www.theguardian.com/business/2015/nov/06/nearly-157000-had-data-breached-in-talktalk-cyber-attack.

[80] S Farrell, 'TalkTalk Counts Costs of Cyber-Attack', 2 February 2016, *the Guardian*, www.theguardian.com/business/2016/feb/02/talktalk-cyberattack-costs-customers-leave.

All in all, where companies fall victim to economic espionage, the economic security of the host state is undermined and its national security threatened.[81] In fact, such is the severity of the threat posed by economic espionage to national security that some commentators refer to it 'as a new form of war in the post-cold war period'.[82] As we have already seen, where national security is compromised a threat to international peace and security emerges. Significantly, because of the widespread use of cyberspace to store commercial information and given the ease and speed with which this information can be accessed by malicious actors, cyber-enabled economic espionage 'amplifies'[83] this threat to international peace and security: '[e]conomic [cyber] espionage has the capacity to cripple states' economies and de-stabilize the global economic order at a rapid pace, potentially risking the peace and security of the international community'.[84]

The US in particular has expressed its concern at the economic cost of economic cyber espionage, and has identified the negative effect that this activity has upon the maintenance of national security as well as international peace and security. By 2012, the Head of the US National Security Agency and US Cyber Command estimated that economic cyber espionage had resulted in American companies losing $250 billion in stolen information and another $114 billion in related expenses, representing the 'greatest transfer of wealth in history'.[85]

[81] 'Trade secret theft threatens to diminish U.S. competitiveness around the globe and puts U.S. jobs at risk. The reach of trade secret theft into critical commercial and defense technologies poses threats to U.S. national security interests as well'; Office of the United States Trade Representative, *2017 Special 301 Report* (2017) 18. 'The theft of trade secrets from US companies by foreign economic rivals undermines the corporate sector's ability to create jobs, generate revenues, foster innovation, and lay the economic foundation for prosperity and national security'; *Office of the National Counterintelligence Executive* (n 39) 3. '[I]nformation theft undermines America's competitiveness, impedes its economic recovery, and ultimately threatens the national security'; Michal (n 67) 416. According to O'Hara, economic cyber espionage 'threatens not only the economic standing of the United States in the global economy, but its national security as well'; O'Hara (n 78) 241. In the words of the EU, 'the increase of economic espionage and state-sponsored activities in cyberspace poses a new category of threats for EU governments and companies'; Joint Communication to the European Parliament, the Council, the European Economic and Social Committee and the Committee of the Regions, *Cybersecurity Strategy of the European Union: An Open, Safe and Secure Cyberspace* (2013) 3, www.eeas.europa.eu/archives/docs/policies/eu-cyber-security/cybsec_comm_en.pdf.

[82] I Erdoğan, 'Economic Espionage as a New Form of War in the Post-Cold War Period' (2009) 2 *USAK Yearbook of International Politics and Law* 265. Another commentator explains that economic espionage can be 'compared to warfare since both challenge the security and stability of sovereign nations'; Danielson (n 71) 507.

[83] 'Foreign economic collection and industrial espionage against the United States represent significant and growing threats to the nation's prosperity and security. Cyberspace – where most business activity and development of new ideas now takes place – amplifies these threats'; *Office of the National Counterintelligence Executive* (n 39) i.

[84] Lotrionte (n 64) 489. '[E]conomic cyber espionage is not only a domestic concern. Just as it harms the United States' economy, economic cyber espionage also threatens international trade and, over time, stands to have a destabilizing impact on the global economic order'; CP Skinner, 'An International Law Response to Economic Cyber Espionage' (2014) 46 *Connecticut Law Review* 1165, 1170.

[85] J Rogin, 'NSA Chief: Cybercrime Constitutes the "Greatest Transfer of Wealth in History"', 9 July 2012, *Foreign Policy*, www.foreignpolicy.com/2012/07/09/nsa-chief-cybercrime-constitutes-the-greatest-transfer-of-wealth-in-history/. This is not just an American problem. In 2011, the UK reported that

These figures are corroborated by a 2013 report by the Commission on the Theft of American Intellectual Property, which estimated that the damage caused to the US economy by the cyber-enabled theft of intellectual property exceeds $300 billion a year.[86]

The US alleges that China is a prolific perpetrator of economic cyber espionage.[87] Indeed, the scale of Chinese economic cyber espionage was laid bare in a 2013 report by the cyber security company Mandiant, which revealed that China was regularly exploiting cyberspace 'to steal large volumes of valuable intellectual property, including technology blueprints, proprietary manufacturing processes, test results, business plans, pricing documents, partnership agreements, emails and contact lists from victim organizations' leadership'.[88]

The economic impact of Chinese cyber espionage upon the US is startling. In 2011, Congressman Dana Rohrabacher suggested that Chinese economic espionage cost the US tens of billions of dollars a year:

> I would say the American people would be outraged to understand that tens of billions of dollars that have been taken from them in order for research and development in our country has ended up in the hands of an economic and military adversary like Communist China.[89]

the theft of intellectual property cost the UK economy approximately £7.5 billion per annum; A Detica Report in Partnership with the Office of Cyber Security and Assurance in the Cabinet Office, *The Cost of Cyber-Crime – Full Report* (2011) 2, www.gov.uk/government/uploads/system/uploads/attachment_data/file/60943/the-cost-of-cyber-crime-full-report.pdf. According to the 2011 report by the Office of the National Counterintelligence Executive, Germany's Federal Office for the Protection of the Constitution (BfV) estimates that German companies lose $28 billion – $71 billion and 30,000–70,000 jobs per year from foreign economic espionage and South Korea estimated that it lost $82 billion from economic espionage in 2008; *Office of the National Counterintelligence Executive* (n 39) B-1.

[86] DC Blair and JM Huntsman Jr, *The IP Commission Report: The Report of the Commission on the Theft of American Intellectual Property* (2013) 2, www.ipcommission.org/report/ip_commission_report_052213.pdf.

[87] According to FBI Director James Comey, '[f]or too long, the Chinese government has blatantly sought to use cyber espionage to obtain economic advantage for its state-owned industries'; quoted in Department of Justice Office of Public Affairs, *U.S. Charges Five Chinese Military Hackers for Cyber Espionage Against U.S. Companies and a Labour Organization for Commercial Advantage*, 19 May 2014, www.justice.gov/opa/pr/us-charges-five-chinese-military-hackers-cyber-espionage-against-us-corporations-and-labor.

[88] Mandiant, *APT 1: Exposing One of China's Cyber Espionage Units* (2013) 20, www.fireeye.com/content/dam/fireeye-www/services/pdfs/mandiant-apt1-report.pdf.

[89] *Communist Chinese Cyber-Attacks, Cyber-Espionage and Theft of American Technology*, Hearing Before the Subcommittee on Oversight and Investigations of the Committee on Foreign Affairs House of Representatives (2011) 47 (statement of Congressman Dana Rohrabacher) www.fas.org/irp/congress/2011_hr/china-cyber.pdf. 'What has been happening over the course of the last five years is that China – let's call it for what it is – has been hacking its way into every corporation it can find listed in Dun & Bradstreet … Every corporation in the US, every corporation in Asia, every corporation in Germany. And using a vacuum cleaner to suck data out in terabytes and petabytes. I don't think you can overstate the damage to this country that has already been done'; Richard Clarke, former special adviser on cyber security to US President George W Bush, quoted in 'China Accused of Massive Economic Espionage', 14 December 2011, *Sydney Morning Herald*, www.smh.com.au/business/china-accused-of-massive-economic-espionage-20111214-1otni.html.

Exasperated by the scale of Chinese economic cyber espionage, US Vice President Joe Biden insisted that the 'outright cyber-enabling theft that U.S. companies are experiencing now must be viewed as out of bounds and needs to stop'.[90] Also in response to Chinese economic cyber espionage, a senior official within the Obama administration determined that 'the international community cannot tolerate such activity from any country'.[91]

The US has adopted a wide range of measures to counteract the threat posed by Chinese economic cyber espionage, including indicting Chinese officials before US courts,[92] imposing economic sanctions,[93] improving US inter-agency coordination on cyber-hacking[94] and helping domestic companies strengthen their cyber defences.[95] Moreover, in 2015 the US persuaded China to sign a non-binding agreement whereby both states recognised the adverse impact that economic cyber espionage has upon national security and agreed to abstain from participating in this conduct.[96]

To conclude, if nowadays a direct line can be drawn between the maintenance of a state's economic security and the preservation of international peace and security, for international peace and security to be achieved it is essential that international law clearly prohibits economic espionage and, given its scale and intensity, cyber-enabled economic espionage in particular.

4. Conclusion

What is the impact of political and economic cyber espionage upon international relations? Should political and economic cyber espionage be permitted or prohibited by international law? This chapter has sought to provide answers to these questions.

[90] P Eckert and A Yukhananov, 'U.S.–China Talks Cover Cyber Issues, Currency, Chinese Reform', 10 July 2013, *Reuters*, www.reuters.com/article/us-usa-china-dialogue/u-s-china-talks-cover-cyber-issues-currency-chinese-reform-idUSBRE9690T520130710.

[91] US National Security Adviser Tom Donilon, quoted in M Landler and DE Sanger, 'U.S. Demands China Block Cyberattacks and Agree to Rules', *New York Times*, 11 March 2013, www.nytimes.com/2013/03/12/world/asia/us-demands-that-china-end-hacking-and-set-cyber-rules.html.

[92] Department of Justice Office of Public Affairs (n 87).

[93] E Nakashima, 'U.S. Developing Sanctions Against China Over Cyberthefts', 30 August 2015, *Washington Post*, www.washingtonpost.com/world/national-security/administration-developing-sanctions-against-china-over-cyberespionage/2015/08/30/9b2910aa-480b-11e5-8ab4-c73967a143d3_story.html?utm_term=.04fcdec30226.

[94] United States, *Administration Strategy on Mitigating The Theft of US Trade Secrets* (February 2013) www.justice.gov/criminal-ccips/file/938321/download.

[95] 'White House Requests Input on Legislative Fixes for Trade Secret Theft', 22 March 2013, *Inside U.S. Trade*.

[96] E Nakashima and S Mufson, 'The U.S. and China Agree not to Conduct Economic Espionage in Cyberspace', 25 September 2015, *Washington Post*, www.washingtonpost.com/world/national-security/the-us-and-china-agree-not-to-conduct-economic-espionage-in-cyberspace/2015/09/25/1c03f4b8-63a2-11e5-8e9e-dce8a2a2a679_story.html?noredirect=on&utm_term=.dec18fcdbf55.

This chapter has argued that political espionage represents a threat to the maintenance of international peace and security because it violates the principles of the sovereign equality of states and human dignity, which constitute foundational norms of the international society. Moreover, by violating these fundamental principles, political espionage threatens the maintenance of international peace and security on the basis that it undermines trust and confidence between states, thereby preventing them from effectively addressing the threats and dangers that proliferate within the international society.

This chapter has claimed that economic espionage also threatens the maintenance of international peace and security. Stealing a company's trade secrets compromises its financial success and this has a negative knock-on effect upon the economic wellbeing of the host state. Given that economic security and national security are two sides of the same coin, economic espionage can be regarded as constituting a threat to national security and, by implication, to international peace and security.

Significantly, cyberspace facilitates the commission of political and economic espionage, thus enhancing the threat that this conduct represents to the maintenance of international peace and security. Indeed, these threats will only become more intense as the 'Internet of Things' gathers momentum and as more of our information is stored in cyberspace:

> Over the next several years, the proliferation of portable devices that connect to the Internet and other networks will continue to create new opportunities for malicious actors to conduct espionage. The trend in both commercial and government organizations toward the pooling of information processing and storage will present even greater challenges to preserving the security and integrity of sensitive information.[97]

Considering the above arguments, it is clear that, for international peace and security to be maintained, the international society must implement international legal rules that expressly and unequivocally prohibit political and economic cyber espionage. The status of political and economic cyber espionage under international law will be examined in subsequent chapters.

[97] *Office of the National Counterintelligence Executive* (n 39) i.

3

Cyber Espionage and the Rules of Territorial Sovereignty, Non-Intervention and the Non-Use of Force

1. Introduction

The sovereign equality of states represents the constitutional basis of the international society.[1] 'Sovereignty has different aspects'[2] and states have implemented various international legal rules in order to protect the features that comprise their sovereign equality from different types of intervention.[3] The rule of territorial sovereignty protects the territory of states from external intrusion and confers upon them the exclusive right to perform governmental functions within their territory.[4] The rule of non-intervention protects the *domaine réservé* of states from coercive intervention.[5] The prohibition against the threat or use of force[6] protects the territorial integrity and political independence of states from the threat or use of conduct that inflicts physical damage and, where this damage is serious, international law permits victim states to act in self-defence.[7]

This chapter examines the role played by these general principles of international law in regulating cyber espionage. This chapter is structured as follows.

[1] 'It is safe to conclude that sovereign equality constitutes the linchpin of the whole body of international legal standards, the fundamental premise on which all international relations rest'; A Cassese, *International Law* (Oxford, Oxford University Press, 2005) 48. See also Article 2(1) United Nations Charter 1945.

[2] R Jennings and A Watts, *Oppenheim's International Law: Volume 1, Peace* (London, New York, Longmans, Green & Co, 1996) 382.

[3] 'Sovereignty is at the heart of the international legal system and forms the basis of most rules of international law – including the prohibition on intervention and the prohibition on the use of force'; S Watts, 'International Law and Proposed U.S. Responses to the D.N.C. Hack', 14 October 2016, *Just Security*, www.justsecurity.org/33558/international-law-proposed-u-s-responses-d-n-c-hack/.

[4] *Corfu Channel (United Kingdom of Great Britain and Northern Ireland v Albania)*, Judgment (Merits) [1949] ICJ Rep 4, 35.

[5] *Military and Paramilitary Activities in and against Nicaragua (Nicaragua v United States of America)*, Judgment (Merits) [1986] ICJ Rep 14, para 202.

[6] Article 2(4) UN Charter.

[7] ibid Article 51.

Section 2 analyses the application of the rule of territorial sovereignty to acts of cyber espionage. Section 3 assesses whether acts of cyber espionage contravene the rule of non-intervention. Section 4 considers whether acts of cyber espionage violate the prohibition on the use of force and, if so, whether such conduct gives rise to an armed attack that thereby permits the victim state to respond in self-defence. Section 5 offers conclusions.

2. The Rule of Territorial Sovereignty

Despite isolated protestations to the contrary,[8] the rule of territorial sovereignty is firmly enshrined in customary international law[9] and a well-accepted formulation of this rule was espoused by Judge Max Huber in the *Island of Palmas* arbitral award:

> Sovereignty in the relations between States signifies independence. Independence in regard to a portion of the globe is the right to exercise therein, to the exclusion of any other State, the functions of a State.[10]

The rule of territorial sovereignty therefore confers upon states two different types of sovereign entitlement: first, the right to control access to and egress from their territory and, second, the right to perform governmental functions within their territory.[11] It therefore follows that state conduct that impinges upon the exercise of these sovereign prerogatives represents a violation of the rule of territorial sovereignty which, in turn, constitutes an internationally wrongful act.

[8] In May 2018, the UK rejected the contention that the rule of territorial sovereignty had crystallised as customary international law. In the words of Attorney General Jeremy Wright, '[s]overeignty is of course fundamental to the international rules-based system. But I am not persuaded that we can currently extrapolate from that general principle a specific rule or additional prohibition for cyber activity beyond that of a prohibited intervention. The UK Government's position is therefore that there is no such rule as a matter of current international law'; Attorney General Jeremy Wright, *Cyber and International Law in the 21st Century*, 23 May 2018, www.gov.uk/government/speeches/cyber-and-international-law-in-the-21st-century. For academic support for this view see GP Corn and R Taylor, 'Sovereignty in the Age of Cyber' (2017) 111 *AJIL Unbound* 207.

[9] For a compelling demonstration of the wealth of state practice and *opinio juris* that supports the customary international law status of the rule of territorial sovereignty see MN Schmitt and L Vihul, 'Respect for Sovereignty in Cyberspace' (2017) 95 *Texas Law Review* 1639.

[10] *Island of Palmas*, 2 RIAA (Perm Ct Arb 1928) 829, 838. In his separate opinion in the *Corfu Channel* case, Judge Alvarez stated: 'By sovereignty, we understand the whole body of rights and attributes which a State possesses in its territory, to the exclusion of all other States, and also in its relations with other States'; *Corfu* (n 4) 43 (Separate Opinion of Judge Alvarez).

[11] As von Heinegg explains, the rule of territorial sovereignty means that 'the State alone is entitled to exercise jurisdiction, especially by subjecting objects and persons within its territory to domestic legislation and to enforce these rules. Moreover, the State is entitled to control access to and egress from its territory'; WH von Heinegg, 'Territorial Sovereignty and Neutrality in Cyberspace' (2013) 89 *International Law Studies* 123, 124. See also MN Schmitt, *Tallinn Manual 2.0 on the International Law Applicable to Cyber Operations* (Cambridge, Cambridge University Press, 2017) 20.

At its creation, commentators maintained that pre-existing law (including international law) was inapplicable to cyberspace.[12] Central to their argument was that pre-existing rules had been constructed around notions of territoriality and jurisdiction and, given the a-territorial and borderless nature of cyberspace, they could not exist within or apply to this type of virtual environment. Nowadays, however, '[t]he argument that cyberspace constitutes a law-free zone is no longer taken seriously'.[13] Although cyberspace is a virtual domain, it is nevertheless a man-made environment that 'requires a physical architecture to exist',[14] including fibre-optic cables, copper wires, microwave relay towers, satellite transponders, Internet routers etc. Thus, cyberspace does not exist independently from the physical world but is instead rooted in it. In recognition of this, states have determined that law generally and international law specifically applies to cyberspace.[15] With regard to international law and in particular the rule of territorial sovereignty, in 2013 the UN Group of Governmental Experts on Developments in the Field of Information and Telecommunications in the Context of International Security explained:

> State sovereignty and international norms and principles that flow from sovereignty apply to State conduct of ICT-related activities, and to their jurisdiction over ICT infrastructure within their territory.[16]

This paragraph was repeated in the Group's 2015 report,[17] which went on to explain:

> In their use of ICTs, States must observe, among other principles of international law, State sovereignty, sovereign equality, the settlement of disputes by peaceful means and non-intervention in the internal affairs of other States. Existing obligations under international law are applicable to State use of ICTs.[18]

In light of these developments, it is clear that 'State practice provides sufficient evidence that components of cyberspace are not immune from territorial sovereignty'.[19] Indeed, given this widespread state practice, Rule 2 of the *Tallinn Manual 2.0* explains that '[a] State enjoys sovereign authority with regard to the cyber infrastructure … located within its territory'.[20] A state's territorial

[12] DR Johnson and DG Post, 'Law and Borders: The Rise of Law in Cyberspace' (1996) 48 *Stanford Law Review* 1367.

[13] S Watts, 'Low-Intensity Cyber Operations and the Principle of Non-Intervention' (2014) 14 *Baltic Yearbook of International Law* 137, 142.

[14] PW Franzese, 'Sovereignty in Cyberspace: Can it Exist?' (2009) 64 *Air Force Law Review* 1, 33.

[15] For a discussion see JL Goldsmith, 'Against Cyberanarchy' (1998) 65 *University of Chicago Law Review* 1199.

[16] *Group of Governmental Experts on Developments in the Field of Information and Telecommunications in the Context of International Security*, UN Doc A/68/98, 24 June 2013, para 20.

[17] *Group of Governmental Experts on Developments in the Field of Information and Telecommunications in the Context of International Security*, UN Doc A/70/174, 22 July 2015, para 27.

[18] ibid para 28(b).

[19] von Heinegg (n 11) 126.

[20] The commentary to Rule 2 further notes that a 'State's sovereignty over its territory affords it the right under international law to protect cyber infrastructure and safeguard cyber activity that is located

sovereignty encompasses all cyber infrastructure that is physically located within its territory regardless of whether that infrastructure belongs to or is operated by government institutions, private companies or private individuals[21] and, additionally, it extends to those computer networks and systems supported by that cyber infrastructure.

State-sponsored cyber operations can therefore violate the rule of territorial sovereignty upon two different bases: first, where they intrude into computer networks and systems supported by cyber infrastructure located within another state's territory and, second, where they interfere with or usurp the right of another state to perform inherently governmental functions within its territory.[22] Whether acts of cyber espionage run into conflict with these elements of the rule of territorial sovereignty will now be considered.

2.1. Cyber Espionage and Control Over Cyber Infrastructure

Any non-consensual incursion by one state into the territory of another state violates the rule of territorial sovereignty, regardless of whether that infraction produces damage.[23] In the *Lotus* case, for example, the Permanent Court of International Justice explained that 'the first and foremost restriction imposed by international law upon a State is that – failing the existence of a permissive rule to the contrary – it may not exercise its power *in any form* in the territory of another State'.[24] As Chesterman observes, this interpretation

in, or takes place on, its territory'; *Tallinn Manual 2.0* (n 11) 13. 'Cyber infrastructure located within the territory of a State is thus protected through the State's territorial sovereignty'; B Pirker, 'Territorial Sovereignty and Integrity and the Challenges of Cyberspace' in K Ziolkowski (ed), *Peacetime Regime for State Activities in Cyberspace: International Law, International Relations and Diplomacy* (CCDCOE, 2013) 191.

[21] '[I]t is irrelevant as a matter of international law whether the cyber infrastructure in question is public or private in character, or whether the cyber activities concerned are engaged in by the State's organs or by private individuals or entities. A State's sovereign prerogatives also exist irrespective of the purpose of the cyber infrastructure or, as a general matter, the nationality of its owner'; *Tallinn Manual 2.0*, ibid 13–14. 'It is irrelevant whether the cyber infrastructure protected by the principle of territorial sovereignty belongs to or is operated by government institutions, private entities or private individuals'; von Heinegg (n 11) 129. See also *Microsoft Corporation*, 829 F.3d 197, 201 (2d Cir 2016) (where the Second Circuit held that data belonging to the US company Microsoft but which was stored in a datacentre in Dublin, Ireland, was located in the territory of Ireland and therefore protected by Ireland's territorial sovereignty).

[22] *Tallinn Manual 2.0* (n 11) 20.

[23] '[T]he legal regime applicable to extraterritorial enforcement is quite straightforward. Without the consent of the host State such conduct is absolutely unlawful because it violates that State's right to respect for its territorial integrity'; MT Kamminga, 'Extraterritoriality' (2012) *Max Planck Encyclopedia of Public International Law*, para 22. 'I am not aware of any authority demonstrating that the legality of enforcement jurisdiction [in violation of the rule of territorial sovereignty] depends on the scale of the physical presence'; C Forcese, 'Pragmatism and Principle: Intelligence Agencies and International Law' (2016) 102 *Virginia Law Review Online* 67, 80.

[24] *The Case of the SS 'Lotus' (France v Turkey)*, Judgment [1927] PCIJ (Ser A) No 10 1, 18 (emphasis added).

of the territorial sovereignty rule 'would clearly cover unauthorized entry into territory'.[25]

When examining the application of the rule of territorial sovereignty to territorially intrusive acts of espionage, the *Nicaragua* decision is particularly instructive. In this case, the International Court of Justice (ICJ) had to determine whether the US's use of reconnaissance aircraft within Nicaragua's territorial airspace constituted a violation of international law. Importantly, the Court held that '[t]he principle of respect for territorial sovereignty is also directly infringed by the unauthorized overflight of a State's territory by aircraft belonging to or under the control of the government of another State'.[26]

Numerous decisions of national courts have also concluded that acts of espionage that infringe upon the territory of another state violate the rule of territorial sovereignty.[27] Most notably, in 2008 the Federal Court of Canada publicised its response to a request from the Canadian Security Intelligence Service (CSIS) to approve a warrant under Section 12 of the Canadian Security Intelligence Service Act 1984 to conduct surveillance against individuals located within the territory of other states. Under Canadian law, the Court could only issue the warrant if the activities being authorised were compliant with international law. In refusing to grant the warrant, the Court observed:

> The intrusive activities that are contemplated in the warrant sought are activities that clearly impinge upon the above-stated principles of territorial sovereign equality and non-intervention … By authorizing such activities, the warrant would therefore be authorizing activities that are inconsistent with and likely to breach the binding customary principles of territorial sovereign equality and non-intervention, by the comity of nations. These prohibitive rules of customary international law … have evolved to protect the sovereignty of nation states against interference from other states.[28]

With this jurisprudence in mind, it is well-settled that '[i]n time of peace … espionage and, in fact, any penetration of the territory of a state by agents of

[25] S Chesterman, 'The Spy Who Came in from the Cold War: Intelligence and International Law' (2006) 27 *Michigan Journal of International Law* 1071, 1082.

[26] *Nicaragua* (n 5) para 251.

[27] *Cesare Rossi*, 18 September 1928, Swiss Federal Council, Speech by Federal Agent Motta, Zeitschrift Für Ausländische und Öffentliche Recht, vol 12, 283; *Re Flesche*, Holland, Special Criminal Court, 17 February 1949, International Law Reports, 272; *Yao Lun v Arnold*, Military Tribunal of the Supreme People's Court, China, 23 November 1954, International Law Reports, 111; *Powers case*, Union of Soviet Socialist Republics, Supreme Court, 19 August 1960, International Law Reports, 73–74.

[28] *Re Canadian Security Intelligence Service Act* [2008] FC 301, [2008] 4 FCR 230, paras 50–52. Similarly, in the *Hape* decision the Canadian Supreme Court held that '[t]he power to invade the private sphere of persons and property, and seize personal items and information, is paradigmatic of state sovereignty. These actions can be authorized only by the territorial state'; *R v Hape* [2007] 2 SCC 26 (CanLII) [2007] 2 SCR 292, para 87.

another state in violation of the local law is also a violation of the rule of international law imposing a duty upon states to respect the territorial integrity and political independence of other states'.[29]

The majority of the Experts responsible for drafting the *Tallinn Manual 2.0* agreed that, where a state sends its agents into the territory of another state in order to collect confidential data that is stored on computer networks and systems (namely, close access cyber espionage), a violation of the rule of territorial sovereignty occurs at the moment that the victim state's territory is intruded upon.[30] In light of the above discussion, this assessment is uncontroversial. What is controversial, however, is how the *Tallinn Manual 2.0* Experts interpreted the rule of territorial sovereignty as applying to remotely launched acts of cyber espionage.

As a general matter, the majority of the Experts determined that remotely launched cyber operations only trigger a violation of the rule of territorial sovereignty where they produce real-world physical damage (meaning death or injury to people or damage to physical property) or, at a minimum, destructive effects in cyberspace (meaning the 'loss of functionality' of cyber infrastructure).[31] Following on from this, the majority of the Experts opined that, because cyber espionage involves the collection of confidential information and does not therefore produce destructive effects either offline or online, this type of cyber activity does not qualify as an infringement of the victim state's territorial sovereignty.[32]

[29] Q Wright, 'Espionage and the Doctrine of Non-Intervention in Internal Affairs' in RJ Stanger (ed), *Essays on Espionage and International Law* (Columbus, Ohio State University Press, 1962) 12. Other scholars share this view. Kozik argues that 'sending spies to the territory of another State would be a violation of the territorial sovereignty rule'; AL Kozik, 'The Concept of Sovereignty as a Foundation for Determining the Legality of the Conduct of States in Cyberspace' (2014) 14 *Baltic Yearbook of International Law* 93, 99. 'Though international law does not explicitly condemn wartime espionage, peacetime espionage is regarded as an international delinquency and a violation of international law'; MR Garcia-Mora, 'Treason, Sedition and Espionage as Political Offenses Under the Law of Extradition' (1964) 26 *University of Pittsburgh Law Review* 65, 79–80. '[E]spionage appears to be illegal under international law in time of peace if it involves the presence of agents sent clandestinely by a foreign power into the territory of another state'; I Delupis, 'Foreign Warships and Immunity for Espionage' (1984) 78 *AJIL* 53, 67. '[The rule of territorial sovereignty] negates the general permissibility of strategic observation in foreign territory and indicates the requirement of special consent by the territorial State'; J Kish (D Turns, ed), *International Law and Espionage* (The Hague, Nijhoff, 1995) 84. '[A state may not] send its police officers, even if they are in civilian clothes, into foreign States to investigate crimes or make enquiries affecting investigations in their own country. Nor can it allow spies or informers to operate abroad'; FA Mann, 'The Doctrine of Jurisdiction in International Law' (1964) *Collected Courses of The Hague Academy of International Law* 1, 139 (citations omitted).

[30] *Tallinn Manual 2.0* (n 11) 19, 171.

[31] '[T]he Experts agreed that, in addition to physical damage, the remote causation of loss of functionality of cyber infrastructure located in another State sometimes constitutes a violation of sovereignty, although no consensus could be achieved as to the precise threshold at which this is so due to the lack of expression of *opinio juris* in this regard'; ibid 20–21.

[32] 'The majority of the Experts was of the view that [remote access] exfiltration violates no international law prohibition irrespective of the attendant severity'; ibid 171.

Yet, the *Tallinn Manual 2.0* does not explain why the majority of the Experts considered close access cyber espionage to be unlawful as soon as the responsible state intrudes into the physical territory of the victim state (and regardless of whether that operation causes damage or harm), but remote access cyber espionage that trespasses upon another state's cyber infrastructure is lawful (unless it gives rise to damage or harm). Said differently, the *Manual* does not explain why, if all of the Experts agreed that states exercise sovereignty over the cyber infrastructure located within their territory (see Rule 2 of the *Tallinn Manual 2.0*), the majority of them regarded the rule of territorial sovereignty as providing a state's *sovereign* cyber infrastructure with less protection from intrusion than a state's *sovereign* physical territory.

My view is that states exercise territorial sovereignty over the cyber infrastructure that is physically located within their territory on the same basis and to the same extent that they exercise territorial sovereignty over their physical territory. According to this approach, an act of cyber espionage – or indeed any cyber operation – that penetrates computer networks and systems supported by cyber infrastructure situated within the territory of another state constitutes a violation of that state's territorial sovereignty, irrespective of whether that operation causes damage or harm. Indeed, given that the rule of territorial sovereignty protects all cyber infrastructure located within state territory, acts of cyber espionage violate this rule regardless of whether the computer networks and systems targeted are operated by state organs or private actors. Thus, acts of political and economic cyber espionage transgress the rule of territorial sovereignty and they do so on the basis of the underlying act, that is, the unauthorised intrusion into a domain protected by state sovereignty.

Significantly, state practice supports the contention that remote access cyber espionage contravenes the rule of territorial sovereignty. For example, the Snowden leaks revealed that the US National Security Agency (NSA) had been monitoring communications of individuals in the Bahamas. The operation – codenamed SOMALGET – involved the use of computer operations 'to open a backdoor to the country's cellular telephone network, enabling it to covertly record and store the "full-take audio" of every call made to, from and within the Bahamas – and to replay those calls for up to a month'.[33] Reacting to these revelations, the Bahamian Foreign Affairs Minister stated:

> The Bahamas wishes to underscore … that international law is the standard of conduct of States, [and protects] the primacy of sovereignty, [the] maintenance of territorial integrity, [and] freedom from undue external intrusion and influence.[34]

[33] R Devereaux, G Greenwald and L Poitras, 'Data Pirates of the Caribbean: The NSA is Recording Every Cell Phone Call in the Bahamas', 19 May 2014, *The Intercept*, www.theintercept.com/2014/05/19/data-pirates-caribbean-nsa-recording-every-cell-phone-call-bahamas/.

[34] Quoted in R Rolle, 'Lawyers to Act in N.S.A. Spy Row', 5 June 2014, *Tribune 242*, www.tribune242.com/news/2014/jun/05/lawyers-act-ns-spy-row.

Argentina, Bolivia, Brazil, Uruguay and Venezuela also rejected the NSA's cyber espionage as a violation of their territorial sovereignty. Channelling their views through the Pro-Tempore President of MERCOSUR (a South American trading bloc), a Note Verbale was submitted to the UN Secretary-General '[c]ondemning the acts of espionage carried out by intelligence agencies of the United States of America … [which] constitute unacceptable behaviour that violates our sovereignty'.[35] Separately, the Foreign Minister of Venezuela explained before the Security Council that 'we reject the actions of global espionage carried out by the Government of the United States, which undermine the sovereignty of States' and called upon the UN to 'punish and condemn this violation of international law'.[36] Before the UN General Assembly, Indonesia also recorded its 'strong position against extraterritorial surveillance because it was a violation of international law and the United Nations Charter'.[37]

These determinations are significant because they demonstrate that states have invoked the rule of territorial sovereignty to condemn the US's cyber espionage activities. As scholars note, this state practice 'confirms that transnational access to data, and the "pulling" of data from other countries, without the consent of such other countries, is still seen as clearly contrary to public international law'.[38] For Wrange, this practice demonstrates that 'espionage that involves unauthorized access to servers and other computers in a foreign state generally constitutes illegal interventions into the sovereignty of that state'.[39]

[35] Note Verbale dated 22 July 2013 from the Permanent Mission of the Bolivarian Republic of Venezuela to the United Nations Addressed to the Secretary-General, UN Doc A/67/946, 29 July 2013, 2.

[36] 7015th Meeting, UN Doc S/PV.7015 (Resumption 1), 6 August 2013, 8.

[37] 'Third Committee Approves Text Titled "Right to Privacy in the Digital Age", as it Takes Action on 18 Draft Resolutions', UN Doc GA/SHC/4094, 26 November 2013.

[38] I Brown and D Korff, 'Foreign Surveillance: Law and Practice in a Global Digital Environment' (2014) 3 *European Human Rights Law Review* 243, 249–50.

[39] P Wrange, 'Intervention in National and Private Cyberspace and International Law' in J Ebbesson, M Jacobsson, M Klamberg, D Langlet and P Wrange (eds), *International Law and Changing Perceptions of Security: Liber Amicorum Said Mahmoudi* (Leiden, Brill, Nijhoff, 2014) 322. 'In a cyber context, a mere intrusion into another State's networks to gather information would certainly amount to a violation of sovereignty'; Watts (n 13) 145. '[I]t could well be argued that the intrusion by US officials into data stored on servers located on German soil amounts to a violation of Germany's territorial sovereignty because they are hereby, albeit remotely, exercising US governmental authority on German territory without German consent'; PCR Terry, '"Absolute Friends": United States Espionage against Germany and Public International Law' (2015) 28 *Revue Québécoise de Droit International* 173, 194. The reaction of the US to Russia's alleged hacking of the Democratic National Committee's emails during the 2016 US Presidential campaign focused primarily upon the legality of Russia's *use* of the hacked information to influence the election rather than the cyber espionage itself. However, those commentators that subjected the various aspects of the DNC hack to international law analysis concluded that the theft of confidential information contravened the rule of territorial sovereignty. According to Watts, 'a majority view might regard the D.N.C hacks as violations of U.S. sovereignty, assuming they involved nonconsensual intrusion into cyber systems located in the U.S.'; Watts (n 3).

2.2. Cyber Espionage and the Performance of Inherently Governmental Functions

Given the interconnectedness of cyberspace, states frequently transmit their data through and store their data upon cyber infrastructure that is located within the territory of *other* states. If a state's data is collected while it is resident on another state's cyber infrastructure, the latter state's territorial sovereignty is violated according to the legal arguments developed in the previous section. But does the rule of territorial sovereignty afford legal protection to the state that has authored and compiled the data, even though the data is situated on cyber infrastructure located outside of its territory when it is collected?

In order to comprehensively protect state sovereignty, the rule of territorial sovereignty not only insulates state territory from external intrusion but also confers upon states the right to perform inherently governmental functions within their territory without interference. The objective of this section is to determine whether acts of cyber espionage violate this element of the rule of territorial sovereignty. More specifically, this section assesses whether acts of cyber espionage against a state's data while it is located on foreign cyber infrastructure can be said to interfere with that state's right to perform governmental functions.

What functions can be regarded as inherently governmental cannot be definitively listed because different states possess different functions depending upon their particular political configuration.[40] This being said, there are certain core functions that only a state's government is entitled to perform and these include 'the delivery of social services, the conduct of elections, the collection of taxes, the effective conduct of diplomacy, and the performance of key national defence activities'.[41]

The critical question is whether acts of espionage against data that is integral to the delivery of an inherently governmental function qualify as unlawful interference. Academic opinion is divided on this issue. The *Tallinn Manual 2.0* Experts concluded that a computer operation that 'chang[es] or delet[es] data' that relates to the delivery of a governmental function amounts to unlawful interference.[42] While the Experts did not specifically address the example of cyber espionage, the implication is nevertheless clear: the Experts did not regard the *copying* (as opposed to the 'changing or deleting') of data as constituting interference in the performance of governmental functions. Yet, other commentators argue that:

> It is not the business of other states to gather information on political matters which another state seeks not to communicate. Even under a presumable general transparency obligation, states are not obliged to make all of their internal decision-making processes

[40] *Tallinn Manual 2.0* (n 11) 22.
[41] ibid.
[42] ibid.

> public, because this would completely stall politics. For this reason, extracting intra-governmental exchange of information seems to interfere with state sovereignty in its most traditional sense.[43]

The weight of state practice as well as the jurisprudence of national and international tribunals indicates that espionage does not amount to unlawful interference with the delivery of governmental functions. For example, during the early 1960s the US started deploying satellites into outer space in order to observe activities occurring within the territory of the Soviet Union.[44] The US maintained that '[i]nternational law imposed no prohibition on the observation of the earth from outer space, which was peaceful and did not interfere with other activities on earth or in space'.[45] At least initially, the Soviet Union took the opposite view:

> We cannot agree with the claim that all observation from space, including observation for the purpose of collecting intelligence, is in conformity with international law – a conclusion which could be drawn from the statement made this morning by the representative from the United States. Such observation is just as wrong as when intelligence data are obtained by other means, such as photographs made from the air. The object to which illegal surveillance is directed constitutes a secret guarded by a sovereign State, and regardless of the means by which such an operation is carried out, it is in all cases an intrusion into something guarded by a sovereign State in conformity with its sovereign prerogative. Thus, such observations are in violation of the sovereignty of States.[46]

For the Soviet Union, then, non-territorially intrusive forms of espionage nevertheless violated the rule of territorial sovereignty on the basis that they constituted unlawful interference with the delivery of governmental functions. Importantly, this interpretation of the rule of territorial sovereignty was widely rejected by other states at the time.[47] Perhaps more significantly, towards the end of 1963 'Soviet statements … on the legality of space reconnaissance ceased'[48] and, as its technological capacity increased, it began to deploy its own satellites into outer space for the purpose of reconnaissance.[49] Indeed, it is nowadays well-settled that the use

[43] A Peters, 'Surveillance Without Borders? The Unlawfulness of the NSA Panopticon, Part I', 1 November 2013, EJIL: *Talk!*, www.ejiltalk.org/surveillance-without-borders-the-unlawfulness-of-the-nsa-panopticon-part-i/.

[44] See RA Falk, 'Space Espionage and World Order: A Consideration of the Samos-Midas Program' in Stanger (n 29) chapter 3.

[45] Meeker, US Representative to the Legal Subcommittee of the UN Space Committee, Summary Record of the Seventh Meeting, UN Doc No A/AC.105/C.2/SR.7, 7 June 1962.

[46] Soviet Statement in the General Assembly, First Committee, 17th Session, 1298th Meeting, 3 December 1962. For a similar statement see Timerbaev, USSR Representative to the Legal Subcommittee of the UN Space Committee, Summary Record of the Twentieth Meeting, UN Doc No A/AC.105/C.2/SR.28/13, 3 May 1963 ('All attempts to reconcile the collection of intelligence information by artificial satellites with the principles of international law were completely unfounded').

[47] For a discussion see JR Soraghan, 'Reconnaissance Satellites: Legal Characterization and Possible Utilization for Peacekeeping' (1964) 13 *McGill Law Journal* 458, 475–83.

[48] ibid 473.

[49] UPI Report, New Haven Register, 26 September 1965, section 1, 5 ('Shortly before his ouster, Soviet Premier Nikita S Khrushchev openly boasted that Soviet satellites were constantly photographing military installations in the United States').

of spy satellites does not transgress the territorial sovereignty rule, even where the confidential information collected relates to the performance of another state's inherently governmental functions.[50]

The European Court of Human Rights (ECtHR) and the Federal Court of Canada have also concluded that non-territorially intrusive espionage is compatible with the rule of territorial sovereignty, indicating that they do not regard the theft of confidential data relating to the performance of governmental functions as amounting to unlawful interference. In *Weber*, two individuals petitioned the ECtHR on the grounds that German legislation authorising the interception of electronic communications violated their right to private and family life as protected by Article 8 of the European Convention on Human Rights (ECHR). Although this case concerned the infringement of human rights, it is relevant to the present discussion insofar as Article 8 ECHR required that the impugned German legislation had to be in accordance with the law, which included international law. The ECtHR concluded that the German legislation that permitted the use of surveillance stations upon German soil to intercept electronic communications emanating from other states did not violate the rule of territorial sovereignty. The ECtHR explained:

> Signals emitted from foreign countries are monitored by interception sites situated on German soil and the data collected are used in Germany. In light of this, the Court finds that the applicants failed to provide proof in the form of concordant inferences that the German authorities, by enacting and applying strategic monitoring measures, have acted in a manner which interfered with the territorial sovereignty of foreign States as protected in public international law.[51]

After the refusal of the Federal Court of Canada 2008 to issue a warrant to the CSIS to conduct espionage within the territory of other states, the CSIS reformulated its warrant and requested approval to use listening posts within Canada to intercept communications emanating from foreign territory. Distinguishing its 2008 decision, the Court explained that this 'is not a warrant that authorizes activities abroad but one which authorizes investigative activities to be conducted in Canada which will allow for communications to be listened to and information obtained from Canada'.[52] The presiding judge went on to explain that what 'has been proposed in the present warrant does not, in my view, constitute the enforcement of Canada's laws abroad but rather the exercise of jurisdiction here relating to the protection of Canada's security'.[53] The Court therefore concluded that this formulation of the warrant was in accordance with international law. Put differently, the Court was of the view that espionage is compatible with the rule of

[50] GA Res 41/65, *Principles Relating to Remote Sensing of the Earth from Space* (3 December 1986). Reviewing state practice, Chesterman concludes that '[t]here is no prohibition … on spying from orbit'; Chesterman (n 25) 1085.

[51] *Weber and Saravia v Germany*, Decision, App No 54934/00, ECtHR, 29 June 2006, para 88.

[52] X (Re), [2010] 1 FCR 460, 2009 FC 1058 (CanLII) para 40.

[53] ibid para 66.

territorial sovereignty providing that it does not involve intrusion into the territory of another state, that is, espionage does not amount to interference in the delivery of governmental functions.

Commentators claim that the 2014 *East Timor v Australia* litigation before the ICJ represents 'an interesting indication of the current paradigm shift under international law, whereby some states are, at the very least, finally protesting the legal status quo', namely, that espionage does not constitute unlawful interference in the performance of governmental functions.[54] This case involved Australia sending its agents into the office of an Australian lawyer – which was located within the territory of Australia – and who was acting as legal counsel for East Timor. The Australian agents seized documents and data that contained correspondence between East Timor and its legal counsel and which related to upcoming arbitration between these two states. East Timor applied to the ICJ for a provisional order that would declare '[t]hat the seizure by Australia of the documents and data violated (i) the sovereignty of Timor-Leste' and that 'Australia must immediately return to the nominated representative of Timor-Leste any and all of the aforesaid documents and data, and to destroy beyond recovery every copy of such documents and data that is in Australia's possession or control'.[55]

The ICJ found in favour of East Timor and granted the provisional measures requested. The Court required that Australia ensure the confidentiality of the seized material and that 'Australia shall not interfere in any way in communications between Timor-Leste and its legal advisers',[56] suggesting that this decision 'might be derived from the principle of the sovereign equality of States, which is one of the fundamental principles of the international legal order and is reflected in Article 2, paragraph 1, of the Charter of the United Nations'.[57]

A reasonable reading of this decision is that the ICJ regarded the collection of documents and data containing confidential correspondence between a state and its legal advisers as amounting to unlawful interference with the performance of an inherently governmental function or, more to the point, that Australia's act of espionage constituted a violation of East Timor's territorial sovereignty. If this reading is correct it would be, as Deeks recognises, 'a pretty big deal' because it represents an important 'step in limiting the legality of spying under international law'.[58]

Such a reading must be approached cautiously, however. First, as a provisional award, it is noticeable that the legal reasoning of the ICJ's judgment lacks

[54] N Jupillat, 'From the Cuckoo's Egg to Global Surveillance: Cyber Espionage that Becomes Prohibited Intervention' (2017) 42 *North Carolina Journal of International Law and Commercial Regulation* 933, 961.

[55] *Questions Relating to the Seizure and Detention of Certain Documents and Data (Timor-Leste v Australia)* (Provisional Orders) [2014] ICJ Rep 147, para 2.

[56] ibid para 55.

[57] ibid para 27.

[58] A Deeks, 'Can the ICJ Avoid Saying Something on the Merits About Spying in Timor-Leste vs. Australia?', 12 March 2014, *Lawfare*, www.lawfareblog.com/can-icj-avoid-saying-something-merits-about-spying-timor-leste-vs-australia.

granularity and this makes it difficult to ascertain precisely the reasons why – and the legal basis upon which – the Court awarded provisional measures. Certainly, East Timor requested that the ICJ declare Australia's conduct a violation of its sovereignty and, in order to protect its sovereignty, that Australia be required to ensure the confidentiality of the appropriated information and also abstain from interfering in its communications with its legal advisors in the future. In short, it appeared that East Timor was petitioning the Court to determine that Australia's espionage activities violated its sovereignty. Yet, Sir Elihu Lauterpacht – a member of East Timor's legal representation – explained before the Court that 'this is not a case about spying and espionage. The Court will not have to pronounce on such activities generally.'[59] Indeed, although the Court awarded the provisional measures that East Timor requested, when reasoning its decision the Court appeared to reformulate the legal basis of East Timor's request. The Court noted that '[t]he principal claim of Timor-Leste is that a violation has occurred of its right to communicate with its counsel and lawyers in a confidential manner with regard to issues forming the subject-matter of pending arbitral proceedings and future negotiations between the Parties'.[60] When granting East Timor's request, the Court explained that 'at least some of the rights for which Timor-Leste seeks protection – namely, the right to conduct arbitration proceedings or negotiations without interference by Australia, including the right of confidentiality of and non-interference in its communications with legal advisers – are plausible'.[61] Thus, rather than finding in favour of East Timor on the basis that acts of espionage interfere with the delivery of an inherently governmental function (that is, acts of espionage violate the rule of territorial sovereignty), the Court based its decision on the fact that, through virtue of their sovereignty, states possess a right under international law to maintain a confidential relationship with their legal advisers.

The application of the rule of territorial sovereignty to cyber espionage is further complicated by the reaction of a number of states to the Snowden revelations, which indicate that espionage activities can be regarded as interfering with the delivery of inherently governmental functions. For example, in condemning the US's cyber espionage activities, the Brazilian President Dilma Rousseff explained:

> Tampering in such a manner in the affairs of other countries is a breach of international law and is an affront [to] the principles that must guide the relations among them, especially among friendly nations. A sovereign nation can never establish itself to the detriment of another sovereign nation.[62]

[59] Oral Proceedings, Verbatim Record 2014/1, *Case Concerning Questions Relating to the Seizure and Detention of Certain Documents and Data (Timor-Leste v Australia)*, CR 2014/1 (2014) 15–16.

[60] *East Timor* (n 55) para 27.

[61] ibid para 28.

[62] Quoted in J Borger, 'Brazilian President: US Surveillance a "Breach of International Law"', 24 September 2013, *the Guardian*, www.theguardian.com/world/2013/sep/24/brazil-president-un-

The language used by the Brazilian President – 'tampering in such a manner in the affairs of other countries' – indicates that Brazil regarded the US's conduct as impermissible interference with governmental functions. Similarly, and as we have seen, the Bahamas insisted that the NSA's activities constituted not just a violation of its right to 'territorial integrity' but also its right to 'freedom from undue external intrusion and influence'.[63]

By way of conclusion, perhaps the best view is that, currently and in terms of *lex lata*, espionage does not amount to interference with the delivery of governmental functions. But 'there are signs of a turning tide'.[64] In particular, it appears that the fallout from the Snowden disclosures has given rise to state practice which, albeit embryonic, indicates that espionage is being increasingly regarded as impermissible interference with the performance of governmental functions and, as such, it constitutes a violation of the rule of territorial sovereignty.

3. The Rule of Non-Intervention

The rule of non-intervention commands a long pedigree in international law[65] and is undoubtedly 'part and parcel of customary international law'.[66] Identifying whether state action violates the rule of non-intervention is important because of the legal consequences that such a breach entails, principally, the nature, scope and intensity of the countermeasures that can be adopted by the victim state in order to put an end to the unlawful activity.

In clarifying the meaning of the non-intervention rule, the ICJ has explained:

> A prohibited intervention must accordingly be one bearing on matters in which each State is permitted, by the principle of State sovereignty, to decide freely. One of these is the choice of a political, economic, social and cultural system, and the formulation of foreign policy. Intervention is wrongful when it uses methods of coercion in regard to such choices, which must remain free ones.[67]

speech-nsa-surveillance. Brazilian Justice Minister Jose Eduardo Cardozo also described the surveillance as 'an attack on our country's sovereignty'; 'Brazil and Mexico Probe Claims US Spied on Presidents', 2 September 2013, *BBC News*, www.bbc.co.uk/news/world-latin-america-23938909.

[63] Quoted in Rolle (n 34).

[64] D Pun, 'Rethinking Espionage in the Modern Era' (2017) 18 *Chicago Journal of International Law* 353, 367.

[65] Article 8 Montevideo Convention on the Rights and Duties of States 1933; *Declaration on the Inadmissibility of Intervention in the Domestic Affairs of States and the Protection of Their Independence and Sovereignty*, UN Doc A/RES/20/2131, 21 December 1965; *Declaration on Principles of International Law Concerning Friendly Relations and Co-operation Among States in Accordance with the Charter of the United Nations*, Principle C, UN Doc A/RES/25/2625, 24 October 1970; *Declaration on the Inadmissibility of Intervention and Interference in the Internal Affairs of States*, UN Doc A/RES/36/103, 9 December 1981.

[66] *Nicaragua* (n 5) para 202.

[67] ibid para 205.

There are two conditions precedent for establishing a violation of the rule of non-intervention. The first condition relates to the domain within which intervention takes place and the second describes the type of intervention that is required.[68]

3.1. *Domaine Réservé*

Intervention is defined through the matrix of sovereignty. To establish unlawful intervention, the conduct in question must impinge upon matters that a state is freely entitled to determine on the basis that they fall within its sovereign competence (its *domaine réservé*). The subject matter that constitutes a state's *domaine réservé* is defined residually as that which '[is] not, in principle, regulated by international law'.[69] Identifying the totality of sovereign prerogatives that are susceptible to intervention is difficult because what is included (or remains) within a state's *domaine réservé* is not fixed and depends upon the content of international law as it reacts to developments within international relations.[70] This being said, the ICJ has offered examples of matters that fall within the *domaine réservé*, such as the choice of political, economic, social and cultural system and the formulation of foreign policy but these are not exhaustive.[71]

Generally, states possess the sovereign authority to determine for themselves what information they choose to disclose in pursuit of their foreign, economic and domestic policy objectives. As Peters explains, private communications between government officials is a good example of a matter that falls squarely within a state's *domaine réservé*.[72] Yet, under international law, states may have an obligation to disclose certain types of information or, in other words, international law divests states of their sovereign right to keep that information secret. As we saw in chapter 1, states may become party to a treaty that obliges them to disclose certain types of information to other treaty members or even to the international society as a whole. If a state refuses to comply with such an obligation, it commits a violation of international law. If another state has a legal right to access that confidential information and, in order to acquire access, commits espionage, it is difficult to see how this conduct constitutes interference in that state's *domaine réservé* within the meaning of the non-intervention rule (although it may, depending upon the circumstances, violate another rule of international law).

[68] M Jamnejad and M Wood, 'The Principle of Non-Intervention' (2009) 22 *Leiden Journal of International Law* 345, 347.
[69] *Nationality Decrees in Tunis and Morocco*, PCIJ Rep Series B No 4 (1923) 23.
[70] ibid.
[71] *Nicaragua* (n 5) para 205.
[72] 'Nonpublic communications among government figures (including Chancellor Angela Merkel's telephone calls with other public officials) certainly belong to this *domaine réservé*'; A Peters, 'Privacy, *Rechtsstaatlichkeit*, and the Legal Limits on Extraterritorial Surveillance' in RA Miller (ed), *Privacy and Power: A Transatlantic Dialogue in the Shadow of the NSA Affair* (Cambridge, Cambridge University Press, 2017) 164.

Similarly, a state may store information on cyber infrastructure physically located in a foreign state and those states may conclude agreements stipulating which state possesses sovereign authority over that data.[73] If the terms of an agreement transfer authority over that information to the host state, the state that originally produced that information no longer maintains a sovereign right to keep that information secret and, in the event that it is subject to espionage, it is precluded from claiming that its *domaine réservé* has been interfered with. It is important to stress that much will depend upon the exact terms of the agreement. As said, it is the content of international law that determines whether a matter falls within the protected confines of a state's *domaine réservé*.

3.2. Coercion

To establish a violation of the rule of non-intervention there must be *intervention* in the state's *domaine réservé*. It is imperative to distinguish intervention from interference because, while intervention in the domestic affairs of another state is unlawful, interference is permissible because it is regarded as an inevitable by-product of an increasingly globalised world order where states are constantly interacting.[74]

The dividing line between intervention and interference is whether the impugned conduct is coercive: '[t]he element of coercion … defines, and indeed forms the very essence of, prohibited intervention'.[75] Coercion denotes 'imperative pressure'[76] that subordinates the will of the state in order for the entity exercising coercion to realise certain objectives or, in Oppenheim's words, intervention is 'dictatorial interference … in the affairs of another State for the purpose of maintaining or altering the actual condition of things'.[77]

[73] For example, Estonia and Luxembourg entered into an agreement which determines that, in certain circumstances, Estonia continues to exercise sovereignty over its data when it is resident on cyber infrastructure located within Luxembourg; 'Estonia to Open the World's First Data Embassy in Luxembourg', 21 June 2017, *Estonian World*, www.estonianworld.com/security/estonia-open-worlds-first-data-embassy-luxembourg/.

[74] Unless, of course, a state interferes with the performance of an *inherently governmental function* of another state. As we saw in section 2.2 of this chapter, this conduct transgresses the rule of territorial sovereignty.

[75] *Nicaragua* (n 5) para 205.

[76] WM Reisman, *Nullity and Revision: The Review and Enforcement of International Judgments and Awards* (New Heaven, Yale University Press, 1971) 839–40.

[77] L Oppenheim (H Lauterpacht, ed) *International Law: A Treatise* (London, New York, Longmans, Green & Co, 1955) 305. For Jamnejad and Wood, coercion is imposed where 'action is taken by one state to secure a change in the policies of another'; Jamnejad and Wood (n 68) 347–48. According to Joyner, '[c]oercion in inter-State relations involves the government of one State compelling the government of another State to think or act in a certain way by applying various kinds of pressure, threats, intimidation or the use of force'; CC Joyner, 'Coercion' (2006) *Max Planck Encyclopaedia of Public International Law*, para 1. For the *Tallinn Manual 2.0* Experts, '[t]he key is that the coercive act must

Commentators overwhelmingly conclude that espionage does not qualify as coercive because it does not compel a state to act or to abstain from acting in a particular way.[78] As Ziolkowski explains:

> A forbidden intervention in domestic affairs requires the element of coercion of the other State. Scholars assert that illegal coercion implies massive influence, inducing the affected State to adopt a decision with regard to its policy or practice which it would not entertain as a free and sovereign State. It is clear that clandestine information gathering as such will not fulfil such requirements.[79]

Alternatively, there are a few commentators that argue that political cyber espionage results in the imposition of coercion against the victim state. The basis of their argument is that, unless otherwise prescribed by international law, states are entitled to keep information secret. Where another state accesses and copies a state's secret information, the victim state's autonomous decision-making capacity is undermined because the confidentiality of that information is removed without its consent. In this sense, cyber espionage possesses a coercive element because it forces the hand of the victim state. In response to the NSA's cyber espionage activities against Germany, Terry argues:

> [A]t a basic level there can be little doubt that this requirement [of coercion] is met. After all, it is self-evident that it is a State's prerogative and sovereign right, as part of its foreign policy, to decide what information it shares with other States, whether these are allies or foes. A sovereign government has the right to develop its domestic and foreign affairs policies unobserved by a foreign power. By denying the German government that right, the USA forces Germany to-unwittingly-disclose what it, as a sovereign State, has decided not to disclose in pursuit of its foreign, trade or domestic policy goals. By trying to obtain internal communications which the German government obviously did not want to share with the USA, Germany is robbed of the opportunity of making a sovereign decision on whom it wants to share these secret government deliberations with.[80]

have the potential for compelling the target State to engage in an action that it would otherwise not take (or refrain from taking an action it would otherwise take)'; *Tallinn Manual 2.0* (n 11) 319.

[78] Although the use of information after it has been collected to exercise influence over another state may be coercive; I Kilovaty, 'Doxfare: Politically Motivated Leaks and the Future of the Norm on Non-Intervention in the Era of Weaponized Information' (2017) 9 *Harvard National Security Journal* 146.

[79] K Ziolkowski, 'Peacetime Cyber Espionage – New Tendencies in Public International Law' in Ziolkowski (n 20) 433 (citations omitted). There was consensus among the *Tallinn Manual 2.0* Experts that '[c]yber espionage *per se* … does not qualify as intervention because it lacks a coercive element'; *Tallinn Manual 2.0* (n 11) 323. '[T]he obtaining of information in itself falls short of coercive or dictatorial interference, and would not constitute 'intervention' in the legal sense'; T Gill, 'Non-Intervention in the Cyber Context' in Ziolkowski (n 20) 224. 'Both in the cyber context and physical context, a mere intrusion into another state's networks to gather information would not violate the norm of non-intervention without some indication that such collection was used to coercively influence the target state'; C Lotrionte, 'Countering State-Sponsored Cyber Economic Espionage under International Law' (2015) 40 *North Carolina Journal of International Law and Commercial Regulation* 443, 508. '[T]he NSA's surveillance did not seek to pressure – or "coerce" – the states in which the programs operated to make specific policy choices or take specific actions'; Peters (n 72) 164.

[80] Terry (n 39) 197. Banks asks 'does the contemporary use of state-sponsored espionage to steal trade secrets and intellectual property constitute intervention? Is a breach of the norm measured by

Conceptually, the argument that political cyber espionage is coercive because it usurps the decision of the victim state to keep information secret is persuasive. The fact of the matter, however, is that such an approach is not supported by state practice and, from the perspective of *lex lata*, it can be concluded that espionage does not possess the requisite coercive element to trigger a violation of the rule of non-intervention.[81]

4. The Prohibition on the Use of Force

Article 2(4) UN Charter and its customary international law counterpart[82] impose an obligation upon states to 'refrain in their international relations from the threat or use of force against the territorial integrity or political independence of any state'. Establishing whether cyber espionage contravenes the prohibition on the use of force is important because of the consequences that flow from its violation. States such as the US maintain that any use of force amounts to an 'armed attack' within the meaning of Article 51 UN Charter. According to this view, any act that qualifies as a use of force engages the victim state's right to self-defence.[83] This is not the mainstream approach, however, and the preponderance of authority submits that it is only those uses of force that are sufficiently 'grave'[84] in terms of their 'scale and effects'[85] that qualify as an armed attack under Article 51.[86] Yet, commentators argue that even if self-defence is unavailable in relation to uses of force not amounting to an armed attack, in such circumstances states are nevertheless entitled to take resort to proportionate forcible (as well as non-forcible) countermeasures.[87]

Whether cyber espionage violates the use of force prohibition depends upon the definition of the term 'force'. Force is not defined by Article 2(4) UN Charter and in the years following the signing of this agreement there was an 'acrimonious'

the impact of the intervention, whether virtual or physical? Certainly cyber surveillance or espionage targeting government activities interferes with the internal affairs of the victim state'; WC Banks, 'Cyber Espionage and Electronic Surveillance: Beyond the Media Coverage' (2017) 66 *Emory Law Journal* 513, 520. Wright claims that 'espionage into official secrets' is 'doubtless interference' in the domestic affairs of a state and thus constitutes unlawful intervention; Wright (n 29) 5.

[81] The careful reader will notice that I have previously argued that cyber espionage does possess a coercive element and thus violates the non-intervention rule: R Buchan, 'Cyber Espionage and International Law' in N Tsagourias and R Buchan (eds), *Research Handbook on International Law and Cyberspace* (Cheltenham, Edward Elgar, 2015). Upon reflection, it seems that there is insufficient state practice to conclude that espionage imposes coercion upon the victim state in the sense required by the rule of non-intervention.

[82] *Nicaragua* (n 5) para 188–90.

[83] US Department of Defense, Office of the General Consul, *Law of War Manual* (June 2015) para 16.3.3.1.

[84] *Nicaragua* (n 5) para 191.

[85] ibid para 195.

[86] ibid para 191.

[87] *Oil Platforms (Islamic Republic of Iran v US)*, Judgment (Merits) [2003] ICJ Rep 161, para 12 (Separate Opinion of Judge Simma).

debate as to the meaning of this concept.[88] In particular, debate centred on whether Article 2(4) prohibits the use of armed force or whether its scope is broader and includes the imposition of economic and political coercion.[89] Since the end of the Cold War these debates have largely subsided, with a consensus emerging around an interpretation of Article 2(4) that prohibits armed force only.[90]

Brownlie defines armed force as the use of a weapon to inflict physical damage, by which he means 'destruction to life and property'.[91] In the words of Dinstein, a use of force is an act of 'violence'.[92] Thus, state conduct that produces physical damage within another state constitutes a use of force within the meaning of Article 2(4) UN Charter, even if that damage is brought about by cyber means.[93] While acting as Legal Adviser to the US State Department, Harold Koh explained:

> In analyzing whether a cyber operation would constitute a use of force, most commentators focus on whether the direct physical injury and property damage resulting from the cyber event looks like that which would be considered a use of force if produced by kinetic weapons. *For example, cyber activities that proximately result in death, injury, or significant destruction would likely be viewed as a use of force.*[94]

However, due to the international society's growing reliance upon cyberspace, malicious cyber operations can inflict significant harm even if they do not produce physical damage. In light of this, commentators have sought to progressively develop the definition of the concept of force, expanding the scope of Article 2(4) to include cyber operations that produce non-physical damage that is comparable in effects to physical damage.[95]

The *Tallinn Manual 2.0* Experts were of the view that it is 'less clear' as to whether the notion of force can be interpreted to include cyber operations that

[88] RD Kearney and RE Dalton, 'The Treaty on Treaties' (1970) 64 *AJIL* 495, 534–35.

[89] 6 UNCIO Docs 334, 609 (1945) Doc 2, 617(e)(4), 3 UNCIO Docs 251, 253–54 (1945). See also the debate in the General Assembly; UN GAOR Special Comm on Friendly Relations, UN Doc A/AC/AC.125/SR.110 to 114 (1970).

[90] 'The term does not cover any possible kind of force, but is, according to the correct and prevailing view, limited to armed force'; A Randelzhofer, 'Article 2(4)' in B Simma (ed), *The Charter of the United Nations: A Commentary* (Oxford, Oxford University Press, 2002) 117.

[91] I Brownlie, *International Law and the Use of Force by States* (Oxford, Clarendon Press, 1963) 362.

[92] 'It does not matter what specific means – kinetic or electronic – are being used to bring it about, but the end result must be that violence occurs or is threatened'; Y Dinstein, *War, Aggression and Self-Defence* (Cambridge, Cambridge University Press, 2017) 90 (citations omitted).

[93] 'Acts that injure or kill persons or physically damage or destroy objects are uses of force'; *Tallinn Manual 2.0* (n 11) 333. See generally M Roscini, *Cyber Operations and the Use of Force in International Law* (Oxford, Oxford University Press, 2014) 52–55.

[94] HH Koh, 'International Law in Cyberspace' (2012) 54 *Harvard International Law Journal Online* 1, 3–4 (citations omitted).

[95] '[A traditional definition of Article 2(4) UN Charter] emphasizes death or physical injury to people and destruction of physical property as its criteria for the definitions of "use of force" and "armed attack." But modern society depends on the existence and proper functioning of an extensive infrastructure that itself is increasingly controlled by information technology. Actions that significantly interfere with the functionality of that infrastructure can reasonably be regarded as uses of force, whether or not they cause immediate physical damage'; National Research Council, *Technology, Policy, Law and Ethics Regarding U.S. Acquisition and Use of Cyberattack Capabilities* (WA Owens, KW Dam and HS Lin, 2009) 7–9.

produce harmful effects in cyberspace but which do not cause physical damage.[96] This being said, 'the International Group of Experts took notice of an approach that seeks to assess the likelihood that States will characterise a cyber operation as a use of force'.[97] For the Experts, the factors that could be used to indicate that a harmful but not physically destructive cyber operation is sufficiently serious to violate Article 2(4) UN Charter include: the severity of the attack; its immediacy, directness and invasiveness; whether it is of a military character; and the level of state involvement.[98] While all these factors would have to be weighed in the balance when determining whether the Article 2(4) threshold is met, the Experts note that '[s]everity is the most significant factor in the analysis' and that, when assessing severity, 'the more consequences impinge on critical national interests, the more they will contribute to the depiction of a cyber operation as a use of force'.[99]

Undoubtedly, states regard certain types of confidential information as forming part of their critical national infrastructure[100] (an obvious example being the launch codes of nuclear weapons) and, where this information is deprived of its confidentiality, they consider their critical national interests to be adversely affected. If we accept a definition of the concept of force to include cyber operations that impinge upon critical national interests, it opens up the possibility that acts of cyber espionage can trigger a violation of the Article 2(4) prohibition. According to Melnitzky:

> The severity of the problem of data theft is simply too great and its effects are too harmful … The scale of theft is unprecedented … Prior to the Internet, looting on such a scale could only have been accomplished by a military occupation. The effects-based approach requirement that a cyberattack must cause damage only previously possible by traditional military force is therefore satisfied.[101]

Indeed, if this expansive reading of Article 2(4) UN Charter is accepted, it may even be the case that the impact of cyber espionage upon critical national interests is so grave that it qualifies as an armed attack within the meaning of Article 51 UN Charter, thereby engaging the victim state's right to self-defence.

I reject this broad interpretation of the concept of force. Instead, I agree with Waxman's observation that there is currently significant divergence between states as to how Article 2(4) UN Charter applies to malicious cyber operations, thus 'impeding formation of a stable international consensus' on the meaning

[96] *Tallinn Manual 2.0* (n 11) 333.
[97] ibid.
[98] ibid 334–36.
[99] ibid 334.
[100] According to the US, '[critical national infrastructure includes] systems and assets, *whether physical or virtual*, so vital to the United States that the incapacity or destruction of such systems and assets would have a debilitating impact on security, national economic security, national public health or safety, or any combination of those matters'; Patriot Act 2001, Public Law 107–56 (26 October 2001) section 1016(e) (emphasis added).
[101] A Melnitzky, 'Defending America against Chinese Cyber Espionage Through the Use of Active Defenses' (2012) 20 *Cardozo Journal of International and Comparative Law* 537, 566.

of the term force beyond conduct that causes real-world, physical damage.[102] Consequently, arguments that are designed to dilate the scope of the term force to include conduct that produces non-physical harm must be regarded as articulations of *lex ferenda* rather than *lex lata*:

> In light of the ever-increasing reliance of society on computers and computer networks, many readers, like the author, will find the 'physical consequences' standard [of Article 2(4) UN Charter] too narrow. But it does represent the lex lata, that is, the law that presently exists.[103]

Thus, given that acts of cyber espionage result in the copying of confidential data and do not produce physical damage, they do not contravene the use of force prohibition: 'the type of surveillance described in the classified documents disclosed by Edward Snowden, lacking as it did any injury to people or property, would not likely rise to the level to constitute a use of force'.[104] Certainly, 'no government regards cyber espionage of any kind as a prohibited use of force'.[105] If cyber espionage does not amount to a use of force then, a fortiori, it cannot constitute an armed attack within the meaning of Article 51 UN Charter.[106]

5. Conclusion

This chapter has examined the application of the rules of territorial sovereignty, non-intervention and the non-use of force to cyber espionage. This chapter has concluded that the latter two rules have little role to play in regulating cyber

[102] MC Waxman, 'Cyber-Attacks and the Use of Force: Back to the Future of Article 2(4)' (2011) 36 *Yale Journal of International Law* 421, 425–26. For Dinstein, 'when studied in context, the term "force" in Article 2(4) must denote violence'; Dinstein (n 92) 90.

[103] MN Schmitt, '"Attack" as a Term of Art in International Law: The Cyber Operations Context' in C Czosseck, R Ottis and K Ziolkowski (eds), *International Conference on Cyber Conflict* (CCDCOE, 2012) 288.

[104] CS Yoo, 'Cyber Espionage or Cyberwar? International Law, Domestic Law, and Self-Protective Measures' in JD Ohlin, K Govern and C Finkelstein (eds), *Cyberwar: Law and Ethics for Virtual Conflicts* (Oxford, Oxford University Press, 2015) 179. 'Computer-based espionage, intelligence collection, or even some preemptive cyber-operations or countermeasures designed to disable an adversary's threatening capabilities, for example, would generally not constitute prohibited force because these activities do not produce destructive consequences analogous to a kinetic military attack'; Waxman (n 102) 434–35. '[C]yber espionage cannot be deemed either a "threat" or "use of [armed] force" in the meaning of Article 2(4) of the UN Charter, nor an "armed attack" pursuant to Article 51 of the UN Charter'; Ziolkowski (n 79) 456.

[105] DP Fidler, 'Economic Cyber Espionage and International Law: Controversies Involving Acquisition of Trade Secrets through Cyber Technologies', 29 March 2013, *ASIL Insights*, www.asil.org/insights/volume/17/issue/10/economic-cyber-espionage-and-international-law-controversies-involving. 'Nations seem to agree that espionage, among other activities, is not enough to count as a use of force'; A Wortham, 'Should Cyber Exploitation Ever Constitute a Demonstration of Hostile Intent That May Violate UN Charter Provisions Prohibiting the Threat or Use of Force?' (2012) 64 *Federal Communications Law Journal* 643, 652.

[106] '[A]cts of cyber intelligence gathering … do not qualify as armed attacks'; *Tallinn Manual 2.0* (n 11) 341.

espionage. As cyber espionage describes the copying of confidential information, it lacks the requisite coercive element to trigger a violation of the non-intervention rule and does not produce the physical damage necessary to infringe the prohibition on the use of force.

States exercise territorial sovereignty over computer networks and systems supported by cyber infrastructure physically located within their territory. Where states engage in computer operations that penetrate foreign computer networks and systems in search of confidential information, they violate the victim state's territorial sovereignty. Cyber espionage violates the rule of territorial sovereignty regardless of whether the computer networks and systems infiltrated are operated by state organs or private actors or whether the information sought is of a political or economic nature.

There are limits to the utility of the rule of territorial sovereignty when it comes to regulating cyber espionage. States invariably store data on and transmit data through computer networks and systems supported by cyber infrastructure located within foreign territory. If data is accessed and copied while it is located upon foreign cyber infrastructure, it is clear that the state to which the data belongs cannot claim that its sovereign cyber infrastructure has been intruded upon.[107] The rule of territorial sovereignty also protects the right of states to perform inherently governmental functions within their territory without interference. However, as we have seen, this element of the rule of territorial sovereignty provides states with little protection against cyber espionage because, to date, the international society has refused to accept that the unauthorised collection of confidential information amounts to interference with the exercise of governmental functions.

[107] '[I]n cases where confidential data of one state is located in the cloud outside its territory, the state will face difficulties in justifying control over such data'; MT Veber and MK Dine, 'Big Data and Economic Cyber Espionage: An International Law Perspective' in A Završnik (ed), *Big Data, Crime and Social Control* (London, Routledge, 2017) 199.

4

Cyber Espionage and Diplomatic and Consular Law

1. Introduction

The Edward Snowden disclosures revealed that the United States (US) had directed its cyber espionage activities against diplomatic missions and consular posts located within the US. According to one document, the US had identified 38 diplomatic missions and consular posts within its territory as 'targets' (as they were ominously referred to) for espionage, including missions and posts belonging to traditional adversaries (such as Middle Eastern states) and to long-standing allies (France, Greece, Italy etc).[1]

Moreover, the Snowden leaks revealed that the US had utilised its diplomatic missions and consular posts to obtain confidential data belonging to those states within which they were based.[2] For sure, the exploitation of diplomatic missions and consular posts for the purpose of cyber espionage is not a practice isolated to the US. For example, in November 2013 the Indonesian government summoned the Australian Ambassador to Indonesia to a meeting to explain reports that Australia's diplomatic mission in Jakarta had been used to conduct espionage (and in particular cyber espionage). Indeed, the Australian media further reported that Australian diplomatic missions and consular posts in Bangkok, Beijing, Dili, Hanoi, Kuala Lumpur and Port Moresby had also been used to conduct espionage.[3]

Diplomatic and consular law is codified in the widely ratified Vienna Convention on Diplomatic Relations (VCDR) 1961 and the Vienna Convention on Consular Relations (VCCR) 1963.[4] The objective of this chapter is to assess the

[1] E MacAskill and J Borger, 'New NSA Leaks Show How US is Bugging its European Allies', 30 June 2013, *the Guardian*, www.theguardian.com/world/2013/jun/30/nsa-leaks-us-bugging-european-allies.

[2] 'Embassy Espionage: The NSA's Secret Spy Hub in Berlin', 27 October 2013, *Spiegel*, www.spiegel.de/international/germany/cover-story-how-nsa-spied-on-merkel-cell-phone-from-berlin-embassy-a-930205.html.

[3] B Jabour, 'Indonesia Summons Australian Envoy Over Embassy Spying Claims', 1 November 2013, *the Guardian*, www.theguardian.com/world/2013/nov/01/indonesia-summons-australian-ambassador-embassy-spying-claims.

[4] The Vienna Conventions are considered to be reflective of customary international law; *United States Diplomatic and Consular Staff in Tehran (United States of America v Iran)*, Judgment [1980] ICJ Rep 3, para 45 ('The Vienna Conventions, which codify the law of diplomatic and consular relations,

application of these regimes to cyber espionage.[5] Section 2 analyses whether diplomatic and consular law effectively protects confidential information belonging to diplomatic missions and consular posts from cyber espionage. Section 3 assesses whether it is permissible under diplomatic and consular law for diplomatic missions and consular posts to be used as a platform to commit cyber espionage. Additionally, this section considers whether the personal immunities enjoyed by diplomatic and consular officials under the VCDR and the VCCR mean that they cannot be held responsible for acts of cyber espionage that violate the national laws of the receiving state. Section 4 offers conclusions.

2. Cyber Espionage Against Diplomatic Missions and Consular Posts

A key function of diplomatic missions is to represent the political interests of the sending state.[6] In contrast, consular posts take responsibility for less politically sensitive matters, such as assisting nationals in the receiving state, promoting trade between private actors within the sending and receiving states and facilitating cultural exchange.[7]

Cyberspace is 'indispensable' to the performance of diplomatic and consular functions, enabling diplomatic missions and consular posts to store and transmit huge amounts of information instantaneously.[8] Notwithstanding the benefits of cyberspace to diplomacy, the technological vulnerabilities associated with this domain render the information stored within it, and the communications that occur across it, susceptible to interception and appropriation.[9] Recognising that

state principles and rules essential for the maintenance of peaceful relations between States and accepted throughout the world by nations of all creeds, cultures and political complexions').

[5] Other international legal regimes have been implemented in order to regulate diplomatic and consular relations, such as the Vienna Convention on Special Missions 1969. Due to space limitations, these frameworks will not be addressed in this chapter. However, many of the provisions contained in the VCDR and the VCCR are replicated in these treaties and, consequently, much of the analysis that follows in this chapter can provide useful insights into how they apply to cyber espionage.

[6] For the functions of diplomatic missions see Article 3 VCDR.

[7] For the functions of consular posts see Article 5 VCCR.

[8] 'Communication is vital to diplomacy. The nature of the Internet has rendered it an indispensable means of communication in this modern age and has given rise to the burgeoning of what we have termed "Internet diplomacy"'; W-M Choi, 'Diplomatic and Consular Law in the Internet Age' (2006) 10 *Singapore Year Book of International Law* 117, 118.

[9] 'Technological evolution has certainly improved the performance of diplomatic and consular functions. However, there is also a dark side to such evolution – modern technology provides both more opportunities and more tools for forbidden information surveillance and intelligence gathering'; R Värk, 'Diplomatic and Consular Privileges and Immunities in Case of Unfriendly Cyber Activities' (2014) 14 *Baltic Yearbook of International Law* 125, 125. 'Technological developments that allow for the fast and uncomplicated distribution of data have been introduced to diplomatic correspondence and negotiations, increasing both efficiency and vulnerability'; S Duquet and J Wouters, 'Diplomacy,

secrecy is an essential part of diplomatic and consular relations, the VCDR and the VCCR provide a number of legal protections that enable diplomatic missions and consular posts to maintain confidentiality over their information and communications. However, these rules were developed long before the advent of cyberspace and our task is to assess whether they apply to the online activities of diplomatic missions and consular posts and, in particular, whether they afford protection against cyber espionage.

2.1. The Inviolability of Diplomatic and Consular Premises

2.1.1. Premises

The inviolability of diplomatic and consular premises constitutes 'a bedrock principle'[10] of diplomatic and consular law and is enshrined in Article 22 VCDR and Article 31 VCCR. Turning first to diplomatic missions, Article 22(1) VCDR declares that '[t]he premises of the mission shall be inviolable. The agents of the receiving State may not enter them, except with the consent of the head of the mission.' Article 30(1) VCDR further provides that '[t]he private residence of a diplomatic agent shall enjoy the same inviolability and protection as the premises of the mission'. The premises of the diplomatic mission extend to 'the buildings or parts of buildings and the land ancillary thereto, irrespective of ownership, used for the purposes of the mission including the residence of the head of the mission'.[11] In essence, diplomatic premises encompass the entire territorial space belonging to the diplomatic mission, including areas such as the garden and car park.[12]

By defining the scope of the diplomatic premises expansively and by designating them as inviolable, the objective of Article 22(1) VCDR is to establish 'a protective ring' around the diplomatic mission and safeguard it from unauthorised access,[13] thereby allowing the mission to perform its functions without fear of intrusion. The immediate question is whether the computer networks and systems used by diplomatic missions to store and transmit confidential data form part of the 'premises' of the mission within the meaning of Article 22(1) VCDR and thus benefit from inviolability.

Secrecy and the Law' (March 2015) Working Paper No 151, *Leuven Centre for Global Governance Studies* 1, 4.

[10] MN Schmitt, *Tallinn Manual 2.0 on the International Law Applicable to Cyber Operations* (Cambridge, Cambridge University Press, 2017) 212.

[11] Article 1(i) VCDR.

[12] J d'Aspremont, 'Premises of Diplomatic Missions' (2009) *Max Planck Encyclopedia of Public International Law*, para 4.

[13] 'Inviolability involves the placing of a protective ring around the ambassador, the embassy and its archives and documents which neither the receiving state nor the courts of the receiving state may lawfully penetrate … Inviolability, like other diplomatic immunities, is a defence against an attempt to exercise state power'; *R (Bancoult No 3) v Secretary of State for Foreign and Commonwealth Affairs* [2014] EWCA Civ 708, [2014] 1 WLR 2921, para 58.

As I argued in chapter 3, states exercise territorial sovereignty over the cyber infrastructure that is physically located within their territory and also over the computer networks and systems that this infrastructure supports. Diplomatic missions are not separate legal entities but are instead organs of their sending state and are thus an embodiment of their sovereignty. By analogy, it can be said that the inviolability conferred by Article 22(1) VCDR extends to cyber infrastructure located upon the premises of the diplomatic mission and this includes the computer networks and systems that this infrastructure supports, even though they exist virtually.[14] However, computer systems and networks that are supported by cyber infrastructure that is located *outside* of the diplomatic mission do not constitute part of its premises and do not therefore benefit from the protection afforded by Article 22(1) VCDR (although the data they hold may be nevertheless protected by other provisions of the VCDR).

Whether the premises of diplomatic missions enjoy absolute inviolability has been subject to debate. For example, while the Harvard Draft Convention on Diplomatic Privileges and Immunities appeared to recognise the absolute inviolability of diplomatic premises, its commentary explains that it:

> does not undertake to provide for well-known exceptions in practice, as when the premises are on fire or when there is imminent danger that a crime of violence is about to be perpetrated upon the premises. In such cases it would be absurd to wait for the consent of a chief of mission in order to obtain entry upon the premises. Like acts of God and force majeure these are necessarily implied as exceptions to the specific requirement of prior consent for entry. Whether or not the circumstances are sufficiently extraordinary to justify non-observance of the rule would be a matter for diplomatic reclamation.[15]

In a similar vein, the International Law Commission's (ILC) Special Rapporteur Emil Sandström's original draft of Article 22(1) VCDR (Draft Article 12) provided for an exception to the general rule of inviolability 'in an extreme emergency, in order to eliminate a grave and imminent danger to human life, public health or property, or to safeguard the security of the State. In such emergencies the authorization of the Ministry of Foreign Affairs must, if possible, be obtained.'[16] If this approach had been accepted it would yield significant implications for the inviolability of the premises of diplomatic missions because concepts such as human life, public health, public property and national security are capacious and malleable. In particular, it would open up the possibility that where diplomatic premises are used to launch acts of political cyber espionage, the interests of national security would permit the receiving state to enter the mission and put an end to this damaging conduct.

[14] Rule 39 of the *Tallinn Manual 2.0* explains that '[c]yber infrastructure on the premises of a diplomatic mission or consular post is protected by the inviolability of that mission or post'; *Tallinn Manual 2.0* (n 10).

[15] 26 *AJIL* (1932 Supp) 52. cp Genet (1931) vol I, 542.

[16] Diplomatic Intercourse and Immunities, Report by Special Rapporteur Emil Sandström, UN Doc A/CN.4/91, 21 April 1950, 11.

Crucially, the proposition that diplomatic premises possess a qualified inviolability has been decisively rejected. During its discussions of diplomatic intercourse and immunities in the late 1950s, the ILC determined that state practice did not recognise any exceptions to the inviolability of diplomatic premises, except where the receiving state obtained the consent of the head of mission. Although there was evidence that receiving states had entered diplomatic premises in times of emergency (for example, where there was a fire), it was agreed that entry was not performed unilaterally but instead at the invitation of the head of mission. For this reason, the ILC deleted the Special Rapporteur's 'emergency exception' from Draft Article 12.[17]

Whether diplomatic premises can be entered in times of emergency was also debated at length at the Vienna conference. States such as Ireland and Japan proposed an amendment to the ILC's draft articles that would enable receiving states to take 'such measures as are essential for the protection of life and property in exceptional circumstances of public emergency and danger'.[18] However, this amendment was rejected by other states, which concurred with the ILC's assessment that diplomatic premises are absolutely inviolable. It is therefore clear that, under Article 22(1) VCDR, 'no exception is allowed to the general rule of inviolability of mission premises'.[19]

One further issue requires consideration. If a diplomatic mission engages in internationally wrongful conduct, can the receiving state adopt countermeasures that are otherwise in contravention of Article 22(1) VCDR in order to induce the sending state into complying with its international law obligations? For example, can the receiving state engage in cyber espionage and appropriate confidential data with the view to cajoling the sending state into law-compliance? Given the potential for countermeasures to aggravate tensions and further destabilise international peace and security, their availability is subject to very strict conditions. A consideration of these conditions is unnecessary given that in the *Tehran Hostages* case the International Court of Justice (ICJ) unambiguously ruled out the use of countermeasures within the context of diplomatic relations. As the ICJ explained, the VCDR is a 'self-contained régime'[20] and thus provides its own mechanisms for remedying violations of its rules.[21]

[17] See Draft Article 20(1), ILC, *Draft Articles on Diplomatic Intercourse and Immunities, with Commentaries* (1958). For a discussion see E Denza, *Diplomatic Law: Commentary on the Vienna Convention on Diplomatic Relations* (Oxford, Oxford University Press, 2016) 118–19.

[18] United Nations Conference on Diplomatic Intercourse and Immunities, Official Records, vol II (1962) 24, UN Doc A/CONF.20/C.1/L.163.

[19] Y Bao, 'The Protection of Public Safety and Human Life vs the Inviolability of Mission Premises' in P Behrens (ed), *Diplomatic Law in a New Millennium* (Oxford, Oxford University Press, 2016) 151.

[20] *Tehran Hostages* (n 4) para 86.

[21] The most potent remedy available to the receiving state is to declare diplomatic agents or even the entire mission *persona non grata*; Article 9 VCDR (for a similar provision in the context of consular posts see Article 23 VCCR).

There is one exception. Where a diplomatic mission engages in conduct that qualifies as a 'grave'[22] use of force under Article 2(4) United Nations (UN) Charter – that is, an 'armed attack' within the meaning of Article 51 UN Charter – this engages the receiving state's right to self-defence and it is thereby permitted to undertake measures against and within the premises of the diplomatic mission to the extent that they are necessary to halt and repel the armed attack, including the use of cyber espionage.[23]

To summarise, except in the narrow circumstances of self-defence, the inviolability of diplomatic premises is 'absolute, without automatic exceptions'.[24] Hence, any intrusion into these premises constitutes a violation of Article 22(1) VCDR, regardless of whether the intrusion produces damage or harm.[25] We have already seen that diplomatic premises include computer systems and networks that are supported by cyber infrastructure located on the mission's territory. Thus, a cyber operation that intrudes upon these computer networks and systems in search of confidential data amounts to a violation of Article 22(1) VCDR (unless of course the cyber operation has been consented to by the head of the mission, in which case it would not be properly classified as espionage).

Turning now to consular posts, Article 31(1) VCCR provides that '[c]onsular premises shall be inviolable to the extent provided in this article', and consular premises are defined as 'the buildings or parts of buildings and the land ancillary thereto, irrespective of ownership, used exclusively for the purposes of the consular post'.[26]

As with diplomatic premises, there seems little difficultly in concluding that cyber infrastructure physically located within the territory of the consular post forms part of the consular premises within the meaning of Article 31(1) VCCR, as do computer networks and systems supported by that infrastructure. But note that the definition of consular premises is restricted to those areas of consular

[22] *Military and Paramilitary Activities in and against Nicaragua (Nicaragua v United States of America)*, Judgment (Merits) [1986] ICJ Rep 14, para 191.

[23] As an illustration, in 1984 a group of anti-Gaddafi protesters had gathered outside the Libyan Embassy in London. Shots were fired at the protesters and British policewoman Yvonne Fletcher was killed. The UK concluded that the shot had been fired from the Libyan Embassy and subsequently surrounded it. Although coming under pressure to enter the Embassy and apprehend those responsible, the UK respected the inviolability of the mission and instead severed diplomatic ties with Libya. Subsequently, the House of Commons Foreign Affairs Committee examined the events surrounding the shooting and the Legal Advisor to the Foreign and Commonwealth Office made it clear to the Committee that the government's view was that where diplomatic missions are used to launch armed attacks the receiving state is justified in forcibly entering the mission in the exercise of its inherent right to self-defence; Foreign Affairs Committee (UK), 'The Abuse of Diplomatic Immunities and Privileges', HC Paper 127 (1984–85) paras 88–95. See generally JS Beaumont, 'Self-Defence as a Justification for Disregarding Diplomatic Immunity' (1991) 29 *Canadian Yearbook of International Law* 391, 398 and *Tallinn Manual 2.0* (n 10) 214. For a fuller discussion of the doctrine of self-defence see chapter 8.

[24] Värk (n 9) 130.

[25] This was the view of the majority of the Experts responsible for drafting the *Tallinn Manual 2.0*, even though a '[a] few of the Experts … were of the view that a violation of this Rule requires the receiving State's physical presence in the mission'; *Tallinn Manual 2.0* (n 10) 213.

[26] Article 1(j) VCCR.

posts that are used *exclusively* for the purpose of consular functions. If parts of consular posts are dual use in the sense that they are used for both consular and non-consular functions, they are not used exclusively for the purpose of consular functions and, consequently, they do not qualify as consular premises and do not enjoy inviolability under Article 31(1) VCCR (although items within the consular post (such as official correspondence) may benefit from other protections afforded by the VCCR). Thus, computer rooms and computer networks and systems that are used for consular purposes but are also used for purposes not pursuant to consular functions (for example, to engage in cyber espionage which, as we shall see below, is not a permissible function of a consular post) do not constitute consular premises and do not possess inviolability under Article 31(1) VCCR.

Significantly, unlike diplomatic premises, consular premises are not conferred absolute inviolability.[27] Article 31(2) VCCR provides:

> The authorities of the receiving State shall not enter that part of the consular premises which is used exclusively for the purpose of the work of the consular post except with the consent of the head of the consular post or of his designee or of the head of the diplomatic mission of the sending State. The consent of the head of the consular post may, however, be assumed in the case of fire or other disaster requiring prompt protective action.

Three issues require discussion. First, Article 31(2) VCCR provides that the receiving state may enter consular premises (and parts thereof) even where they are used exclusively to undertake work of the consular post 'in the case of fire or any other disasters requiring prompt protective action'. In such instances, the consent of the head of the post is assumed.[28] The question becomes under what circumstances can it be said that a disaster is occurring within consular premises? Certainly, the ambit of Article 31(2) VCCR is not limited to natural disasters given that fires can be started deliberately by human beings. For the present author, the crux of the matter is that there are events occurring within consular premises that pose such a serious threat to the safety of its inhabitants and infrastructure that the situation can be regarded as a disaster. If so, the receiving state is justified in entering consular premises in order to protect the premises, their inhabitants and their contents. If this interpretation is correct, a disaster occurs, for example, where critical cyber infrastructure belonging to a consular post is infected with malware and this malware is affecting the functionality or availability of that infrastructure.[29] Likewise, a disaster occurs where

[27] 'It should be highlighted that the inviolability of consular premises is less comprehensive than that of diplomatic premises'; d'Aspremont (n 12) para 38.

[28] Although this assumption can be rebutted, of course, for example where the head of the mission makes it clear that he or she refuses consent.

[29] '[W]e are living in a different time, one in which not only natural disasters but also artificial disasters such as cyber terror and computer viruses may paralyze the functions of consular posts if not promptly dealt with … It is certainly true that a situation involving cyber terrorism or widespread computer virus requires prompt protective action'; Choi (n 8) 122.

the computer networks and systems of a consular post are infected with spyware and critical data is being appropriated. However, given that the purpose of Article 31(2) VCCR is to provide the receiving state with the exceptional power to *protect* consular premises from disaster, this provision does not allow the receiving state to classify as a disaster those situations where consular officials are utilising consular premises to concoct and launch malicious activities (such as cyber espionage) that only pose a threat to actors and interests located outside of the consular post.[30]

Second, even if a disaster is unfolding within consular premises, the receiving state is only permitted to undertake 'protective action'. Thus, if a disaster is underway and the receiving state exploits these circumstances in order to conduct cyber espionage and obtain confidential information belonging to the consular post, such conduct cannot be regarded as protective and is unlawful.[31] However, if the receiving state can demonstrate that cyber espionage is necessary to protect confidential data from damage or destruction due to a disaster occurring within consular premises, such conduct is permissible under Article 31(2) VCCR.

Third, it is worth pointing out that, as with diplomatic premises, a receiving state cannot invoke countermeasures against a consular post in the event that it commits an internationally wrongful act. An important qualification is that, if consular premises are used to launch an armed attack against the receiving state, under Article 51 UN Charter the receiving state is entitled to exercise its right to self-defence and undertake measures (such as cyber espionage) against and within the premises of the consular post to the extent necessary to thwart the attack.

2.1.2. The 'Special Duty' to Protect Premises

Article 22(2) VCDR provides that '[t]he receiving State is under a special duty to take all appropriate steps to protect the premises of the mission against any intrusion or damage and to prevent any disturbance of the peace of the mission or impairment of its dignity'. Article 31(3) VCCR imposes an identical obligation upon receiving states in relation to consular premises.[32]

This duty applies to state and non-state actors that threaten the inviolability of diplomatic and consular premises. In the *Tehran Hostages* case, the US complained that Iran had failed to protect the premises of its diplomatic mission from student protesters who had forcibly entered the mission, ransacked it and taken dozens of personnel hostage. Citing a violation of Article 22(2) VCDR,

[30] '[S]ituations in which the mission or post itself generates cyber disaster to the outside are not covered [by Article 31(2) VCCR]. This is obvious since the purpose of the exception is to protect the premises of the consular post, not to protect premises beyond'; ibid, 123 (citations omitted).

[31] ibid.

[32] Rule 40 of the *Tallinn Manual 2.0* explains that '[a] receiving State must take all appropriate steps to protect cyber infrastructure on the premises of a sending State's diplomatic mission or consular post against intrusion or damage'; *Tallinn Manual 2.0* (n 10).

the ICJ determined that the 'Iranian government failed to take appropriate steps to protect the premises, staff, and archives of the United States mission against attack by militants, and to take steps to prevent or stop the attack'.[33] Note that the duty upon the receiving state is to protect diplomatic and consular premises from intrusion or damage regardless of the source of the threat. Thus, this duty applies irrespective of whether the malicious activity that threatens the inviolability of diplomatic and consular premises – cyber espionage, for example – is concocted and launched by state or non-state actors operating within the receiving state's territory or from the territory of a third state.

Crucially, the special duty contained within Article 22(2) VCDR and Article 31(3) VCCR is an obligation of due diligence. Due diligence is a general standard conditioning the performance of international legal obligations and its scope and content has received extensive consideration by national and international tribunals.[34]

Knowledge is the 'decisive element of due diligence'[35] and it is only where a state has knowledge of a threat that the obligation to suppress or mitigate that threat is triggered.[36] Just because a threat emanates from within a state's territory does not mean that it is automatically assumed to have known of the threat. In the *Corfu* case, the ICJ held that 'it cannot be concluded from the mere fact of the control exercised by a State over its territory and waters that that State necessarily knew, or ought to have known', of the threats that existed within its territory.[37]

Where a state has actual knowledge of a threat, the duty of due diligence is obviously activated. Knowledge can be also imputed given the circumstances prevailing at the time. For example, in the *Corfu* case the ICJ held that Albania was subject to a duty to protect or at least to warn vessels of the mines within its territorial waters even if it could not be demonstrated that Albania actually knew of the existence of the mines. Given that Albania kept 'a jealous watch on its territorial waters'[38] and that the mines were located so close to Albania's coastline that

[33] *Tehran Hostages* (n 4) para 6. See also *Case Concerning Armed Activities on the Territory of the Congo (Democratic Republic of the Congo v Uganda)*, Judgment [2005] ICJ Rep 168, para 342 ('The Vienna Convention on Diplomatic Relations not only prohibits any infringements of the inviolability of the mission by the receiving State itself but also puts the receiving State under an obligation to prevent others – such as armed militia groups – from doing so').

[34] For a discussion see R Pisillo-Mazzeschi, 'The Due Diligence Rule and the Nature of International State Responsibility' (1993) 35 *German Yearbook of International Law* 9.

[35] K Bannelier-Christakis, 'Cyber Diligence: A Low-Intensity Due Diligence Principle for Low-Intensity Cyber Operations' (2014) 14 *Baltic Yearbook of International Law* 23, 28.

[36] '[A] State's obligation to prevent, and the corresponding duty to act, arise at the instant that the State learns of, or should normally have learned of, the existence of a serious risk that genocide will be committed'; *Application of the Convention on the Protection and Punishment of the Crime of Genocide (Bosnia v Serbia)*, Judgment [2007] ICJ Rep 1, para 431.

[37] *Corfu Channel (United Kingdom of Great Britain and Northern Ireland v Albania)*, Judgment (Merits) [1949] ICJ Rep 4, 18.

[38] ibid 19.

'[t]he laying of a minefield in these waters could hardly fail to have been observed by the Albanian coastal defences',[39] the Court concluded that Albania 'must have known'[40] that the mines had been deployed and thus must have been aware of the threat that they represented to passing vessels.

The preparedness of the ICJ to presume knowledge derives from the fact that one cannot deny knowledge of facts that are widely known.[41] Thus, while cyber espionage is usually committed in secret, it may be nevertheless widely known that spyware is rampant upon the receiving state's cyber infrastructure and that this is likely to impinge upon the premises of a diplomatic mission or consular post, that is, their computer networks and systems. Alternatively, it may be widely known that malicious actors are planning to launch acts of cyber espionage against diplomatic or consular premises because, for example, the threat of cyber espionage has been widely discussed online or it has been reported by cyber security companies or within the media more generally. In these circumstances, it is assumed that the state must have known of the threat.

Importantly, case law reveals that knowledge can be constructed in light of the circumstances prevailing at the time.[42] In *Corfu* it was explained that:

> It is true, as international practice shows, that a State on whose territory or in whose waters an act contrary to international law has occurred, may be called upon to give an explanation. It is also true that that State cannot evade such a request by limiting itself to a reply that it is ignorant of the circumstances of the act and its authors.[43]

The adequacy of constructive knowledge therefore places an obligation upon receiving states to make themselves aware of threats to diplomatic and consular premises. But states are only expected to identify those threats that are reasonably discernible in the circumstances. What is reasonably expected of a state depends upon a variety of different factors such as its available resources as well as the source and nature of the threat. For example, with regard to malicious cyber operations such as cyber espionage, states possess different technological capabilities and, while it may be reasonable for one state to utilise its capacity to discover threats operating upon its cyber infrastructure, this may not be reasonable for other less technologically capable states. Moreover, if the threat of cyber espionage against diplomatic and consular premises emanates from outside of the territory of the receiving

[39] ibid 20.

[40] ibid.

[41] *Re Yamashita* No 61, Misc. Supreme Court of the United States 327 US 1; 66 S. Ct. 340; 90 L. Ed. 499; 1946 US LEXIS 3090.

[42] As Tonkin explains, constructive knowledge is adequate because it would be 'incongruous if a state could avoid responsibility by claiming its lack of knowledge if it could have discovered the prohibited activity through diligent detection'; H Tonkin, *State Control Over Private Military and Security Companies in Armed Conflict* (Cambridge, Cambridge University Press, 2011) 67.

[43] *Corfu Channel* (n 37) 18. Similarly, in the *Genocide* case the ICJ explained that 'to incur responsibility … it is enough that the State was aware, or should normally have been aware, of the serious danger that acts of genocide would be committed'; *Bosnian Genocide* (n 36) para 432.

state and especially if the author of that threat is a relatively anonymous non-state actor, it may not be reasonable to expect the receiving state to be aware of the threat.

Where they are aware of a threat, receiving states are under an obligation to take all reasonable measures to protect diplomatic and consular premises from intrusion, damage, disturbance and impairment of their dignity. If the threat is actualised and receiving states have knowledge of this, there is an obligation upon them to do all that is reasonably possible to ameliorate its harmful effects and thus protect diplomatic and consular premises. Moreover, if reasonable in the circumstances, the receiving state must take enforcement action against the culprits, with the objective of punishing them for their activities and also deterring likeminded individuals or entities from engaging in such conduct in the future.[44]

The special duty upon receiving states to protect diplomatic and consular premises is an obligation to act diligently and is thus 'not absolute'.[45] A state is not required to succeed in achieving a particular result but must instead 'deploy adequate means, to exercise best possible efforts, to do the utmost, to obtain [the] result'.[46] The speed at which acts of cyber espionage can be devised and perpetrated will therefore have a significant bearing upon whether a state can be reasonably expected to protect diplomatic and consular premises against such conduct. Similarly, it is reasonable that states will dedicate less resources to the suppression of threats of cyber espionage that are embryonic and speculative than to those that are imminent and pressing.[47] It is also relevant that states possess different levels of technological capacity. This is important because the due diligence standard imposes differentiated responsibilities upon states depending upon their particular capabilities. In short, a state with advanced cyber capabilities is reasonably expected to provide diplomatic and consular premises with greater levels of protection than less cyber-capable states.[48]

2.1.3. Furnishings, Property and Means of Transport

Article 22(3) VCDR provides that '[t]he premises of the mission, their furnishings and other property thereon and the means of transport of the mission shall be immune from search, requisition, attachment or execution'. Although diplomatic premises are inviolable under Article 22(1) VCDR, Article 22(3) VCDR 'has value of its own' insofar as it ensures that if the receiving state enters diplomatic premises (with the consent of the head of mission, for example), the furnishings, property

[44] *Janes* (*US v Mexico*) 4 RIAA 82 (1926) para 4.

[45] *Tallinn Manual 2.0* (n 10) 217.

[46] *Responsibilities and Obligations of States Sponsoring Persons and Entities with Respect to Activities in the Area, Seabed Disputes Chamber of the International Tribunal for the Law of the Sea* (Advisory Opinion) [2011] para 110.

[47] ibid para 117.

[48] *Armed Activities* (n 33) para 301.

and means of transport on those premises remain immune from search, requisition, attachment or execution.[49]

Cyber infrastructure located within the premises of a diplomatic mission is regarded as property of that mission and the data resident upon that cyber infrastructure (and the computer networks and systems that it supports) is thus protected against acts of cyber espionage (that is, 'search' and 'requisition') by Article 22(3) VCDR. Similarly, Article 22(3) VCDR protects against cyber espionage laptops, tablets and mobile phones that are physically located upon the mission's premises, which would include devices belonging to the mission and its staff (including privately owned devices) as well as devices belonging to visitors. Providing devices remain physically upon diplomatic premises, there is no doubt that they are immune from search, requisition, attachment or execution even though their functionality and utility depend upon cyber infrastructure that is not located physically within diplomatic premises, such as where laptops connect to the Internet via private Internet Service Providers or where satellite phones are used and rely upon satellites owned and operated by third parties. As Article 22(3) VCDR explains, this provision accords protection to the premises of a diplomatic mission and the furnishings and other property 'thereon'.

Does the use of the term 'thereon' mean that Article 22(3) VCDR does not protect furnishings and property located outside of the diplomatic premises? My view is that Article 22(3) VCDR affords such items protection providing there is a sufficiently close nexus between the property in question and the performance of diplomatic functions. Although this does not necessarily comport with a literal reading of Article 22(3) VCDR, two reasons support this broader interpretation of this provision.

First, while treaty provisions must be conferred their ordinary meaning, such interpretations must be compatible with the object and purpose of the treaty.[50] This is significant in the context of the VCDR because a failure to protect property and furnishings when they are located outside of the mission's premises 'runs counter to the object and purpose of the VCDR',[51] which is to enable diplomatic missions to fulfil their functions by providing their premises and property with protection from interference. When being used for diplomatic work, moveable objects such as the head of mission's laptop or mobile phone are just as integral to the functioning of the mission when they are located outside of diplomatic premises as when they are located within these premises. Given the proliferation of portable devices in the modern era, diplomatic missions would be unable to effectively perform their functions if their portable devices enjoy a revolving door of protection that depends on whether they happen to be located within or outside the territorial confines of the mission.

[49] *Draft Articles on Diplomatic Intercourse and Immunities* (n 17) 95.
[50] Article 31(1) Vienna Convention on the Law of Treaties 1969.
[51] K Kittichaisaree, *Public International Law and Cyberspace* (Cham, Springer, 2017) 251.

Second, given that the moveable personal property of diplomatic agents is inviolable wherever it is located,[52] it must surely be the case that the property of the mission is also inviolable while it is outside of the mission and in the hands of a diplomatic agent.[53] Indeed, state practice supports such an interpretation of Article 22(3) VCDR because it is now well-accepted that bank accounts belonging to the mission are protected even though they are supported entirely by cyber infrastructure located outside of the mission's premises.[54]

With regard to the protection afforded to means of transport, this conventionally refers to motorcars, vans and motorbikes that are used by diplomatic officials to travel to and from the mission.[55] However, by logical extension, means of transport can also include computer hardware (such as flash drives) and software (for example, zip files sent electronically) given that they are used primarily as a means of transporting information that is vital to the performance of diplomatic functions. Cyber espionage against such assets is therefore prohibited.

In relation to consular posts, Article 31(4) VCCR provides that '[t]he consular premises, their furnishings, the property of the consular post and its means of transport shall be immune from any form of requisition for purposes of national defence or public utility. If expropriation is necessary for such purposes, all possible steps shall be taken to avoid impeding the performance of consular functions, and prompt, adequate and effective compensation shall be paid to the sending State.' Consular premises, property, furnishings and means of transport enjoy a similar *type* of protection to that of diplomatic missions but, critically, the *extent* of the protection they receive is not identical.[56] Most notably, while there is a presumption against expropriation, the wording of Article 31(4) VCCR nevertheless makes it clear that consular premises, property, furnishings and means of transport can be expropriated where it is necessary for national defence or public utility.

Turning to the focus of this chapter, cyber espionage against confidential consular data – that is, the 'expropriation' of consular property within the meaning of Article 31(4) VCCR – is permissible where necessary to protect national security or public utility. In order to ensure that the discharge of consular functions

[52] Article 30(2) VCDR ('His [the diplomatic agent's] papers, correspondence and, except as provided in paragraph 3 of article 31, his property, shall likewise enjoy inviolability').

[53] '[I]t would be incongruent to conclude that property of a diplomatic mission is violable once removed from the premises, whereas the private property of a diplomatic agent enjoys inviolability, wherever located'; *Tallinn Manual 2.0* (n 10) 215.

[54] *Alcom v Republic of Colombia* [1984] AC 580 (12 April 1984); US Department of State Office of the Legal Advisor, *Digest of United States Practice in International Law* (2000) 548. See generally Denza (n 17) 128–31. As the *Tallinn Manual 2.0* explains, '[a] majority of the Experts was of the view that such property [located outside of diplomatic premises] enjoys inviolability under this Rule [Rule 39, which confers inviolability to cyber infrastructure on the premises of a diplomatic mission]'; *Tallinn Manual 2.0* (n 10) 215.

[55] US State Department, *Circular Note to Chiefs of Mission* (22 December 1993).

[56] The ILC's draft of Article 31(4) VCCR (Draft Article 30) was identical to Article 23(3) VCDR but the final wording of this provision was altered by the states at the Vienna conference; ILC, *Draft Articles on Consular Relations, with Commentaries* (1961).

is not needlessly disrupted, two requirements must be met. First, there must be a threat to national security or public utility, which essentially requires that there is a real and pressing threat to the receiving state's critical interests such as its defence, security or, more generally, its public services. For example, cyber espionage undertaken by a consular post that prevents the receiving state from relying upon information relating to the functioning of its air defence system would qualify as a threat justifying expropriation. Second, acts of cyber espionage committed by the receiving state must be rationally connected to averting or alleviating the threat to national security or public utility. In other words, the expropriation of consular data must serve a protective function.

2.2. The Inviolability of Archives and Documents

Article 24 VCDR explains that '[t]he archives and documents of the mission shall be inviolable at any time and wherever they may be'.[57] In relation to consular posts, Article 33 VCCR provides that 'the consular archives and documents shall be inviolable at all times and wherever they may be'. Archives and documents will almost always form part of the official correspondence of diplomatic missions and consular posts which, as we shall see below, is also inviolable. In this sense, Article 24 VCDR and Article 33 VCCR provide the archives and documents of a diplomatic mission and consular post with 'overlapping protection'.[58]

Article 24 – and the VCDR generally – does not define what constitutes archives or documents of the diplomatic mission. However, Article 1(1)(k) VCCR explains that consular archives include 'all the papers, documents, correspondence, books, films, tapes and registers of the consular post, together with the ciphers and codes, the card-indexes and any article of furniture intended for their protection or safe keeping'. To ensure congruency between the protection afforded to the archives of consular posts and to the archives of diplomatic missions, the meaning of the term archives within Article 24 VCDR must be interpreted in line with the definition of this term as provided by Article 1(1)(k) VCCR.[59]

Article 1(1)(k) VCCR does not refer to information that is compiled and stored electronically, which is unsurprising given that the VCCR was drafted long before cyberspace was used to store and transmit electronic information. Yet, Article 1(1)(k) VCCR is not intended to provide an exhaustive definition of the notion of archives and it would be incompatible with the object and purpose of the VCCR (and also the VCDR) to deprive consular (and diplomatic) documents of

[57] Moreover, Article 30(1)–(2) VCDR extends inviolability to the correspondence, papers, property and private residence of diplomatic agents.

[58] Värk (n 9) 131.

[59] *Shearson Lehman Brothers Inc v Maclaine Watson & Co Ltd* (No 2) [1988] 1 WLR 16; [1988] 1 All ER 116 (where the UK House of Lords used the definition of 'archives' provided by Article 1(1)(k) VCCR to interpret the concept of 'archives' under Article 24 VCDR).

their inviolability on the basis that they are compiled in electronic format.[60] In the context of the VCDR, the UK Supreme Court explained that '[t]he draftsmen of article 24 were thinking in terms of physical documents. But retrievable electronic files are also documents and may be part of an archive'.[61] Moreover, the authors of the *Tallinn Manual 2.0* had little hesitation in determining that the inviolability conferred by Article 24 VCDR and Article 33 VCCR 'include[s] hard drives, flash drives, and other media on which electronic documents are stored'.[62] The *Manual* further explains that inviolability encompasses 'not only final materials in electronic form, but also related drafts, negotiating documents, and other similar material that are amassed and deliberately preserved by diplomatic missions or consular posts in the course of their activities'.[63] Private submissions (such as passport and visa applications) to the diplomatic mission or consular post are also covered by Article 24 VCDR and Article 33 VCCR on the basis that, once officially received, they become part of the archives and documents of that mission or post.[64] Electronic archives and documents are therefore protected from cyber espionage by Article 24 VCDR and Article 33 VCCR.

Article 24 VCDR and Article 33 VCCR explain that the archives and documents of a diplomatic mission and consular post enjoy inviolability 'wherever they may be', that is, regardless of whether they are physically located within or outside of the diplomatic mission or consular post.[65] Consequently, archives and documents that are resident on cyber infrastructure owned and operated by another state or a private actor are inviolable, for example where archives and documents are stored on a private email server (such as Google Mail) or on Cloud computing (such as Google Drive and Dropbox).

Moreover, archives and documents of the diplomatic mission and consular post possess inviolability 'at any time' (or, in the words of the VCCR, 'at all times'),

[60] Denza and Foakes explain that the term archive 'is normally understood to cover any form of storage of information or records in words or pictures and to include modern forms of storage such as tapes, sound recordings and films, or computer disks'; E Denza and J Foakes, *Satow's Diplomatic Practice* (edited by Sir Ivor Roberts) (Oxford, Oxford University Press, 2017) 238, para 13.31. See further Denza (n 17) 161 (explaining that rather than attempting to list all modern methods of information storage, 'it is probably better simply to rely on the clear intention of Article 24 to cover all physical items storing information').

[61] *R (on the application of Bancoult No 3) v the Secretary of State for Foreign and Commonwealth Affairs* [2018] UKSC 3; [2018] 1 WLR 973, para 68.

[62] *Tallinn Manual 2.0* (n 10) 220.

[63] ibid.

[64] ibid.

[65] Indeed, Article 24 VCDR refers to archives and documents 'of the mission' rather than 'within the mission'. 'Article 24 stipulates that the archives and documents shall be inviolable at any time and 'wherever they may be'. It is clear that this last phrase is meant to cover circumstances where a building other than embassy premises is used for storage of the archives; and also the circumstances in which an archived document has been, for example, taken there by a member of the Secretariat staff for overnight work – or even inadvertently left by him on the train or in a restaurant'; R Higgins, *Problems and Process: International Law and How We Use It* (Oxford, Clarendon Press, 1995) 88–89.

even if diplomatic and consular premises lose their diplomatic or consular status and thus their inviolability.[66] That archives and documents are inviolable at any time is important in the cyber context given that electronic records are difficult to destroy and can exist in perpetuity.

This does not mean, however, that archives and documents retain their inviolability forever. In the *Bancoult No 3* case a sensitive diplomatic cable produced by the US Embassy in London cast doubt on the legality of the UK's decision to impose a Marine Protected Area (MPA) around the Chagos Islands. The Supreme Court found that in all probability the cable, which at one point in time formed part of the archive of the mission, was accessed and appropriated while it was in the possession of the US State Department in Washington DC. The individual responsible for extracting the cable then passed it to the whistleblower website Wikileaks and it was eventually published by *the Guardian* newspaper. A key question that the Supreme Court had to address was whether the appellants, who were seeking to have the UK's decision to impose the MPA declared unlawful, could use the contents of this cable as evidence against the UK government in court. The Supreme Court reaffirmed the long-standing view[67] that if the cable constituted part of the archives of the diplomatic mission it was inviolable under Article 24 VCDR and thus inadmissible as evidence.

The Supreme Court concluded that when the US Embassy in London transmitted the cable to the US State Department in Washington DC (and elsewhere) it did not attach any reservations to or place any limitations upon its use or distribution but was simply designated as confidential. Lord Mance, with whom Lord Neuberger, Lord Clarke and Lord Reed agreed, explained that documents 'must constitute or remain part of the mission archive' in order to be inviolable and that '[i]n these circumstances, once the document reached the State Department or any other addressee, it was, so far as appears and in the form in which it was there held, a document in the custody of the Federal Government of the United States … and not part of the London Embassy archive'.[68] As Lord Sumption noted, the fact that access to the cable was no longer under the control of the US Embassy – 'whether directly or by virtue of the terms on which the mission transmitted the document to another governmental entity' – meant that it was no longer part of the Embassy's archives.[69] As such, the cable was not inviolable and could be used as evidence in court. In light of this, it can be said that, providing a diplomatic mission (and, by extension, a consular post) possesses control over its documents in the sense that it retains (physical or virtual) access to them, they are inviolable wherever they may be located and at any time. Consequently, cyber espionage against such documents is prohibited.

[66] Article 45(a) VCDR; Article 27(1)(a) VCCR.
[67] *Shearson Lehman Brothers* (n 59).
[68] *Bancoult No 3* (2018) (n 61) para 20.
[69] ibid para 68.

Additionally, the Supreme Court held that documents forming part of the archives of a diplomatic mission (and presumably a consular post) that fall into the possession of a third party retain their inviolability under Article 24 VCDR.[70] The important caveat is that documents are only inviolable to the extent that they remain private and confidential, that is, they are not publicly available. In *Bancoult No 3*, the Supreme Court determined that because 'the cable has been put into the public domain by Wikileaks and the newspaper articles which followed … the cable has as a result lost its inviolability'.[71] Thus, materials only form part of the archives and documents of a diplomatic mission or consular post and enjoy legal protection against acts of cyber espionage while they retain their confidentiality.

2.3. Freedom of Communication

Freedom of communication is essential in order for diplomatic missions and consular posts to discharge their functions. For this reason, Article 27(1) VCDR requires that '[t]he receiving State shall permit and protect free communication on the part of the mission for all official purposes. In communicating with the Government and the other missions and consulates of the sending State, wherever situated, the mission may employ all appropriate means, including diplomatic couriers and messages in code or cipher.' Article 35(1) VCCR imposes a similar obligation upon receiving states in relation to consular posts.

According to Article 27(2) VCDR and Article 35(2) VCCR, 'official correspondence' is 'inviolable'. These provisions explain that official correspondence means 'all correspondence' relating to the functions of the diplomatic mission and consular post. '[A]ll correspondence' indicates that all official correspondence sent and received by diplomatic missions and consular posts is protected against interference, including correspondence sent and received by modern forms of communication such as mobile phones, emails and online software utilised for communication purposes (such as Skype and WhatsApp):[72] 'Communication through these means shall always be confidential and inviolable, despite the fact that these means of communication did not exist at the time when the VCDR was signed or entered into force.'[73]

Given the vulnerabilities associated with sending information through the post and electronically, sending states and diplomatic missions and consular

[70] ibid para 21. *Tallinn Manual 2.0* (n 10) 223 ('The Experts were of the view that the inviolability of a diplomatic mission's or consular post's archives, documents, and official correspondence survives even if the material is stolen or obtained by a third party (including another State) using improper means and then provided, or otherwise made available, to a State obligated to respect its inviolability').

[71] *Bancoult No 3* (2018) (n 61) para 21.

[72] Although where a diplomatic mission or consular post wishes to use a wireless transmitter, it can only do so with the consent of the receiving state; see Articles 27(1) VCDR and 35(1) VCCR.

[73] JEF Puig, 'Contemporary Developments Relating to the Inviolability of Mission Premises' in Behrens (n 19) 175.

posts sometimes prefer to send sensitive correspondence to each other in hard copy, placing that information in a bag that remains in the physical possession of a trusted courier. Different levels of protection are accorded to diplomatic and consular bags.[74]

With regard to diplomatic bags, Article 27(3) VCDR determines that '[t]he diplomatic bag shall not be opened or detained' and Article 27(4) VCDR explains that 'packages constituting the diplomatic bag must bear visible external marks of their character and may contain only diplomatic documents or articles intended for official use'.

Articles 27(3) and 27(4) VCDR do not stipulate the size, shape or weight of the 'packages constituting the diplomatic bag'. State practice reveals that the concept of the diplomatic 'bag' is not defined literally to mean a suitcase, briefcase or rucksack but, instead, is interpreted broadly to include photocopying machines, cipher equipment, computers and even building materials.[75] Although there is no state practice as to whether official correspondence that is compiled and transmitted electronically can qualify as a diplomatic bag, such an interpretation is in line with the expansive definition that states have accorded to this concept.[76]

Diplomatic bags must exhibit a 'visible external mark of their character'. More specifically, state practice reveals that under Article 27(4) VCDR a diplomatic bag must have a seal affixed to it by the competent authority of the sending state or diplomatic mission, exhibit a tag or label that is addressed to the head of mission, consular post or Ministry of Affairs and carry the official stamp of the sending state or diplomatic mission.[77] In essence, what is required is that the sender takes steps to ensure that the bag can be visibly identified as a genuine communication from the sending state or the diplomatic mission. Emails or other forms of online communication can comply with the requirements set out in Article 27(4) VCDR.[78] Electronic messages will invariably (and even necessarily) exhibit the address of the sender and this can be used to verify that it has originated from the sending state or diplomatic mission. Online communications can also have subject lines that reveal their provenance and attached files can be given names that indicate their diplomatic status. Moreover, online communications can be accompanied by electronic signatures that act as 'seals' in the sense that they authenticate the diplomatic status of the sender.

[74] Note that information contained in a diplomatic and consular bag is inviolable on the basis that it constitutes 'official correspondence' of the mission or post under Article 27(2) VCDR and Article 35(2) VCCR.

[75] Denza (n 17) 194.

[76] Choi (n 8) 127.

[77] Note No A622/02 of 31 October 2002, sent to diplomatic missions in London. The US also stipulates that seals and tags must be used to identify a diplomatic bag; Diplomatic Note 03-54 of 28 August 2003.

[78] For an alternative view see PG Labat and N Burke, 'The Protection of Diplomatic Correspondence in the Digital Age' in Behrens (n 19) 214 ('An attempt to expand the concept of the diplomatic bag to cover electronic documents may be both unnecessary and incompatible with the essence of the concept').

Article 27(3) VCDR does not confer upon the diplomatic bag inviolability but instead provides that it must not be 'opened or detained'. This provision certainly proscribes acts of cyber espionage that penetrate electronic communications in order to access and copy confidential information. There has been debate as to whether diplomatic bags can be scanned such as when their courier is passing through airport security. This is interesting in the cyber context given that software now exists that enables online messages and electronic files to be scanned.

The prevailing view is that diplomatic bags can be scanned providing that this process does not result in their contents being revealed: 'the scanning must not be of a kind which would reveal the contents of the communications which are being transmitted in the bag'.[79] Thus, the use of sniffer dogs against diplomatic bags is acceptable because it does not result in the bag being opened or detained. By extension, the use of 'sniffer software' to examine the *external* features of an electronic message in order to determine its source (such as its IP address) and to authenticate the email addresses of the sender and receiver is lawful.[80] However, the use of technologically advanced scanners (such as millimetre wave scanners and x-rays) that penetrate inside the diplomatic bag (or at least parts of it) are prohibited because the result is, in effect, that the bag is opened.[81] On the same basis, the use of software to scan online electronic communications and their attachments for particular words, phrases, images or computer code is unlawful.

Article 35(3) VCCR provides similar protection to consular bags as to diplomatic bags in the sense that '[t]he consular bag shall be neither opened nor detained'. Unlike with the diplomatic bag, Article 35(3) VCCR explains that 'if the competent authorities of the receiving State have serious reason to believe that the bag contains something other than the correspondence, documents or articles' of the consular post, 'they may request that the bag be opened in their presence by an authorized representative of the sending State'. If this request is refused, this does not give the receiving state authority to open and search the consular bag (email, zip file etc). Instead, the inviolability of the bag must be preserved and, at most, the bag 'shall be returned to its place of origin'.[82]

[79] ILC Yearbook 1988, vol II, Part 1, 157.

[80] Choi (n 8) 131. Although see Labat and Burke who argue that 'the concept of diplomatic bag … cannot encompass electronic documents because its ordinary meaning implies physicality. Any attempt to redefine that concept to include a form of "virtual diplomatic bag" is neither reasonable nor necessary'; Labat and Burke (n 78) 215.

[81] According to Draft Article 28 of the ILC's Draft Articles on the Status of the Diplomatic Courier and the Diplomatic Bag Not Accompanied by Diplomatic Courier and Draft Optional Protocols 1989, diplomatic bags 'shall be exempt from examination directly or through electronic or other technical devices'. In arriving at this conclusion, the ILC explained in its commentary to Draft Article 28 that it was concerned that 'the evolution of technology had created very sophisticated means of examination which might result in the violation of the confidentiality of the bag'; ILC Yearbook 1989, vol II, Part 2, 43.

[82] Article 35(3) VCCR.

Article 40(3) VCDR and Article 54(3) VCCR impose an obligation upon third party states to afford official correspondence and communications as well as diplomatic and consular bags that are 'in transit … the same inviolability and protection as the receiving State is bound to accord' under these conventions. Third party states are therefore prohibited from intercepting the official correspondence of diplomatic missions and consular posts that is transiting through their territory, including electronic correspondence passing through their cyber infrastructure. The majority of the *Tallinn Manual 2.0* Experts interpreted Article 40(3) VCDR and Article 54(3) VCCR as requiring that third party states must abstain from interfering with official correspondence that is 'in transit' as opposed to that which is 'at rest'.[83] But this does not mean that official correspondence is unprotected when it is at rest in foreign jurisdictions, such as when data is stored on servers within other states. Instead, at rest official correspondence invariably forms part of the documents or archives of a diplomatic mission or consular post and, as we have seen above, Article 24 VCDR and Article 33 VCCR provide these documents and archives with comprehensive protection, namely, that they are inviolable at all times and wherever they are located (which includes electronic data at rest in foreign territory). Once the inviolability provisions of the VCDR and VCCR are taken together, it emerges that electronic information relating to the performance of the functions of diplomatic missions and consular posts is afforded considerable international legal protection against acts of cyber espionage.

3. The Use of Diplomatic Missions and Consular Posts for Cyber Espionage

Diplomatic and consular law imposes a number of obligations upon diplomatic missions and consular posts when operating within the territory of the receiving state. First, Article 41(1) VCDR explains that diplomatic officials are under a duty 'to respect the laws and regulations of the receiving State'. This duty is imposed upon consular officials verbatim by Article 55(1) VCCR. The obligation to comply with local law includes the full gamut of national law including criminal law, contract law, labour law, traffic law etc. Diplomatic and consular officials must therefore familiarise themselves with national law and streamline their conduct in accordance with its stipulations. Given that almost all states adopt national laws (and usually criminal laws) that prohibit espionage – which includes cyber-enabled espionage – such conduct inevitably gives rise to a violation of Article 41(1) VCDR and Article 55(1) VCCR.[84]

[83] *Tallinn Manual 2.0* (n 10) 221–22.

[84] As Peters explains, '[i]t is therefore important that the secret surveillance, in probably all affected states, constitutes a crime. Most states criminalise both the spying out of state secrets (by tapping intergovernmental communication) and spying on private communication, e.g. through illegal tapping

Second, Article 41(1) VCDR explains that diplomatic staff 'have a duty not to interfere in the internal affairs of that [the receiving] State', an obligation that is also imposed upon consular officials under Article 55(1) VCCR. This duty is broader than the obligation to respect local laws and 'serves a more political purpose'.[85] In the context of this chapter, the question is whether cyber espionage amounts to interference in the internal affairs of the receiving state. This requires a consideration of two elements: first, whether the act of espionage pertains to matters that fall within the receiving state's internal affairs (its *domaine réservé*) and, if it does, second, whether espionage constitutes interference in those affairs.

The subject matter that falls within a state's internal affairs is defined residually as that which is free from international legal regulation. What constitutes a state's *domaine réservé* therefore depends upon the content of the international legal obligations that are applicable to a particular state at a particular time.[86] As The Netherlands explains in relation to the application of Article 41(1) VCDR:

> There are no international guidelines for the application of Article 41 paragraph 1, and we doubt whether it would be at all possible to develop such guidelines, given the fact that views on what should, or should not, be regarded as inadmissible interference in the internal affairs of a receiving State vary from place to place from time to time.[87]

It is therefore not possible to concretely identify the matters that fall within a state's sovereign prerogative but, with regard to cyber espionage, the crux of the matter is whether international law confers upon the receiving state the sovereign right to keep information private and confidential.

The obligation upon diplomatic missions and consular posts to abstain from interfering in the internal affairs of the receiving state is broader than the rule of non-intervention that is contained within customary international law. As we saw in chapter 3, the customary obligation upon states not to intervene in each other's internal affairs does not prohibit espionage because intervention requires coercion, and espionage is not coercive. But Article 41(1) VCDR and Article 55(1) VCCR proscribe *interference*, which is a lower threshold than intervention. Although states have not agreed a precise definition of what is interference within the meaning of Article 41(1) VCDR and Article 55(1) VCCR, state practice nevertheless indicates that acts of espionage and in particular cyber espionage constitute unlawful interference.[88] For example, the Snowden leaks revealed that the UK

of telephone conversations'; A Peters, 'Surveillance Without Borders: The Unlawfulness of the NSA Panopticon, Part II', 4 November 2013, EJIL: *Talk!*, www.ejiltalk.org/surveillance-without-borders-the-unlawfulness-of-the-nsa-panopticon-part-ii/.

[85] S Duquet and J Wouters, 'The Legal Duties of Diplomats Today: The Continuing Relevance of the Vienna Convention' (January 2015) Working Paper No 146, *Leuven Centre for Global Governance Studies* 1, 8.

[86] *Nationality Decrees in Tunis and Morocco*, PCIJ Rep Series B No 4 (1923) 24.

[87] A Memorandum of Reply by the Netherlands Government for its Parliament, quoted in Denza (n 17) 379.

[88] In July 1985, Liberia expelled the entire Soviet diplomatic mission for acts of espionage that it regarded as amounting to 'gross interference' in its internal affairs; US Department of State, Expulsions

diplomatic mission in Berlin had committed cyber espionage against Germany. A diplomatic row ensued and the German Foreign Office formally reminded the UK Ambassador to Germany that 'intercepting communication[s] from within diplomatic buildings represented a violation of international law'.[89] Venezuela also condemned the US's use of its diplomatic mission in Caracas to conduct acts of cyber espionage against the Venezuelan government as 'grave violations of international law'.[90]

Third, Article 41(3) VCDR provides that '[t]he premises of the mission must not be used in any manner incompatible with the functions of the mission as laid down in the present Convention or by other rules of general international law or by any special agreements in force between the sending and the receiving State'. Similarly, Article 55(2) VCCR prohibits the use of 'consular premises … in any manner incompatible with the exercise of consular functions'.

Both the VCDR and the VCCR prescribe the functions of diplomatic missions and consular posts. According to Article 3 (1)(d) VCDR[91] and Article 5(c) VCCR,[92] a permissible function of diplomatic missions and consular posts is to collect information relating to the activities and events occurring within the receiving state. Importantly, both of these provisions explain that only 'lawful means' can be used to collect information. This certainly requires that the means used to collect information are acceptable under the national law of the receiving state and, additionally, it requires that they are compatible with the stipulations of international law more generally.[93]

It has already been noted that cyber espionage will most likely violate the national law of the receiving state. Thus, the use of diplomatic and consular premises to conduct cyber espionage is not a permissible function of diplomatic

of Soviets Worldwide, 1986, January 1987, 4, www.insidethecoldwar.org/sites/default/files/documents/Department%20of%20State%20Report%20on%20Expulsion%20of%20Soviet%20Officials%20World-wide%201986%20January%201987.pdf.

[89] P Oltermann, J Borger and N Watt, 'Germany Calls in UK Ambassador over Spy Claims', *the Guardian*, 5 November 2013, www.theguardian.com/world/2013/nov/05/germany-summons-uk-ambassador-spy-claims-berlin.

[90] Telesur, 'Venezuela Demands US Identify Spies', 19 November 2016, www.telesurtv.net/english/news/Venezuela-Demands-US-Identify-Spies-20151119-0029.html.

[91] Article 3(1)(d) VCDR provides that a function of diplomatic missions is '[a]scertaining by all lawful means conditions and developments in the receiving State, and reporting thereon to the Government of the sending State'.

[92] Article 5(c) VCCR provides that a function of consular posts is 'ascertaining by all lawful means conditions and developments in the commercial, economic, cultural and scientific life of the receiving State, reporting thereon to the Government of the sending State and giving information to persons interested'.

[93] It is well accepted that the requirement that information can only be collected through 'lawful means' requires adherence to international as well as domestic law: 'the word "unlawful" should be interpreted expansively so as to include not only unlawfulness under domestic law but also unlawfulness under international law. The modern approach to expressions such as these is to construe them autonomously, i.e. not as pure *renvois* to domestic law, in order to contribute to a universal understanding of the treaty provision'; Peters (n 84). In fact, Article 41(3) VCDR specifically requires that diplomatic premises must be used compatibly with 'general international law'.

missions or consular posts and this activity is prohibited by Article 41(3) VCDR and Article 52(2) VCCR.[94] Indeed, in the *Tehran Hostages* case the ICJ explicitly stated that acts of 'espionage' by diplomatic officials constitute 'abuses of their functions' and cannot be regarded as a lawful means through which information can be collected.[95]

In terms of international law, and as I have argued in chapter 3, acts of cyber espionage that penetrate computer systems and networks supported by cyber infrastructure physically located within another state's territory violate international law, specifically, the rule of territorial sovereignty. As such, the use of cyber espionage by diplomatic missions and consular posts to collect information from computer networks and systems supported by cyber infrastructure located within the receiving state (as well as from cyber infrastructure located within other states)[96] cannot be regarded as a 'lawful means' of information collection. Such conduct therefore constitutes an impermissible function of diplomatic missions and consular posts and is unlawful.

3.1. Immunities for Diplomatic and Consular Officials

Although diplomatic and consular officials must respect the laws and regulations of the receiving state, they nevertheless benefit from a number of privileges and immunities. As was mentioned previously, most states prohibit espionage (and so cyber espionage) by way of their national criminal law. Yet, under Article 31(1) VCDR, '[a] diplomatic agent shall enjoy immunity from the criminal jurisdiction of the receiving State' and, pursuant to Article 29 VCDR, '[t]he person of a diplomatic agent shall be inviolable. He shall not be liable to any form of arrest or detention'.

The rationale that underpins the conferral of diplomatic immunity from criminal jurisdiction is that it is necessary to enable the effective functioning of the mission, rather than to serve the personal benefit of the diplomat.[97] The upshot of this is that diplomatic officials only enjoy procedural immunity from the criminal

[94] 'I believe that diplomats commit acts contrary to international law if they gather *secret* information. Their task may be to collect information from various sources in the host state, but they have a duty not to overstep a certain mark beyond which their activities become treacherous and hostile to the host state. Once they attempt to amass "secret" information i.e., information not commonly available or classified as secret by authorities in the host state, diplomats overstep the line of legality in international law'; I Delupis, 'Foreign Warships and Immunity for Espionage' (1984) 78 *AJIL* 53, 69.

[95] *Tehran Hostages* (n 4) para 84.

[96] 'A separate issue is whether it is permissible for a sending State to use the premises of its diplomatic mission or consular post, without the consent of the receiving State, as a base to engage in cyber espionage directed at a third State, whether that espionage occurs against the third State's organs located in the receiving State or beyond it. A majority of the International Group of Experts concluded that such practices are prohibited … since they are inconsistent with accepted diplomatic functions'; *Tallinn Manual 2.0* (n 10) 229.

[97] '[I]t is now the "functional necessity" theory which provides the most convincing explanation of much of the modern law of diplomacy'; C Wickremasinghe, 'Immunities Enjoyed by Officials of

jurisdiction of the receiving state and do not possess substantive immunity for violations of national criminal law.[98] Thus, diplomatic officials are legally required to adhere to national criminal law but, in the event of transgression, the receiving state cannot exercise its jurisdiction.[99] As the UK explained in a Memorandum on Diplomatic Immunity that it distributed to all new diplomats taking up posts in London:

> [M]embers of diplomatic missions and their families are expected to respect the laws and regulations of the United Kingdom. Diplomatic immunity in no way absolves members of diplomatic missions or their families from their duty to obey the law. The police investigate all allegations that the law has been broken and report the results to the Foreign and Commonwealth Office. The Foreign and Commonwealth Office draw these to the attention of the Head of Mission (or sometimes a senior official).[100]

Consular officials also enjoy immunity from the criminal jurisdiction of the receiving state but, according to Article 43(1) VCCR, this immunity only exists 'in respect of acts performed in the exercise of consular functions',[101] that is, they only possess immunity for official acts. As we have seen, cyber espionage is not a permissible function of a consular post. In relation to non-official acts such as cyber espionage, Article 41(1) VCCR provides that consular officials 'shall not be liable to arrest or detention pending trial, except in the case of a grave crime and pursuant to a decision by the competent judicial authority'. What is a grave crime is not defined in the VCCR but it is clear from the ILC commentary to Article 41(1) VCCR that it must be serious:

> The privilege under this paragraph is granted to consular officials by reason of their functions. The arrest of a consular official hampers considerably the functioning of the consulate and the discharge of the daily tasks – which is particularly serious inasmuch as many of the matters calling for consular action will not admit of delay (e.g., the issue of visas, passports and other travel documents; the legalization of signatures on commercial documents and invoices; various activities connected with shipping, etc.). Any such step would harm the interests, not only of the sending State, but also of the receiving State, and would seriously affect consular relations between the two States. It would therefore be inadmissible that a consular official should be placed under arrest or detention pending trial in connexion with some minor offence.[102]

Fundamentally, the concern is that the arrest and detention of consular officials would interfere with the work of the consular post and that such disruption cannot

States and International Organizations' in M Evans (ed), *International Law* (Oxford, Oxford University Press, 2014) 380–81.

[98] '[I]t is elementary law that diplomatic immunity is not immunity from legal liability, but immunity from suit'; *Empson v Smith* (English Court of Appeal) [1966] 1 QB 426, 438. Of course, states remain responsible for acts of cyber espionage that are internationally wrongful under the VCDR and the VCCR, regardless of the immunities enjoyed by diplomatic and consular officials.

[99] Although note that Article 32(1) VCDR provides that diplomatic immunity can be waived by the sending state and, where this occurs, national courts (including national criminal courts) can exercise jurisdiction and bring prosecutions.

[100] Quoted in Denza (n 17) 375–76.

[101] Again, immunity can be waived by the sending state; Article 45(1) VCCR.

[102] *Draft Articles on Consular Relations, with Commentaries* (n 56) 116.

be justified where the offence is minor.[103] Of course, states hold different views as to what crimes can be regarded as grave.[104] With regard to the crime of espionage, most states regard this as grave, not least because they impose severe punishments for such conduct including long prison sentences and even the death penalty. Thus, it can be reliably concluded that consular officials engaging in cyber espionage do not enjoy immunity from criminal prosecution and can be arrested and detained before trial providing that this is pursuant to a decision of a competent judicial authority.

4. Conclusion

The driving force behind diplomatic and consular law is the recognition that the exchange of diplomatic missions and consular posts is crucial to the maintenance of international peace and security.[105] At the same time, this legal framework is cognisant of the threats faced by states when they send their officials into the jurisdiction of another state and also the dangers that such officials represent to the receiving state. The objective of diplomatic and consular law is to balance the interests of the sending and receiving states and, through the implementation of binding rules, to reduce the risks faced by both.[106] This is achieved, on the one hand, by conferring inviolability upon the premises, property, archives, documents and correspondence of diplomatic missions and consular posts and, on the other, by requiring that diplomatic missions and consular posts respect the national laws of the receiving state, only exercise clearly defined functions and do not engage in activities that interfere in the internal affairs of the receiving state. As this chapter has revealed, these rules prohibit receiving states from conducting cyber espionage against diplomatic missions and consular posts and proscribe sending states from utilising their diplomatic missions and consular posts for the purpose of cyber espionage.

[103] D Akande, 'Immunity of Consular Officials – The Arrest by the US of an Indian Deputy Consul-General', 20 December 2013, EJIL: *Talk!*, www.ejiltalk.org/immunity-of-consular-officials-the-arrest-by-the-us-of-an-indian-deputy-consul-general/.

[104] For example, in the US a grave crime under Article 41(1) VCCR has been interpreted to mean a felony; US v Cole, 717 F. Supp. 309, 323 n. 5 (E.D. Pa. 1989). In the UK, a '"grave crime" shall be construed as meaning any offence punishable (on a first conviction) with imprisonment for a term that may extend to five years or with a more severe sentence'; Article 1(2) Consular Relations Act 1968.

[105] 'Convinced that respect for the principles and rules of international law governing diplomatic and consular relations is a basic prerequisite for the normal conduct of relations among States and for the fulfilment of the purposes and principles of the Charter of the United Nations'; GA Res A/69/121 (18 December 2014). '*Believing* that an international convention on diplomatic intercourse, privileges and immunities would contribute to the development of friendly relations among nations'; Preamble VCDR.

[106] As the ICJ explained, 'on the one hand, [diplomatic law] lays down the receiving State's obligations regarding the facilities, privileges and immunities to be accorded to diplomatic missions and, on the other, foresees their possible abuse by members of the mission and specifies the means at the disposal of the receiving State to counter any such abuse'; *Tehran Hostages* (n 4) para 86.

5

Cyber Espionage and International Human Rights Law

1. Introduction

Edward Snowden's disclosures revealed that, in addition to conducting cyber espionage against other states, the United States (US) National Security Agency (NSA) had been collecting confidential information belonging to individuals from across the globe.[1] Individuals were targeted on the basis that they were suspected of being involved in terrorist-related activities as well as other criminal enterprises such as drug- and people-trafficking. As we shall see, however, the surveillance methods employed by the NSA were so pervasive that they invariably resulted in the collection of confidential information belonging to non-suspects (for want of a better word).[2]

While international law is primarily concerned with the regulation of inter-state relations, this regime has come to recognise the prominent role that non-state actors play within the international society and has thus endowed them with certain rights and responsibilities.[3] Most notably, through the implementation of treaties and the incremental development of state practice, a sophisticated international legal framework has emerged that imposes conventional and customary obligations upon states to respect fundamental human rights.

The objective of this chapter is to examine whether cyber espionage targeted against individuals violates international human rights law. Space limitations preclude an assessment of how all international human rights regimes apply to

[1] The lesson learned from the Snowden disclosures was not that states engage in espionage but that '[w]here once we might have thought of international spying as government versus government, today it's government versus individual across the globe'; JS Granick, *American Spies: Modern Surveillance, Why Should You Care, and What To Do About It* (Cambridge, Cambridge University Press, 2017) 24.

[2] 'Nine of 10 account holders found in a large cache of intercepted conversations, which former NSA contractor Edward Snowden provided in full to The Post, were not the intended surveillance targets but were caught in a net the agency had cast for somebody else'; B Gellman, J Tate and A Soltani, 'In the NSA-Intercepted Data, Those Not Targeted Far Outnumber the Foreigners Who Are', 5 July 2014, *the Washington Post*, www.washingtonpost.com/world/national-security/in-nsa-intercepted-data-those-not-targeted-far-outnumber-the-foreigners-who-are/2014/07/05/8139adf8-045a-11e4-8572-4b1b969b6322_story.html?utm_term=.73d1872566c6.

[3] K Parlett, 'The Individual and Structural Legal Change in the International System' (2012) 1 *Cambridge Journal of International and Comparative Law* 60, 60.

cyber espionage. Instead, this chapter focuses upon the International Covenant on Civil and Political Rights (ICCPR) 1966 and the European Convention on Human Rights (ECHR) 1950. The ICCPR is prioritised for international legal analysis because it is widely ratified and, moreover, many of its provisions are considered to be reflective of customary international law (including, most importantly, the right to privacy).[4] The ECHR is singled out for assessment because on multiple occasions the European Court of Human Rights (ECtHR) – the international court entrusted with interpreting and applying the ECHR – has examined how online surveillance impacts upon human rights and the Court has therefore generated a rich and interesting jurisprudence on this topic.

This chapter is organised as follows. Section 2 examines whether a state's human rights obligations under the ICCPR and the ECHR apply extraterritorially, a matter that has long vexed international lawyers and which takes on added significance in cyberspace given the a-territorial nature of this domain. Section 3 identifies the right to privacy as a fundamental human right under the ICCPR and the ECHR and examines to what extent it protects online data from state interference. Section 4 recognises that privacy is not an absolute right and that its enjoyment can be limited where necessary to meet legitimate societal needs, and considers under what circumstances the right to privacy can be permissibly curtailed in the context of online surveillance. Section 5 provides conclusions.

2. The Extraterritorial Application of Human Rights Treaties

Article 29 Vienna Convention on the Law of Treaties (VCLT) 1969 is typically regarded as the starting point for determining the spatial application of treaties, not least because it sits under the title of 'the territorial scope of treaties'. Article 29 provides that '[u]nless a different intention appears from the treaty or is otherwise established, a treaty is binding upon each party in respect of its entire territory'.

This provision is often interpreted as raising the presumption that treaties are only applicable within the territory over which the state holds sovereign title, although this presumption can be rebutted where the terms of the treaty indicate that it is intended to apply beyond state territory.[5] Yet, such a reading of Article 29 is 'unfounded'[6] because, as the *travaux préparatoires* of this provision

[4] A Peters, 'Privacy, *Rechtsstaatlichkeit*, and the Legal Limits on Extraterritorial Surveillance' in RA Miller (ed), *Privacy and Power: A Transatlantic Dialogue in the Shadow of the NSA Affair* (Cambridge, Cambridge University Press, 2017) 147.

[5] See, for example, Russia's submission to the International Court of Justice in *Case Concerning Application of the International Convention on the Elimination of All Forms of Racial Discrimination (Georgia v Russia)*, CR 2008/23, 39.

[6] M Milanovic, *Extraterritorial Application of Human Rights Treaties: Law, Principles, and Policy* (Oxford, Oxford University Press, 2013) 10.

illustrate, the drafters did not intend for it to determine the spatial application of treaties but instead to confirm that, unless otherwise indicated, treaties apply evenly and uniformly throughout state territory.[7] When it comes to ascertaining whether a treaty applies extraterritorially what is required is an:

> interpretation of that particular treaty and of what its States parties actually wanted to achieve … It is thus through interpreting each provision in the treaty (while bearing in mind the treaty as a whole) that we can tell whether and how it can apply to territory and it is only then that we can ask where it applies.[8]

Human rights treaties usually contain provisions that determine the territorial scope of the human rights obligations they impose upon member states. With regard to the ICCPR, Article 2(1) provides that '[e]ach State Party to the present Covenant undertakes to respect and to ensure to all individuals within its territory and subject to its jurisdiction the rights recognized in the present Covenant'. In relation to the ECHR, Article 1 explains that 'High Contracting Parties shall secure to everyone within their jurisdiction the rights and freedoms defined in Section 1 of this Convention'.

Where a state commits cyber espionage against an individual located within its territory, the ICCPR and the ECHR apply on the basis that the individual is both within its territory and (*ipso facto*) subject to its jurisdiction, even if the data collected is resident on cyber infrastructure located outside of its territory.[9] But what about the situation where a state conducts cyber espionage against an individual that is located within foreign territory, as is often the case with politically and economically motivated cyber espionage? The answer to this question requires a detailed analysis of Article 2(1) ICCPR and Article 1 ECHR.

2.1. ICCPR

The interpretation of Article 2(1) ICCPR has generated much controversy. The US has long maintained that the text of the Covenant precludes the application of this agreement to individuals that are not located within territory over which it holds sovereign title.[10] This approach is justified on the basis that

[7] International Law Commission, 'Draft Articles on the Law of Treaties with Commentaries' (1966) 2 *Yearbook of the International Law Commission* 187, 214.

[8] M Milanovic, 'The Spatial Dimension: Treaties and Territory' in CJ Tams, A Tzanakopoulos and A Zimmermann, with AW Richford (eds), *Research Handbook on the Law of Treaties* (Cheltenham, Edward Elgar, 2016) 191–92.

[9] '[A] State's human rights law obligations attach when the communications of an individual who is located in its territory are intercepted abroad by that State or when the State acquires access to the individual's data that is stored electronically beyond its borders'; MN Schmitt, *Tallinn Manual 2.0 on the International Law Applicable to Cyber Operations* (Cambridge, Cambridge University Press, 2017) 183–84.

[10] Human Rights Committee, *Consideration of Reports Submitted by States Parties Under Article 40 of the Covenant, Third Periodic Report of States Due in 2003: United States of America*, UN Doc CCPR/C/

Article 31(1) VCLT 1969 requires that treaty provisions are interpreted 'in accordance with the ordinary meaning' of their terms. Applying this rule, the US contends that Article 2(1) must be read conjunctively: the ICCPR only applies to persons that are both within its territory *and* subject to its jurisdiction.

This interpretation of Article 2(1) is problematic. While Article 31(1) VCLT provides that a treaty provision must be accorded its 'ordinary meaning', it goes on to explain that this meaning can only be ascribed to a treaty provision where it is congruent with the 'object and purpose' of that treaty. This is important in the context of the ICCPR because the Preamble to this agreement affirms 'the equal and inalienable rights of all members of the human family' and recognises 'that these rights derive from the inherent dignity of the human person'. The universality of human rights is therefore at the heart of the ICCPR, contradicting the US view that the human rights obligations contained within the Covenant are territorially constrained. Moreover, Article 5(1) is suggestive of the Covenant's extraterritorial capacity when it explains that 'nothing in the present Covenant may be interpreted as implying … any right to engage in any activity … aimed at the destruction of any rights … to a greater extent than is provided for in the present Covenant'.

If the application of Article 31(1) VCLT renders the meaning of a treaty provision 'ambiguous or obscure', Article 32 VCLT permits recourse to the provision's *travaux* for clarification. The US relies on the *travaux* to support its view that a state only incurs obligations under the ICCPR in relation to individuals that are both within its territory and subject to its jurisdiction.[11] It is correct that in 1950 Eleanor Roosevelt, chief US delegate during the drafting of the ICCPR, insisted that Article 2(1) be framed conjunctively. However, this insistence was designed to respond to the specific and exceptional circumstances prevailing at that time, namely, the long-term US occupation of large swathes of enemy territory after the conclusion of the Second World War.[12] In this sense, the concern of the US was to avoid assuming obligations under the Covenant to protect its nationals abroad against third states or to legislate for the people of occupied territories. Thus, 'the preparatory work is remarkably unhelpful when it comes to any first principles regarding the interpretation of Article 2(1)'[13] and, as such, cannot be read as precluding the extraterritorial application of the Covenant as a general matter.

In contrast to the US's approach, international tribunals and human rights bodies have consistently determined that the ICCPR imposes obligations upon

USA/3, 28 November 2005, Annex I, 109 (where the US noted the 'inescapable conclusion that the obligations assumed by a State Party to the International Covenant on Civil and Political Rights (Covenant) apply only within the territory of the State Party').

[11] US Department of State (Matthew Waxman), *Report Concerning the International Covenant on Civil and Political Rights (ICCPR): Opening Statement to the UN Human Rights Committee*, 17 July 2006, www.2001-2009.state.gov/g/drl/rls/70392.htm.

[12] UN Doc E/CN.4/SR.138 (1950) paras 33–34.

[13] M Milanovic, 'Human Rights Treaties and Foreign Surveillance: Privacy in the Digital Age' (2015) 56 *Harvard International Law Journal* 81, 103. 'The *travaux* emphatically do not offer us what we most need – a set of first principles as to the proper interpretation of Article 2(1)'; Milanovic (n 6) 225.

state parties 'in respect of acts done by a State in the exercise of its jurisdiction outside of its own territory'.[14] In light of this jurisprudence, it seems well-settled that Article 2(1) ICCPR must be read disjunctively: states owe human rights obligations under the Covenant to those persons that are either located within their territory *or* subject to their jurisdiction. Yet, this raises the question as to the circumstances in which a state's jurisdiction can be established under the ICCPR when it operates extraterritorially.

The ICJ has adopted a spatial model for establishing state jurisdiction under the ICCPR, determining that states only owe human rights obligations extraterritorially to those persons located within territory over which they exercise effective control (such as occupied territory).[15] However, 'the territorial control thesis was destined to disappoint in light of the simple fact that States are capable of violating the rights of individuals abroad without fully controlling the territory or situs on which those violations occurred'.[16] In response, the Human Rights Committee (HRC) has adopted a personal model for establishing state jurisdiction under the ICCPR, which is a broader doctrine that allows for the extraterritorial application of the Covenant to those circumstances where states exercise authority and control over individuals (as opposed to territorial areas). For example, in the *Lopez* case the HRC had to consider the kidnapping of a Uruguayan trade union activist by Uruguayan secret service agents in Buenos Aires, Argentina. Finding Uruguay in violation of its human rights obligations, the HRC explained that the application of the ICCPR depends upon the 'relationship between the individual and the State' and without regard to 'the place where the violation occurred'.[17] In the *Celiberti* case, Uruguay abducted a Uruguayan citizen of Italian nationality while she was visiting Brazil. The HRC held that Uruguay's obligations under the ICCPR were operative on the basis that 'it would be unconscionable to so interpret the responsibility under article 2 of the Covenant as to permit a State party to perpetrate violations of the Covenant on the territory of another State, which violations it could not perpetrate on its own territory'.[18] More generally, in General Comment 31 the HRC explained that the Covenant applies 'to those within the power or effective control of the forces of a State Party acting outside its territory, regardless of the circumstances in which such power or effective control was obtained'.[19]

As the *Lopez* and *Celiberti* cases reveal, a state indisputably exercises authority and control over a person that is within its physical custody. But given

[14] *Legal Consequences of the Construction of a Wall in the Occupied Palestinian Territory* (Advisory Opinion) [2004] ICJ Rep 136, para 111; Human Rights Committee, *General Comment No. 31, Nature of the General Legal Obligation Imposed on States Parties to the Covenant*, UN Doc CCPR/C/21/Rev.1/Add.13, 26 May 2004, para 10.

[15] *Wall* (n 14); *Armed Activities on the Territory of the Congo (Democratic Republic of Congo v Uganda)*, Judgment [2005] ICJ Rep 168, para 216.

[16] B Van Schaack, 'The United States' Position on the Extraterritorial Application of Human Rights Obligations: Now is the Time for Change' (2014) 90 *International Law Studies* 20, 40.

[17] *Lopez v Uruguay*, Comm No R.12/52, UN Doc Supp No 40 A/36/40 (1981) para 12.2.

[18] *Celiberti v Uruguay*, Comm No 56/1979, UN Doc CCPR/C/OP/1 (1984) para 10.3.

[19] *General Comment No. 31* (n 14) para 10.

that a state can violate human rights even where the individual is not within its physical custody – such as where a state remotely targets a person using aircraft, drones and the like – the HRC later determined that a state can exercise authority and control over a person even in the absence of physical apprehension.[20] In essence, the HRC's approach is that, where states conduct operations against individuals located beyond state borders, state jurisdiction under the Covenant is assumed. This means that, when acting extraterritorially, states are subject to a negative obligation to ensure that their conduct respects the human rights contained within the ICCPR.[21]

This notwithstanding, commentators argue that the Covenant only applies in those circumstances where a state exercises *physical* authority and control over a person: 'The majority [of the *Tallinn Manual 2.0* Experts] was of the view that, in the current state of the law, physical control over territory *or the individual* is required before human rights law obligations are triggered'.[22] If this approach is correct, it means that states cannot exercise their authority and control over individuals by virtual means, thus ruling out the possibility that state jurisdiction under the Covenant can be established with regard to state activities conducted in cyberspace (such as cyber espionage).[23]

This approach is unconvincing in terms of policy and law. From a policy perspective, why should a state's extraterritorial operations in the physical world have to comply with fundamental human rights but not its activities in the virtual world? The argument that states should respect human rights in cyberspace is particularly compelling given that, in a virtual world like cyberspace, states frequently interact with individuals based in foreign territories and often exercise their authority and control over them.

From a legal perspective, the physical control approach is unpersuasive because human rights bodies have recently determined that state jurisdiction under the Covenant can be established where states exercise authority and control over individuals in cyberspace. For example, in 2014 the HRC considered the US's Fourth Periodic Report on its compliance with the ICCPR. After expressing its concern at the NSA's online surveillance activities, the HRC Report urged the US to 'take all necessary measures to ensure that its surveillance activities, *both within*

[20] Human Rights Committee, *Concluding Observations on the Fourth Periodic Report of the United States of America*, UN Doc CCPR/C/USA/CO/4, 23 April 2014, para 9.

[21] '[Relevant jurisprudence] reveals a distinct trend towards an understanding that States' human rights obligations follow their agents and instrumentalities offshore whenever they are in a position to respect – or to violate – the rights of individuals they confront abroad'; Van Schaack (n 16) 32.

[22] *Tallinn Manual 2.0* (n 9) 185 (emphasis added).

[23] '[E]ven if the ICCPR did apply to U.S. extraterritorial activities, surveillance does not naturally amount to "effective control" of a person. Such an interpretation seems strained. Interference with correspondence hardly amounts to effective control of a person in the same manner as physical detention'; D Severson, 'American Surveillance of Non-U.S. Persons: Why New Privacy Protections Offer Only Cosmetic Change' (2015) 56 *Harvard International Law Journal* 465, 495. See also A Deeks, 'An International Legal Framework for Surveillance' (2015) 35 *Virginia Journal of International Law* 291, 311 ('it is not yet accepted that the ICCPR applies to situations in which a state is simply monitoring the electronic data of someone abroad').

and outside the United States, conform to its obligations under the Covenant, including article 17'.[24] In the same year, the Office of the High Commissioner for Human Rights submitted a report to the General Assembly and the Human Rights Council, which determined that states owe human rights obligations to individuals over whom they exercise authority and control in cyberspace:

> [A] State may not avoid its international human rights law obligations by taking action outside of its territory that it would be prohibited from taking "at home" … The notions of "power" and "effective control" are indicators of whether a State is exercising "jurisdiction" or governmental powers, the abuse of which human rights protections are intended to constrain … It follows that digital surveillance therefore may engage a State's human rights obligations if that surveillance involves the State's exercise of power or effective control in relation to digital communications infrastructure, wherever found, for example, through direct tapping or penetration of that infrastructure.[25]

Consequently, it seems clear that where states exercise their authority and control in cyberspace – such as where they undertake acts of cyber espionage against individuals – the ICCPR applies to that conduct regardless of where the targeted individual is geographically located.[26]

2.2. ECHR

At least initially, the ECtHR expressed a strong preference for a spatial model for establishing state jurisdiction under the ECHR, determining that a state's extraterritorial jurisdiction only extends to those individuals located within territory over which it exercises effective control.[27] For instance, in *Banković* the ECtHR insisted upon an 'essentially territorial notion' of state jurisdiction, with 'other bases of jurisdiction being exceptional and requiring special justification in the particular circumstances of each case'.[28] In this case, the ECtHR rejected the applicants' contention that they were within the *espace juridique* (legal space) of Belgium on the basis that when Belgium launched airstrikes against Serbia (a non-ECHR member) it did not exercise effective control over the territory within which the applicants were killed or injured.

With the *Banković* decision coming under intense criticism,[29] in a series of cases in the early 2000s the ECtHR applied the ECHR extraterritorially on the

[24] *Fourth Periodic Report of the USA* (n 20) para 22(a) (emphasis added).

[25] Office of the High Commissioner for Human Rights, *The Right to Privacy in the Digital Age: Report of the Office of the United Nations High Commissioner for Human Rights*, UN Doc A/HRC/27/37, 30 June 2014, paras 33–34 (citations omitted).

[26] 'I submit that human rights treaties apply to most, if not all, foreign surveillance activities'; Milanovic (n 13) 129.

[27] *Loizidou v Turkey*, Preliminary Objections, App No 15318/89, ECtHR, 23 March 1995, para 62.

[28] *Banković v Belgium*, Decision, App No 52207/99, ECtHR, 12 December 2001, para 6.

[29] For a flavour of this criticism see A Orakhelashvili, 'Restrictive Interpretation of Human Rights Treaties in the Recent Jurisprudence of the European Court of Human Rights' (2003) 14 *EJIL* 529.

basis that the state in question exercised authority and control over the individual whose rights had been violated, without assessing whether the state exercised effective control (or indeed any control) over the territory within which the person was located. In the *Öcalan* case, for example, Kenyan security forces handed over a suspected terrorist to Turkish officials in Kenya and the suspect was subsequently mistreated. The Court held that as soon the suspect was handed over to the Turkish authorities and taken into custody 'the applicant was effectively under Turkish authority and therefore within the "jurisdiction" of Turkey'.[30]

This does not mean that a state's extraterritorial jurisdiction under the ECHR can only be established where a person is within its physical custody. An 'even more telling'[31] decision with regard to the ECHR's extraterritorial application is that of *Pad*.[32] This case involved several Iranian individuals who were shot and killed by a Turkish helicopter while it was patrolling the Turkish-Iranian border. It was unclear as to whether the individuals were within Turkish or Iranian territory when they were shot but the Court determined that this was irrelevant 'given that the Government has already admitted that the fire discharged from the helicopters had caused the killing of the applicants' relatives'.[33] In other words, Turkey's jurisdiction was established on the basis that the Turkish forces exercised authority and control over the victims by shooting at them, even though these individuals were not in the physical custody of Turkey and regardless of where they were located.

The 2008 *Liberty* case is important because it concerns online surveillance.[34] This case, which was decided one year after *Pad*, required the ECtHR to determine whether the UK's interception of electronic communications between two Irish non-governmental organisations and a British non-governmental organisation constituted a breach of the ECHR. Admittedly, the ECtHR did not engage in an in-depth discussion of the question of jurisdiction. Instead, the Court *assumed* that the UK possessed jurisdiction and proceeded to examine whether the UK's conduct had violated Convention rights. Moreover, it is noteworthy that the communications between the applicants were intercepted while they were passing through UK cyber infrastructure, which may have influenced the Court when assuming that the UK possessed jurisdiction.[35] However, the fact remains that two of the applicants asserting their human rights had been violated were located outside of British territory at the moment that the alleged human rights abuses occurred. A reasonable reading of this decision is that the ECtHR was of the view

[30] *Öcalan* v *Turkey*, Judgment, App No 46221/99, ECtHR, 12 May 2005, para 91.

[31] Van Schaack (n 16) 45.

[32] *Pad and Others v Turkey*, Decision, App No 60167/00, ECtHR, 28 June 2007.

[33] ibid para 54.

[34] *Liberty and Others v UK*, Judgment, App No 58243/00, ECtHR, 1 July 2008.

[35] In its earlier decision in *Bosphorus*, the Strasbourg Court established state jurisdiction and determined that the ECHR was applicable on the basis that Ireland detained the applicant's property (a plane) while it was located within Irish territory (Dublin airport) even though the applicant (the company that owned the plane) was based in Turkey; *Bosphorus v Ireland*, Judgment, App No 45036/98, ECtHR, 30 June 2005.

that, by intercepting their data, the UK exercised authority and control over the applicants, thus bringing them within the UK's jurisdiction even though they were located within foreign territory.

This line of case law reveals the Court's dissatisfaction with the spatial model for establishing state jurisdiction and its attempt to move towards the personal model preferred by the HRC in the context of the ICCPR. Recognising that its jurisprudence failed to provide clear guidance on when the ECHR applied extraterritorially, in 2011 the ECtHR sought to provide clarification in the *Al-Skeini* case.[36] This case involved UK military personnel shooting and killing an Iraqi national in South Eastern Iraq. The Court reviewed its previous decisions and reaffirmed the *Banković* view that '[a] State's jurisdictional competence under Article 1 [ECHR] is primarily territorial' but held that, 'in exceptional cases', state jurisdiction (and thus the obligations imposed by the ECHR) can apply extraterritorially.[37] The Court then proceeded to set out the exceptional cases that can lead to the extraterritorial application of the ECHR, which included those situations where the state exercises effective control over foreign territory[38] and 'whenever the State through its agents exercises control and authority over an individual'.[39]

As a general matter, it appears that the Court expressed unequivocal support for the personal model for establishing jurisdiction. For the reasons argued above in the context of the ICCPR, this would mean that the ECHR applies not just to those situations where a state exercises physical control over persons but also where it exercises virtual control over them in cyberspace.

The UK was formally declared an occupying power in South Eastern Iraq by Security Council Resolution 1483 (2003). However, the ECtHR avoided the difficult question as to whether the strength of the insurgency meant that the UK did not exercise effective control over the territory in which the applicants were located when they were subject to human rights abuses. Instead, the Court utilised the personal model to determine jurisdiction. But, crucially, when concluding that the UK exercised jurisdiction over the applicants, the Court qualified its prior approval of the personal model by explaining that it could only be used due to the 'exceptional circumstances' of the case, namely, that the UK 'assumed in Iraq the exercise of some of the public powers normally to be exercised by a sovereign government'.[40] Thus, the Court limited the availability of the personal model to those situations where the state in question exercises public powers within foreign territory – which creates a new hybrid model that contains 'a rather bizarre mix

[36] In *Al-Skeini* Judge Bonello described the ECtHR's case law on Article 1 ECHR as 'bedevilled by an inability or an unwillingness to establish a coherent and axiomatic regime'; *Al-Skeini v United Kingdom*, Judgment, App No 55721/07, ECtHR, 7 July 2011, para 4 (Concurring Opinion of Judge Bonello).

[37] ibid para 131.

[38] ibid para 139.

[39] ibid para 137.

[40] ibid para 149.

of the personal model with the spatial one'[41] – with the implication being that outside of these exceptional circumstances the effective control test as outlined in *Banković* represents the only method by which a state's extraterritorial jurisdiction under the ECHR can be established.[42] In this sense, the Court's rejection of the spatial model outlined in *Banković* and its approval of the personal model was 'half-hearted at best'.[43] According to this reasoning of *Al-Skeini*, operations committed through cyberspace (such as cyber espionage) would not engage the jurisdiction of the offending state under the ECHR, unless of course the state was exercising effective control over – or public powers within – the territory that the person was located when he or she was targeted.

The Court's reluctance to fully embrace the personal model for establishing state jurisdiction can be further observed in the *Jaloud* decision.[44] This case concerned a member of the Dutch military who shot and killed an Iraqi national while he was passing through a military checkpoint in South Eastern Iraq, which Dutch forces had set up pursuant to Security Council Resolution 1483. The Court concluded that the ECHR was applicable on the basis that the shooting occurred while the victim was passing through territory (a checkpoint) that Dutch forces exercised authority and control over,[45] as opposed to the fact that the soldier exercised authority and control over the *victim* when shooting him. The *Jaloud* decision therefore appears to reintroduce the element of territorial control into the test for determining when state jurisdiction can be established extraterritorially, even if the scope of territorial control in this case was very small (a checkpoint) and that The Netherlands was not in effective control of that territory. If this interpretation of *Jaloud* is accurate, the ECHR cannot apply to state-sponsored cyber operations (including acts of cyber espionage) due to the fact that these operations occur within an a-territorial environment, that is, cyberspace.

Interestingly, Sari offers an alternative reading of *Jaloud* and concludes that, properly interpreted, this decision does not necessarily limit the extraterritorial application of the ECHR to *territorial* spaces under a state's authority and control. As Sari explains:

> Checkpoints do not have to be fixed or permanent. They can be mobile and set up at short notice. Consequently, what exactly distinguishes them from a foot patrol: is a patrol not a moving checkpoint? Checkpoints may be set up not only on land, but also at sea and in the air. Could one aircraft intercepting another one not conceivably be said to enforce a checkpoint?[46]

[41] M Milanovic, 'Al-Skeini and Al-Jedda in Strasbourg' (2012) 23 *EJIL* 121, 131.

[42] '[A] contrario, had the UK not exercised such public powers, the personal model of jurisdiction would not have applied. In other words, *Banković* is according to the Court still perfectly correct in its result'; ibid 130.

[43] ibid 129.

[44] *Jaloud v The Netherlands*, Judgment, App No 47708/08, ECtHR, 20 November 2014.

[45] ibid para 152.

[46] A Sari, 'Jaloud v Netherlands: New Directions in Extra-Territorial Military Operations', 24 November 2014, EJIL: *Talk!*, www.ejiltalk.org/jaloud-v-netherlands-new-directions-in-extra-territorial-military-operations/.

To extend Sari's analysis, do checkpoints have to be physical? Where a state appropriates confidential data in cyberspace, is it not essentially establishing and enforcing a type of (electronic) checkpoint insofar as it arrogates to itself the power to determine whether or not that data is interfered with? The point being made is that, while in *Jaloud* the Court shied away from endorsing the personal model for establishing jurisdiction, the boiled down effect of this decision seems to be that state jurisdiction under the ECHR can be established whenever state agents exercise their authority and control over individuals.

What conclusions can be gleaned from above? The jurisprudence of the ECtHR certainly indicates a tentative move towards a more permissive approach to establishing extraterritorial jurisdiction, even if it has not unambiguously adopted the HRC's personal model.[47] But the Court's jurisprudence is inconsistent and convoluted. Under the influence of the HRC and other human rights tribunals,[48] as well as the influential work of UN human rights bodies such as the Office of the High Commissioner, the ECtHR is likely to come under mounting pressure to (finally and unequivocally) endorse the personal model, allowing state jurisdiction to be established whenever and wherever states exercise their authority and control over individuals, even where that authority is exercised virtually through the medium of cyberspace.

3. The Right to Privacy

Article 17 ICCPR explains that 'no one shall be subjected to arbitrary or unlawful interference with his privacy, family, home or correspondence', whereas Article 8 ECHR protects 'the right to respect for private and family life, his home and his correspondence'. Human rights bodies have been reluctant to formulate an exhaustive definition of the right to privacy, instead preferring to interpret the scope of this right on a case-by-case basis.[49] That being said, their jurisprudence indicates that they adopt a broad interpretation of the concept of privacy,[50] with

[47] 'Even the ECtHR is gradually bending toward the reasoning of its sister interpretive bodies [such as the HRC]'; Van Schaack (n 16) 32. For a similar view see M Milanovic, 'Jurisdiction and Responsibility: Trends in the Strasbourg Court' in A van Aaken and I Motoc (eds), *The ECHR and General International Law* (Oxford, Oxford University Press, 2018).

[48] The Inter-American Commission has long adopted the personal model for establishing jurisdiction; *Armando Alejandre Jr et al v Cuba*, Case 11, 589, Inter-American Commission HR, Report No 86/99, OAS/Ser.L/V/II.104 (1999) para 25 ('The fact that the events took place outside Cuban jurisdiction does not limit the Commission's competence *ratione loci* because, as previously stated, when agents of a state, whether military or civilian, exercise power and authority over persons outside national territory, the state's obligation to respect human rights continues – in this case the rights enshrined in the American Declaration'). For a more recent example see *Franklin Guillermo Aisalla Molina v Ecuador-Colombia*, Case IP-02, Inter-American Commission HR, Report No 112/10, OEA/Ser.L/V/II.140 Doc 10 (2010) para 99.

[49] *Peck v United Kingdom*, Judgment, App No 44647/98, ECtHR, 28 January 2003, para 57 '(Private life is a broad term not susceptible to exhaustive definition').

[50] Milanovic (n 13) 132.

it encompassing not just a negative right for persons to be left alone but, more generally, a positive entitlement to 'establish details of their identity as individual human beings'[51] and to 'develop relationships with other human beings and the outside world'.[52]

Information that enables individuals to establish and maintain a personal and professional life is protected from interference by the right to privacy, regardless of whether it is confidential or publicly available.[53] Nowadays, it is uncontested 'that the same rights that people have offline must also be protected online'[54] and that states must 'respect and protect the right to privacy, including in the context of digital communication'.[55] Consequently, the state-sponsored collection of confidential information stored online and the interception of private communications that take place through cyberspace (email, video chat etc) incontrovertibly constitutes a violation of the right to privacy.[56]

Given that this book examines the application of international law to political cyber espionage and also economic cyber espionage, it is necessary to consider whether companies possess fundamental rights under these agreements and in particular the right to privacy. At first glance this line of argument may seem specious and counter-intuitive – surely it is only human beings that can possess human rights?[57] Indeed, the HRC has expressly ruled out the possibility that companies are beneficiaries of the rights recognised by the ICCPR.[58]

Yet, the ECtHR has on numerous occasions determined that companies can be the bearer of fundamental rights under the ECHR.[59] The Court justifies this approach on the basis that: Article 1 of the Convention explains that 'everyone' is entitled to protection of the rights delineated in the agreement, indicating a broad scope that is inclusive of natural and legal persons; the *travaux* reveal that the drafters of the ECHR always intended to protect non-natural persons such as companies;[60] and that Article 34 ECHR explains that '[t]he Court may receive

[51] *Mikulić v Croatia*, Judgment, App No 53176/99, ECtHR, 7 February 2002, para 54.

[52] *Pretty v United Kingdom*, Judgment, App No 2346/02, ECtHR, 29 April 2002, para 61.

[53] *Shimovolos v Russia*, Judgment, App No 30194/09, ECtHR, 21 June 2011, para 65.

[54] Human Rights Council, *The Promotion, Protection and Enjoyment of Human Rights on the Internet*, UN Doc A/HRC/20/L.13, 29 June 2012, para 1.

[55] UN General Assembly, *The Right to Privacy in the Digital Age*, UN Doc A/RES/68/167, 18 December 2013, para 4(a).

[56] 'Surveillance, whether electronic or otherwise, interceptions of telephonic, telegraphic and other forms of communication, wire-tapping and recording of conversations should be prohibited'; Human Rights Committee, *General Comment No. 16: Article 17 (Right to Privacy), The Right to Respect of Privacy, Family, Home and Correspondence, and Protection of Honour and Reputation*, UN Doc HRI/GEN/1/Rev.9 (Vol I), 8 April 1988, para 8. *Liberty* (n 34) para 56 ('Telephone, facsimile and email communications are covered by the notion of "private life" and "correspondence" within the meaning of Article 8').

[57] For an interesting discussion of the theoretical basis for companies possessing human rights under the ECHR see A Grear, *Redirecting Human Rights: Facing the Challenge of Corporate Legal Humanity* (Basingstoke, Palgrave Macmillan, 2010) chapter 2.

[58] 'The beneficiaries of the rights recognized by the Covenant are individuals'; *General Comment No. 31* (n 14) para 9.

[59] *Comingersoll v Portugal*, Judgment, App No 35382/97, ECtHR, 6 April 2000, paras 33–35.

[60] For a discussion see M Emberland, *The Human Rights of Companies: Exploring the Structure of ECHR Protection* (Oxford, Oxford University Press, 2006) 4, 35–36.

applications from any person, non-governmental organization or groups of individuals', with companies falling within the definition of 'non-governmental organisations'.

This does not mean that companies enjoy the rights prescribed by the Convention *in toto*. Instead, when determining whether Convention rights apply to legal persons, what is required is an appreciation of the nature of the right under consideration and whether it is capable of being possessed by a legal person. For example, several judges on the ECtHR have expressly determined that companies cannot possess the right to life under Article 2 ECHR or the right to freedom from torture and inhuman or degrading treatment or punishment under Article 3 ECHR.[61]

Significantly, in *Société Colas Est* the ECtHR explained 'the time has come to hold that in certain circumstances the rights guaranteed by Article 8 of the Convention may be construed as including the right to respect for a company's registered office, branches or other premises'.[62] In this case, the Court concluded that the French government's raid on the offices of three companies violated their right under Article 8(1) ECHR to have their 'home' respected. While the Court has not explicitly determined that companies possess the right to private life under Article 8(1) ECHR, if offices can be regarded as a company's 'home' under this provision it is reasonable to assume that information belonging to a company forms part of its 'private life'.[63]

[61] *Comingersoll* (n 59) Concurring Opinion of Judge Rozakis Joined by Judges Sir Nichols Bratza, Caflisch and Vajić ('I accept that a number of provisions of the Convention may be inapplicable to companies or other juristic persons (for example, Articles 2 and 3)').

[62] *Société Colas Est v France*, Judgment, App No 37971/97, ECtHR, 16 April 2002, para 41.

[63] Article 1 of Protocol 1 to the ECHR expressly confers the right to 'peaceful enjoyment of possessions' to '[e]very natural or legal person' ie, companies. Whether this provision protects companies against economic cyber espionage depends upon whether trade secrets constitute 'possessions' within the meaning of Article 1 of Protocol 1. For the Court, items constitute 'possessions' providing they can be ascribed objective economic value, regardless of whether they are physical or non-physical in nature; *Kopecký v Slovakia*, Judgment, App No 44912/98, ECtHR, 28 September 2004, para 41. Data per se is not a possession under Article 1 of Protocol 1. However, if the substance of that data possesses objective economic value, it can be regarded as a possession. For example, data that pertains to items that give rise to rights of restitution under national law possess economic value and are thus possessions of the company, such as the contents of legally enforceable contracts and patent-protected intellectual property; *Anheuser-Busch Inc v Portugal*, Judgment, App No 73049/01, ECtHR, 11 January 2007, paras 76–78. Certain types of company information can be regarded as possessing objective economic value – for instance, patented research designs – and thus Article 1 of Protocol 1 can provide a company that has been the victim of economic cyber espionage with a cause of action. However, the majority of company information that is the target of espionage is unlikely to possess objective economic value as understood by Article 1 of Protocol 1. Consider, for example, profit and loss accounts, employee details, customer lists and marketing strategies. Nevertheless, the Court has explained that an item can be regarded as a possession even if it does not possess economic value at the point at which it is interfered with, providing the item's owner can demonstrate a reasonable and legitimate expectation that economic value will attach to the item at some future point; *Kopecký* (n 63) paras 47–48. Yet, most trade secrets are unlikely to give rise to a reasonable and legitimate expectation that they will acquire economic value. As an example, while effective marketing strategies are key to revenue generation, it is difficult to see how strategies can engender a legitimate expectation to a future economic benefit. After all, strategies can be successful or unsuccessful and thus may or may not yield profit. The mere 'hope' that an item will become economically valuable does not transform it into a possession; *Kopecký*, ibid para 35. In light of this, most trade secrets cannot be regarded as company possessions under

As a preliminary matter, it is interesting to consider the US view that the mere collection of data does not constitute interference with the right to privacy, such as when information is obtained and stored but not read or even where data is read but this is performed by an algorithm (that uses selectors to search electronic data for key terms such as 'bomb' or 'jihadist') rather than a human being.[64] This is a narrow interpretation of the notion of interference and it runs counter to the views of the HRC and the ECtHR.[65] For these bodies, the collection of information in and by itself constitutes an interference with the right to privacy because it undermines personal autonomy and it prevents individuals from forging relationships with others.

Moreover, Senators Dianne Feinstein and Saxby Chambliss, when acting as Co-Chairs of the US Senate Intelligence Committee, argued that the collection of metadata (as opposed to content data) does not interfere with the right to privacy.[66] This distinction is not persuasive because access to metadata can produce detailed insights into a person's identity and behaviour and, especially when aggregated in significant amounts, can be more revealing than content data.[67] It is for this reason that human rights bodies have consistently determined that the right to privacy protects metadata as well as content data,[68] such as

Article 1 of Protocol 1 and are more likely to benefit from the legal protection afforded by the right to privacy under Article 8 ECHR, which is why Article 8 is the focus of this chapter. Note that while shares are possessions under Article 1 of Protocol 1 and the Court has recognised that shareholders can bring claims independently of the company where state action adversely affects the value of shares, such claims can only be brought in the 'exceptional' scenario where it is 'impossible' for the company to bring a claim on its own behalf; *Agrotexim and Others v Greece*, Judgment, Series A 330-A, ECtHR, 24 October 1995, para 66. Unhelpfully, the Court has not provided any guidance on when it is 'impossible' for a company to vindicate its legal rights.

[64] US Department of Defense, *Procedures Governing the Activities of DOD Intelligence Components that Affect United States Persons*, DOD 5240 1-R (1982) C2.2.1. See also JR Clapper with A Mitchell, 'Director James R Clapper Interview with Andrea Mitchell, NBC News Chief Foreign Affairs Correspondent', *Office of the Director of National Intelligence*, 8 June 2013, www.dni.gov/index.php/newsroom/speeches-interviews/speeches-interviews-2013/item/874-director-james-r-clapper-interview-with-andrea-mitchell.

[65] The HRC explains that '[communications must be] delivered to the addressee without interference and without being opened or otherwise read'; *General Comment No. 16* (n 56) para 8. See also *Shimovolos* (n 53) para 65.

[66] E O'Keefe, 'Transcript: Dianne Feinstein, Saxby Chambliss Explain, Defend NSA Phone Records Program', 6 June 2013, *the Washington Post*, www.washingtonpost.com/news/post-politics/wp/2013/06/06/transcript-dianne-feinstein-saxby-chambliss-explain-defend-nsa-phone-records-program/?utm_term=.c171058830eb.

[67] 'From the perspective of the right to privacy, this distinction [between content and metadata] is not persuasive. The aggregation of information commonly referred to as "metadata" may give an insight into an individual's behaviour, social relationships, private preferences and identity that go beyond even that conveyed by accessing the content of a private communication'; *The Right to Privacy in the Digital Age* (n 25) para 19.

[68] The seminal case is *Malone v United Kingdom*, Judgment, App No 8691/79, ECtHR, 2 August 1984, para 84.

GPS coordinates[69] and the times, dates, contacts, language, and lengths of voice and video calls over the Internet.[70]

4. Restricting the Right to Privacy

The right to privacy is not absolute and its enjoyment can be justifiably restricted. This is explicitly recognised by Article 17 ICCPR, which explains that it is only 'arbitrary or unlawful' interferences with the right to privacy that are prohibited, and in Article 8 ECHR, which determines that the right to privacy can be limited where it is 'in accordance with the law' and 'necessary in a democratic society'.

While these two agreements adopt different terminology, a close examination of the jurisprudence of the HRC and the ECtHR reveals that the conditions that must be met in order for states to permissibly limit the enjoyment of the right to privacy are more or less identical.[71] In fact, the HRC has adopted the 'necessary in a democratic society' vernacular when determining whether Covenant rights can be restricted.[72]

A close assessment of the jurisprudence of the HRC and the ECtHR reveals that these bodies use three criteria to determine the legality of restrictions to the right to privacy under Article 17 ICCPR and Article 8 ECHR: the measure must be (i) in accordance with the law; (ii) necessary to achieve a legitimate aim; and (iii) proportionate to that aim.[73]

4.1. In Accordance with the Law

Both the HRC and the ECtHR have repeatedly determined that a measure must exhibit three distinct qualities in order for it to regarded as being in accordance with the law: the law must be (i) accessible; (ii) its effects foreseeable; and (iii) its application subject to oversight.[74]

[69] *Uzun v Germany*, Judgment, App No 35623/05, ECtHR, 2 September 2010, paras 11–12.

[70] *Kennedy v United Kingdom*, Judgment, App No 26839/05, ECtHR, 18 May 2010, para 118; *Liberty* (n 34) paras 43–45; *The Right to Privacy in the Digital Age* (n 25) para 19.

[71] 'In practice this test [the one used by the HRC to determine whether interferences with Article 17 ICCPR are lawful] aligns itself with the term employed in the European Convention, namely, that restrictions on rights "must be necessary in a democratic society"'; Peters (n 4) 157.

[72] Human Rights Committee, *General Comment No. 27: Article 12 (Freedom of Movement)*, UN Doc CCPR/C/21/Rev.1/Add.9, 2 November 1999, para 11.

[73] *Weber and Saravia v Germany*, Decision, App No 54934/00, ECtHR, 29 June 2006, paras 92–95; *Fourth Periodic Report of the USA* (n 20) para 22 ('measures should be taken to ensure that any interference with the right to privacy complies with the principles of legality, proportionality and necessity, regardless of the nationality or location of the individuals whose communications are under direct surveillance'); *The Right to Privacy in the Digital Age* (n 25) para 23 ('the overarching principles of legality, necessity and proportionality' must be adhered to when restricting the right to privacy under Article 17 ICCPR).

[74] In the context of Article 8 ECHR see *Szabò v Hungary*, Judgment, App No 37138/14/14, ECtHR, 12 January 2016, para 59 and the references therein. With regard to Article 17 ICCPR see Human

4.1.1. Accessible

Legal measures that infringe human rights (including the right to privacy) must be publicly accessible because it is an integral element of the rule of law that the public is able to familiarise itself with the law and understand its content.[75] In *Malone*, the ECtHR stressed that while there was no legal prohibition against the tapping of telephone meters in UK law, Article 8(2) ECHR nevertheless required that the state provide clear legal authority for the activity that gives rise to a breach of Article 8(1) ECHR.[76]

Accessibility is problematic in the context of espionage because states have been reluctant to adopt legal frameworks that expressly regulate the conduct of their intelligence agencies. At least historically, the intelligence community operated largely according to government agency protocols and informal codes of conduct that were never made available to the public. Importantly, the requirement of accessibility means that 'secret rules and secret interpretations – even secret judicial interpretations – of law do not have the necessary qualities of law'.[77]

This being said, various high profile disclosures relating to espionage have put states under significant pressure to improve the transparency and accountability of their intelligence agencies. In response, a number of states have imposed regulatory frameworks upon their intelligence agencies and have publicised them in the same way as any other domestic law, thereby providing their surveillance regimes with the requisite public character to be classified as law.

4.1.2. Foreseeable

The effects of legislation must be foreseeable in order to be lawful, namely, that the relevant law must be sufficiently precise so as to enable the public to comprehend what types of conduct can give rise to surveillance. Human rights bodies have acknowledged that the unanticipated and unpredictable nature of threats to national security make it difficult for states to define in advance and in detail the conduct that can prompt a decision to subject a person to surveillance.[78] For this reason, it is not necessary that surveillance legislation 'set[s] out exhaustively by name the specific offences which may give rise to interception'.[79]

Nonetheless, states cannot confer upon public authorities an 'unfettered power' as to who can be surveilled and when, where and for how long surveillance

Rights Committee, *Concluding Observations on the Seventh Periodic Report of the United Kingdom of Great Britain and Northern Ireland*, UN Doc CCPR/C/GBR/CO/7, 17 August 2015, para 24(b) and the *Fourth Periodic Report of the USA* (n 20) para 22(b).

[75] *Shimovolos* (n 53) paras 67–71.

[76] *Malone* (n 68) para 87.

[77] *The Right to Privacy in the Digital Age* (n 25) para 29.

[78] *Zakharov v Russia*, Judgment, App No 47143/06, ECtHR, 4 December 2015, para 247.

[79] *Kennedy* (n 70) para 159.

can occur.[80] Effective human rights protection requires that legislation must give the public a sufficiently clear indication as to the circumstances in which and the conditions on which public authorities are entitled to resort to measures that interfere with the right to privacy.[81] Accordingly, legislation must specify:

> The nature of the offences which may give rise to an interception order; a definition of the categories of people liable to have their telephones tapped; a limit on the duration of telephone tapping; the procedure to be followed for examining, using and storing data obtained; the precautions to be taken when communicating the data to other parties; and the circumstances in which records may or must be erased or destroyed.[82]

The foreseeability requirement is important in the context of surveillance legislation. While a number of states have devised and implemented laws that place their surveillance activities on a statutory footing, these laws are often broadly drafted and fail to identify the circumstances within which surveillance can occur. Take for example the surveillance laws adopted by the US, which have come under intense scrutiny from human rights lawyers since the Snowden revelations.

The US's surveillance regime is complex and imposes different rules depending upon whether the persons targeted are US nationals and whether they are targeted while located within US territory. In short, US persons located within US territory receive greater protection from US surveillance laws than non-US persons located abroad.[83] Space limitations preclude an assessment of all of these different rules. Instead, the discussion that follows focuses upon those laws that regulate when US intelligence agencies can collect confidential information from non-US persons located abroad, not least because the Snowden disclosures revealed that it was these rules that were frequently invoked by the NSA to justify its cyber espionage activities.

Section 702 of the FISA Amendments Act (FAA) 2008[84] provides US intelligence agencies with the authority to collect Internet and telecommunications content from non-US persons located outside of the US in order to acquire 'foreign intelligence information'. Under Section 702 FAA, the acquisition of information must require assistance from an electronic communications service provider. Given the interconnectedness of cyberspace and the potential for private information belonging to US persons to be incidentally collected while surveillance is being undertaken against non-US persons located abroad, Section 702 FAA

[80] *Zakharov* (n 78) para 230.

[81] ibid para 229. Similarly, the HRC explains that 'relevant legislation must specify in detail the precise circumstances on which such interference [with communications privacy] may be permitted'; *General Comment No. 16* (n 56) para 8.

[82] *Weber* (n 73) para 95.

[83] That the US (and other states) provide greater legal protection to nationals than to non-nationals is problematic under international human rights law, which prohibits discrimination on the grounds of nationality; see Article 26 ICCPR and Article 14 ECHR. Due to space limitations, this chapter does not assess how the non-discrimination rule applies to surveillance laws but, for a discussion in the US context, see Severson (n 23).

[84] The FISA Amendments Act 2008 amended the Foreign Intelligence Surveillance Act (FISA) 1978.

implements procedures that are designed to minimise interference with information belonging to US persons.

Executive Order (EO) 12333[85] is a residual legal measure insofar as it provides US intelligence agencies with the authority to collect foreign intelligence from targets located outside of the US where the FAA is inapplicable,[86] that is, where information is collected from non-US persons located within foreign territories but this process does not require the compelled assistance of electronic communications service providers. Section 2.2 of EO 12333 outlines the circumstances in which information can be collected. Inter alia, intelligence agencies are authorised to target: 'information needed to protect the safety of any persons or organizations'; 'information needed to protect foreign intelligence or counterintelligence sources, methods, and activities from unauthorized disclosure'; 'information concerning persons who are reasonably believed to be potential sources or contacts for the purpose of determining their suitability or credibility'; and 'information necessary for administrative purposes'.

As is apparent, the circumstances in which intelligence agencies can engage in surveillance under Section 702 FAA and EO 12333 are broad and, in the words of other commentators, 'vague'.[87] Although in the context of the ECHR, in *Liberty* the ECtHR explained that the circumstances in which surveillance could take place under UK legislation were not sufficiently foreseeable from the wording of the legislation because of the 'very broad classes of communications'[88] that were susceptible to interception. In the words of the impugned domestic law, communications could be intercepted that were designated 'external communications', which basically included any form of telecommunication sent from or received by a person located outside the British Islands. For the Court, '[t]he legal discretion granted to the executive for the physical capture of external communications was, therefore, virtually unfettered' and was thus deemed unlawful.[89] Similarly, in *Szabò* the Court concluded that a Hungarian law that allowed authorities to target 'persons' suspected of being involved in terrorism was unlawful because of 'the absence of clarification in domestic legislation as to how this notion [of persons] is to be applied in practice. For the Court, the category is overly broad.'[90] These cases indicate that those human rights bodies responsible for applying the ICCPR are unlikely to regard Section 702 FAA and EO 12333 as

[85] Executive Order 12333, 46 FR 59941, 3 CFR, 1981 Comp, 200.

[86] President's Review Group on Intelligence and Communications Technologies, Executive Office of the President, *Liberty and Security in a Changing World: Report and Recommendations* (2013) 70, www.obamawhitehouse.archives.gov/sites/default/files/docs/2013-12-12_rg_final_report.pdf.

[87] Peters (n 4) 158. '[EO 12333] provides the intelligence community with vague powers and very little guidance as to how to exercise them'; CJ Wen, 'Secrecy, Standing, and Executive Order 12, 333' (2016) 89 *Southern California Law Review* 1203, 1213.

[88] *Liberty* (n 34) para 64.

[89] ibid.

[90] *Szabò* (n 74) para 67.

providing sufficient details – and thus adequate guidance to the public – as to the types of activities that can give rise to surveillance in order to produce legal effects that are foreseeable.

In response to the Snowden leaks and the perception that US intelligence agencies have free legal rein to intercept confidential information, in January 2014 President Barack Obama published Presidential Policy Directive 28 (PPD-28) with the view to limiting the circumstances in which signals intelligence can be conducted.[91] PPD-28 stipulates that intelligence agencies can only undertake signals intelligence where necessary to detect and counter six types of threat: (1) espionage; (2) terrorism; (3) weapons of mass destruction; (4) cyber security; (5) threats to US or allied military personnel; and (6) transnational criminal threats.[92] In addition, PPD-28 explains that the US will not conduct surveillance 'for the purpose of suppressing or burdening criticism or dissent, or for disadvantaging persons based on their ethnicity, race, gender, sexual orientation or religion'[93] or to acquire economic information belonging to foreign companies.[94]

Importantly, PPD-28 narrows down and clarifies the circumstances in which US intelligence agencies can collect signals intelligence. In my view, PPD-28 provides Section 702 FAA and EO 12333 with the granularity necessary to ensure that these measures produce legal effects that are sufficiently foreseeable, although another commentator argues that 'PPD-28 makes mostly cosmetic changes'.[95] While this Directive is an authoritative statement of government policy, it does not have the status of law. However, in *Kennedy*, the ECtHR accepted that a Code of Practice adopted by the Secretary of State could be taken into account when determining whether the impugned legislation was sufficiently precise even though it did not have the status of law. In arriving at this conclusion, the Court regarded it as important that the Code was a publicly available document that was regarded by the relevant authorities (and indeed national courts) as imposing demonstrable limits upon their ability to carry out surveillance activities.[96] It is therefore important that PPD-28 is a publicly available document and is regarded by US intelligence agencies as forming an integral part of the regulatory framework applicable to the collection of signals intelligence.[97]

[91] *Presidential Policy Directive – Signals Intelligence Activities*, Policy Directive/PPD-28, 17 January 2014, www.obamawhitehouse.archives.gov/the-press-office/2014/01/17/presidential-policy-directive-signals-intelligence-activities. Note that PPD-28 applies only to signals intelligence and not to other methods of information collection.

[92] ibid section 2.

[93] ibid section 1(b).

[94] ibid section 1(c).

[95] Severson (n 23) 486.

[96] *Kennedy* (n 70) para 157.

[97] P Margulies, 'The NSA in Global Perspective: Surveillance, Human Rights, and International Counterterrorism' (2014) 82 *Fordham Law Review* 2137, 2142.

4.1.3. Oversight

National laws that authorise public authorities to undertake surveillance and thus interfere with the right to privacy must provide 'adequate and effective guarantees against abuse'.[98] In the words of the General Assembly, states must:

> [E]stablish or maintain existing independent, effective, adequately resourced and impartial judicial, administrative and/or parliamentary domestic oversight mechanisms capable of ensuring transparency, as appropriate, and accountability for State surveillance of communications, their interception and the collection of personal data.[99]

Two general requirements can be discerned. First, from a procedural perspective, because surveillance is 'a field where abuse is so easy in individual cases and could have such harmful consequences for democratic society as a whole, it is in principle desirable to entrust supervisory control to a judge'.[100] Non-judicial supervisory bodies are therefore acceptable in principle, although it is required that non-judicial bodies must be 'independent of the authorities carrying out the surveillance' and 'vested with sufficient powers and competence to exercise an effective continuous control'.[101] Whether a body is independent and competent is decided on a case-by-case basis but, for indicative purposes, it has been held that 'supervision by a politically responsible member of the executive, such as a Minister of Justice, does not provide the necessary guarantees'.[102]

Oversight of surveillance operations should ideally occur before they are carried out, although this is 'not an absolute requirement *per se*'[103] because emergencies can arise within which there is no opportunity to acquire *ex ante* authorisation. In such circumstances, however, *post factum* review of the lawfulness of the surveillance is essential and must be performed by a judicial body.[104]

[98] *Klass v Germany*, Judgment, App No 5029/71, ECtHR, 6 September 1978, para 50. The ECtHR has also explained that states should notify individuals that they have been subject to surveillance 'since there is in principle little scope for recourse to the courts by the individual concerned unless the latter is advised of the measures taken without his or her knowledge'; *Weber* (n 73) para 135. In this sense, 'subsequent notification of surveillance measures is inextricably linked to … the existence of effective safeguards against the abuse of monitoring powers'; ibid. Crucially, however, the Court stopped short of saying that notification is a legal requirement: 'the fact that persons concerned by secret surveillance measures are not subsequently notified once surveillance has ceased cannot by itself warrant the conclusion that the interference was not "necessary in a democratic society", as it is the very absence of knowledge of surveillance which ensures the efficacy of the interference'; ibid.

[99] UN General Assembly, *The Right to Privacy in the Digital Age*, A/C.3/71/L.39/Rev.1, 16 November 2016, para 5(d).

[100] *Klass* (n 98) para 56. This Court reiterated this view more recently in the *Szabò* decision, explaining that 'control by an independent body, normally a judge with special expertise, should be the rule and substitute solution, the exception warranting close scrutiny'; *Szabò* (n 74) paras 40–41.

[101] *Klass* (n 98) para 56.

[102] *Szabò* (n 74) para 77.

[103] ibid.

[104] In *Szabò* it was held that, while surveillance carried out without prior authorisation by an independent and competent body is acceptable in emergency situations, '[s]uch measures must however be subject to a *post factum* review, which is required, as a rule, in cases where the surveillance was authorised *ex ante* by a non-judicial authority'; *Szabò* (n 74) para 81.

Second, and more substantively, the supervisory body must have the authority to review decisions of public authorities to engage in surveillance and ensure that they are compliant with international human rights law, that is, that any interference with human rights is in accordance with the law, necessary to meet a legitimate aim and proportionate to that aim given the circumstances.

Again using the US as an illustration, let us consider whether Section 702 FAA and EO 12333 are subject to effective oversight. With regard to Section 702 FAA, the FAA confers upon the Foreign Intelligence Service Court (FISC) the authority to oversee the collection of information under this legislation. Following the Snowden leaks, the Obama administration repeatedly asserted that FISC represented an effective oversight mechanism.[105] FISC provides *ex ante* authorisation insofar as it must approve warrants before surveillance can occur under Section 702 FAA. Moreover, there can be little doubt that FISC is an independent and impartial judicial body – it is a recognised court that operates according to rules and procedures and is presided over by a sitting District Court judge.[106]

Problems emerge, however, due to the limited powers that the FAA confers to FISC to ensure that surveillance warrants are human rights compliant. When it comes to issuing surveillance warrants under Section 702 FAA, the role of FISC is to determine whether year-long certificates can be granted to intelligence agencies to pursue surveillance against *categories* of individuals, that is, non-US persons located abroad. Providing that the Court is satisfied that it is 'reasonably believed' by the intelligence agency that only non-US persons located outside of the US will be targeted, and that if the communications of US persons are incidentally collected the intelligence agency will deploy adequate measures to minimise this interference, the warrant must be approved. Crucially, then, Section 702 FAA does not provide FISC with the authority to examine the merits of *individualised* warrants.[107] In other words, FISC cannot assess whether specific surveillance operations against specific persons in breach of their right to privacy are in accordance with the law, necessary to meet a pressing social need and proportionate to the legitimate ends sought.

[105] M Reilly, 'Obama Defends NSA Surveillance Program, Says It's 'Transparent'', 17 June 2013, *The Huffington Post*, www.huffingtonpost.co.uk/entry/obama-nsa-surveillance_n_3455771.

[106] For an overview of the composition of FISC see R Wheeler, 'The Changing Composition of the Foreign Surveillance Court and What if Anything to do About it' (2014) 2 *Lawfare Research Paper Series* 1.

[107] 'Under section 702, the Attorney General and the Director of National Intelligence may authorize annually, with the approval of the Foreign Intelligence Surveillance Court (FISC), intelligence collection targeting categories of non-US persons abroad, without the need for a court order for each individual target'; JR Clapper and EH Holder, *Letter to (US Congress) John Boehner, Harry Reid, Nancy Pelosi and Mitch McConnell about the Re-Authorization of Title VII of the Foreign Intelligence Surveillance Act (FISA) Enacted by the FISA Amendment Act of 2008 (FAA)*, 8 February 2012, 1. This is in stark contrast to warrants sought under Sections 703 and 704 FAA, which are the provisions that regulate under what circumstances surveillance can be conducted against US persons, for which FISC must approve individualised warrants.

In light of the above, it is apparent that the safeguards offered by FISC are 'extremely limited by the text of the statute'[108] and fall short of the high standard of effective oversight required by international human rights law.[109] It should be noted that there are other entities that have a role in overseeing the use of Section 702 FAA surveillance warrants, including the Office of the Director of Compliance, the Office of General Counsel, the Signals Intelligence Directorate's Oversight and Compliance Section and the Director of Civil Liberties and Privacy Office. As we have seen, non-judicial authorities can provide oversight, although only under very specific conditions. With regard to the US example, problems arise because, first, the aforementioned entities are executive bodies and therefore not sufficiently independent from the authorities invoking the surveillance powers and, second, these entities provide *post factum* oversight only and, as we have seen, only judicial bodies are sufficient to provide *post factum* review.

With regard to EO 12333, surveillance is only lawful under this instrument providing the Attorney General determines 'in each case that there is probable cause to believe that the technique [for surveillance] is directed against a foreign power or an agent of a foreign power'.[110] Unlike Section 702 FAA, EO 12333 requires that the Attorney General assesses each individual case and only approves a surveillance warrant where there is probable cause.

Nevertheless, EO 12333 is problematic from a procedural perspective because, while surveillance warrants under EO 12333 require *ex ante* authorisation by the Attorney General, this is a non-judicial body. Non-judicial bodies can provide *ex ante* authorisation but they must be independent of the government. Significantly, the Attorney General is an executive appointment. Thus, and in the words of Senator Dianne Feinstein, former Chair of the Senate Intelligence Committee, '[t]welve-triple-three programs are under the executive branch entirely'.[111] As such, the Attorney General does not provide adequate independent oversight over the issuance of EO 12333 surveillance warrants.

4.2. Legitimate Aim

Restrictions on the right to privacy are only lawful if they serve a legitimate aim. Article 8(2) ECHR enumerates the legitimate grounds upon which privacy can be restricted: where there is a threat to national security, public safety or the economic wellbeing of the country; for the prevention of disorder or crime; and for the protection of health, morals, and the rights and freedoms of others.

[108] Wen (n 87) 1211.

[109] G Greenwald, 'Fisa Court Oversight: A Look Inside a Secret and Empty Process', 19 June 2013, *the Guardian*, www.theguardian.com/commentisfree/2013/jun/19/fisa-court-oversight-process-secrecy.

[110] EO 12333 (n 85) Section 2.5.

[111] Quoted in A Watkins, 'Most of NSA's Data Collection Authorized by order Ronald Reagan Issued', 21 November 2013, *McClatchy*, www.mcclatchydc.com/news/nation-world/national/national-security/article24759289.html.

While Article 17 ICCPR does not list the legitimate grounds for restricting privacy, relevant jurisprudence indicates that these closely align with those specified by Article 8(2) ECHR.[112]

In the context of the ECHR, the ECtHR has accepted that it is necessary for states to possess legislation that authorises public authorities to engage in surveillance:

> [T]he existence of some legislation granting powers of secret surveillance over the mail, post and telecommunications is, under exceptional conditions, necessary in a democratic society in the interests of national security and/or for the prevention of disorder or crime.[113]

This being said, and as this quotation reveals, the Court has circumscribed the scope of the surveillance powers that national laws can confer upon public authorities and how public authorities can utilise these powers in individual operations. In particular, the Court's jurisprudence reveals that persons can be placed under surveillance only where it is 'strictly necessary',[114] that is, where there is a 'reasonable suspicion'[115] that targeted persons are engaged in activities that the state has a legitimate need to suppress.[116] In *Szabò*, for example, the Court held that Hungary's surveillance law was unlawful because it allowed warrants to be issued without the relevant authorities having to 'produce supportive materials or, in particular, a sufficient factual basis' to demonstrate that the persons to be targeted were engaged in illicit activities and, as a result, this obviated the need for an 'evaluation of [the] necessity of the proposed measure'.[117]

In *Szabò* the Court expressed 'serious concern' over national laws and decisions of public authorities that permit the 'strategic, large-scale interception' of communications.[118] Given the requirement of individualised suspicion, mass surveillance for general or exploratory purposes must be considered unnecessary and therefore unlawful.[119] But this does not mean that mass surveillance is inherently unlawful. For example, it may be the case that information belonging to non-suspects is incidentally collected (and thus their right to privacy infringed) as an unintended and inevitable consequence of targeting suspects. Whether this type of targeted but nevertheless mass surveillance is lawful will fall to be determined by the application of the proportionality principle, discussed below.

[112] *Report of the Special Rapporteur on the Promotion and Protection of Human Rights and Fundamental Freedoms While Countering Terrorism*, UN Doc A/69/397, 23 September 2014, para 33.

[113] *Klass* (n 98) para 48; *Szabò* (n 74) para 68.

[114] *Klass* (n 98) para 42.

[115] *Zakharov* (n 78) para 260.

[116] The only instance where a state is permitted to engage in surveillance against persons without a reasonable suspicion that they are engaged in illicit activities is where the state derogates from the human rights treaty and thus suspends its human rights obligations, such as during times of war or public emergency threatening the life of the nation; Article 4(1) ICCPR; Article 15(1) ECHR.

[117] *Szabò* (n 74) para 71.

[118] ibid para 69.

[119] *The Right to Privacy in the Digital Age* (n 25) para 25.

That human rights bodies are averse to the conferral of wide-ranging and open-ended surveillance powers to public authorities has significant implications for the legality of surveillance laws for states such as the US. Section 702 FAA permits surveillance to be undertaken where it is in pursuit of 'foreign intelligence information'. Section 702 FAA does not therefore require public authorities to produce evidence that demonstrates a reasonable suspicion that the targeted person is involved in illicit activities.[120] Note that PPD-28 does limit the use of signals intelligence to counteracting certain harmful activities (terrorism, espionage etc). This being said, this Directive (as with Section 702 FAA) does not require that public authorities only place under surveillance those persons for which there is evidence demonstrating that they are reasonably suspected of being engaged in harmful activities. Put differently, so long as intelligence agencies can furnish evidence indicating that there is a genuine threat that one of these prescribed harmful activities is at risk of occurring, they can undertake surveillance against persons even if there is no evidence implicating them specifically/individually in that harmful activity. In this sense, PPD-28 preserves the capacity of intelligence agencies to engage in non-suspicion based surveillance.[121] Thus, the surveillance powers conferred by Section 702 FAA cannot be regarded as human rights compliant.

As noted previously, EO 12333 provides that surveillance cannot be undertaken unless the Attorney General 'has determined in each case that there is probable cause to believe that the technique is directed against a foreign power or an agent of a foreign power'.[122] In particular, Section 1(1)(d)(1)–(3) EO 12333 requires that when the Attorney General is assessing a surveillance warrant special emphasis must be given to detecting and countering espionage, terrorism and the development, possession, proliferation and use of weapons of mass destruction.

Undoubtedly, these are activities that a state has a legitimate interest in preventing. Moreover, and unlike under Section 702 FAA, surveillance warrants under EO 12333 can only be granted on the basis of individualised suspicion – the Attorney General must be satisfied that there is 'probable cause' (specifically, objective evidence giving rise to a reasonable suspicion) that the targeted person is involved in one of the aforementioned harmful activities. Consequently, the surveillance powers conferred by this Order can be regarded as necessary to meet a pressing social need.

As a final remark, an interesting question is whether acts of economic cyber espionage that violate a company's right to privacy can be justified on the basis

[120] Privacy and Civil Liberties Oversight Board, Report on the Telephone Records Program Conducted under Section 215 of the USA Patriot Act and the Operations of the Foreign Intelligence Surveillance Court (2014) 57.

[121] PPD-28 (n 91) section 2. As the *Tallinn Manual 2.0* Experts noted, 'with respect to the mass collection of electronic communications that is not directed at particular individuals, the requirement that the surveillance be a necessary limitation on the right to privacy looms large'; *Tallinn Manual 2.0* (n 9) 204.

[122] EO 12333 (n 85) Section 2.5.

that they are necessary to safeguard the 'economic well-being of the country' under Article 8(2) ECHR. Certainly, economic cyber espionage cannot be justified simply because it enhances the competitiveness of domestic companies and thus strengthens the national economy in a general sense; these are not legitimate aims for a state to pursue at the expense of human rights protection. However, if a state is facing economic hardship it remains an 'open question'[123] as to whether resort to economic cyber espionage can be regarded as necessary to protect its economic well-being.

4.3. Proportionality

In order to be lawful, legislation authorising surveillance – or a decision of a public authority to utilise this legislation and engage in a particular surveillance operation – must be pursuant to a legitimate societal need and, in addition, it must strike an acceptable balance between the state's obligation to protect society from the various threats and dangers that exist and its duty to protect fundamental human rights.[124] It follows that surveillance is unlawful if the legitimate aim being pursued by the interference can be effectively achieved through the adoption of measures that are less restrictive upon the enjoyment of human rights.[125]

The application of the principle of proportionality is always contextual and depends upon the circumstances of each specific case. However, to balance competing interests it will always be necessary to identify the breadth and severity of the human rights violations produced by the impugned measure and the significance of the legitimate aim that it serves.[126] In short, the more important the legitimate aim, the more acceptable it is to interfere with the enjoyment of human rights. Thus, surveillance limiting the right to privacy is more readily justified as proportionate where the objective is to protect the community from terrorism and drug trafficking, for example, than if the objective is to protect individuals against low level crime and disorder. Moreover, if it is determined that acts of economic cyber espionage are pursuant to the legitimate aim of protecting the economic well-being of the state, such conduct is more likely to be justified as proportionate if the state is facing an imminent threat of economic collapse than if it is merely experiencing a dip in economic performance.

The margin of appreciation has an important role to play in the application of the proportionality principle but the width of the margin conferred to states and

[123] Milanovic (n 13) 136.

[124] *Weber* (n 73) para 108; *Peck* (n 49) para 77.

[125] To be proportionate, measures 'must be appropriate to achieve their protective function; they must be the least intrusive instrument amongst those which might achieve the desired result; and they must be proportionate to the interest to be protected'; Human Rights Committee, *General Comment No 27, Freedom of Movement (Article 12)*, UN Doc CCPR/C/21/Rev.1/Add.9, 2 November 1999, para 14; *Wall* (n 14) para 136.

[126] *Weber* (n 73) para 106.

their public authorities varies and is very much context-dependent. For example, the jurisprudence of human rights bodies indicates that, given the proliferation of terrorism in recent years in combination with the extreme levels of violence that it entails, states and public authorities enjoy a wide margin of appreciation when deciding how to respond to these types of threats to their national security and in determining what is the acceptable cost to society and human rights protection in particular.[127]

This being said, even in areas of high policy, states do not enjoy 'unlimited discretion' in deciding whether the societal benefits conferred by surveillance outweigh the harm it inflicts upon the protection of human rights.[128] This is especially the case where the infringement of human rights is severe and widespread, such as in relation to online surveillance techniques that, while targeting those reasonably suspected of being involved in illicit activities, incidentally collect private information belonging to a significant number of innocent persons. I am not saying that bulk/mass surveillance is *ipso facto* disproportionate.[129] Consider a situation where a state reasonably believes that certain individuals are about to launch a terrorist attack involving the use of chemical weapons. Even if targeted surveillance against these suspects results in the incidental collection of private information belonging to multiple non-suspects, the exceptional nature of the circumstances may nevertheless mean that the interference with human rights is proportionate to averting the threat to national security and public safety. Rather, the point that I am making is that where a state undertakes bulk surveillance it does not benefit from a wide margin of appreciation. Such conduct is only lawful where the state is able to adduce relevant and sufficient evidence that reveals that the threat posed is imminent and severe as well as demonstrating that the duration, scope and intensity of the surveillance does not go beyond what is necessary to avert that threat.[130] This means that the US Upstream surveillance program would struggle to be justified as proportionate because, while targeting persons suspected of being involved in illicit activities, its 'dragnet'[131] approach resulted in the collection of 'voluminous amounts of data about hundreds of millions of innocent people'.[132]

[127] 'The Court reiterates that when balancing the interest of the respondent State in protecting its national security through secret surveillance measures against the seriousness of the interference with an applicant's right to respect for his or her private life, it has consistently recognised that the national authorities enjoy a fairly wide margin of appreciation in choosing the means for achieving the legitimate aim of protecting national security'; *Weber* (n 73) para 106.

[128] *Klass* (n 98) para 49.

[129] Milanovic (n 13) 144.

[130] Report of the Special Rapporteur (n 112) para 52; *The Right to Privacy in the Digital Age* (n 25) para 25.

[131] Granick (n 1) 3.

[132] '[I]n the name of spying on drug dealers and terrorists, the government opportunistically captures voluminous amounts of data about hundreds of millions of innocent people, along with a smattering of the guilty'; ibid 24.

5. Conclusion

This chapter has examined the application of the ICCPR and the ECHR to cyber espionage. A key question in this inquiry is whether, and if so under what circumstances, a state's extraterritorial jurisdiction can be established under these agreements. With regard to the ICCPR, human rights bodies have taken a broad view and determined that whenever states act extraterritorially, including where they target individuals located within foreign territory through the medium of cyberspace, their jurisdiction is established and they must respect the human rights obligations contained within this agreement. While the ECtHR has yet to unambiguously adopt this model for establishing state jurisdiction under the ECHR, its recent case law is nonetheless sympathetic to this approach and is suggestive of a move towards it.

Online surveillance will almost certainly constitute a prima facie violation of the right to privacy. However, states can justify infringements with the right to privacy where they are prescribed by law, pursuant to a legitimate aim and proportionate to the legitimate ends sought. Whether acts of surveillance are justifiable depends upon the content of the legislation and the circumstances surrounding the decision of the intelligence agency to engage in surveillance in each individual operation. This being said, in light of the jurisprudence of various human rights bodies, a number of general observations can be made. First, national laws that do not clearly delineate the circumstances in which surveillance can be undertaken and which allow for persons to be targeted without probable cause are unacceptable. Second, surveillance laws must establish independent and effective oversight bodies that can ensure that surveillance operations are conducted in accordance with the pre-requisites of international human rights law. Third, authorisation to engage in surveillance must be necessary to meet a legitimate societal need and, furthermore, it must not disproportionately impact upon the human rights of the person targeted or those persons incidentally affected by the surveillance.

6

Economic Cyber Espionage and the World Trade Organization

1. Introduction

Since its creation in 1994, the World Trade Organization (WTO) has emerged as the cornerstone of international trade law. The WTO is a multilateral economic institution that comprises numerous treaties that are designed to protect a variety of trade-related rights including intellectual and industrial property rights.

Chapter 3 argued that, where a state engages in economic cyber espionage and in doing so intrudes upon computer networks and systems supported by cyber infrastructure located within the territory of another state, a violation of that state's territorial sovereignty occurs. The advantage of claiming that economic cyber espionage violates WTO law rather than the rule of territorial sovereignty is that such a claim can be pursued through the WTO's Dispute Settlement Body (DSB).[1] The DSB, which exercises its authority according to the WTO's Understanding on Rules and Procedures Governing the Settlement of Disputes (referred to as the Dispute Settlement Understanding (DSU)), is entrusted with resolving disputes that arise between WTO members and all WTO members are under the DSB's jurisdiction. Where a dispute emerges and negotiation at the consultation stage fails,[2] a member can request that the DSB establish a Panel to hear the dispute and this request cannot be refused unless all members of the DSB agree (which essentially confers compulsory jurisdiction on the DSB).[3] After hearing the particulars of a dispute, the Panel produces a report that determines whether a member's conduct is compliant with its WTO obligations. Unless a party to the dispute decides to appeal the Panel report to the Appellate Body, the report passes to the DSB and becomes binding unless its members agree unanimously to reject it.[4] If the Panel report is appealed to the Appellate Body, the Appellate Body's report

[1] 'For those seeking justice internationally, the WTO has a certain appeal because of its powerful law enforcement mechanism'; C Riffel, *Protection Against Unfair Competition in the WTO TRIPS Agreement: The Scope and Prospects of Article 10bis of the Paris Convention for the Protection of Industrial Property* (Leiden Brill, Nijhoff, 2016) 23.

[2] Article 4 DSU.

[3] ibid Article 6.1.

[4] ibid Article 16.4.

is binding and determinative of the dispute unless the DSB members decide by consensus to reject it.[5]

Where a Panel finds a member in violation of a WTO rule and transgression of that rule is ongoing, it recommends that the member bring its conduct into conformity with WTO law.[6] A Panel also has the discretion to 'suggest' to a WTO member how it can implement that recommendation, although this happens rarely.[7] If an offending member is unable to immediately comply with the Panel's recommendation, the DSB provides it with a 'reasonable period of time' within which to adjust its conduct and comply with WTO law.[8] If this time period lapses and the violation has not been rectified, the prevailing party may request compensation, although this request can be refused by the offending member.[9] If compensation is not forthcoming and the violation remains ongoing, the complainant can request that the DSB 'suspend the application to the Member concerned of concessions or other obligations under the covered agreements'.[10] In essence, the suspension of concessions is where the complainant is permitted to engage in trade retaliation (such as raising tariffs on imports from the offending member), conduct that but for the violation of WTO law would be unlawful. Under Article 22.4 DSU, countermeasures (as they are otherwise known)[11] sanctioned by the DSB 'shall be equivalent to the level of nullification or impairment' sustained by the victim member.[12]

That the WTO can be used to combat economic cyber espionage has been greeted with considerable alacrity in recent years. Private companies have encouraged the use of the WTO to suppress and deter economic cyber espionage.[13] In May 2014, US Senator Chuck Schumer sent a letter to the US Trade Representative Michael Froman, urging him to 'initiate a case at the World Trade Organization (WTO) against China for state-backed cyber espionage against American businesses and workers'.[14] While he was the US Ambassador to China, Max Baucus echoed these sentiments and suggested that the WTO provides an effective legal

[5] ibid Article 17.14.

[6] ibid Article 19.1.

[7] ibid.

[8] ibid Article 21.3.

[9] 'Compensation is voluntary'; ibid Article 22.1.

[10] ibid Article 22.2.

[11] WTO countermeasures should not be confused with countermeasures as understood by the law on state responsibility.

[12] Countermeasures must be aimed 'at eliminating the effects of measures on the trade of a given Member'; *Brazil – Export Financing Programme for Aircraft: Recourse to Arbitration by Brazil under Article 22.6 of the DSU and Article 4.11 of the SCM Agreement*, Decision by the Arbitrators (adopted 28 August 2000) WT/DS46/ARB, para III.68(b).

[13] JP Farwell and D Arakelian, 'China Cyber Charges: Take Beijing to the WTO Instead', 20 May 2014, *The National Interest*, www.nationalinterest.org/blog/the-buzz/china-cyber-charges-take-beijing-the-wto-instead-10496.

[14] Senator Schumer, *Press Release: Schumer Calls on US Trade Representative to File WTO Suit in Response to Chinese Cyber-Attacks*, 22 May 2014, www.schumer.senate.gov/Newsroom/record.cfm?id=351779.

forum to address the threat posed by economic cyber espionage.[15] In 2014, the Office of the US Trade Representative (USTR) produced its annual Special 301 Report, which explained that Chinese 'theft of trade secrets remains a significant concern'[16] and noted that 'the United States will not hesitate to use the WTO dispute settlement procedures, as appropriate', to confront economic cyber espionage.[17]

International legal scholars have been far more skeptical about the utility of the WTO in addressing economic cyber espionage.[18] In short, they argue that there are a number of unassailable hurdles that preclude members from taking recourse to the WTO where companies within their jurisdiction fall victim to economic cyber espionage. For Fidler, the use of the WTO to counter economic cyber espionage is 'not convincing legally or politically'.[19]

The objective of this chapter is to take a fresh look at whether the WTO provides an effective legal institution to tackle the threat represented by economic cyber espionage. In doing so, this chapter adheres to the following structure. Section 2 examines whether economic cyber espionage constitutes a 'measure' as understood by the DSU and is thus capable of legal challenge before the DSB. Section 3 analyses whether acts of economic cyber espionage result in the nullification or impairment of a benefit under a WTO agreement, a pre-requisite in order for a measure to be justiciable before a Panel. Section 4 assesses whether economic cyber espionage violates Article 10*bis* of the Paris Convention 1967 and Article 39.2 of the Agreement on Trade-Related Aspects of Intellectual Property Rights (TRIPS) 1994,[20] these being the two rules of WTO law that are most likely to apply to economic cyber espionage. If economic cyber espionage is not formally violative of a WTO rule, section 5 goes on to consider whether this conduct can instead form the basis of what are known as non-violation complaints. Section 6 offers conclusions.

[15] 'Ambassador Baucus Hints at WTO Case Against China on Cyber Espionage', 4 July 2014, *Inside U.S. Trade*.

[16] Office of the United States Trade Representative, *2014 Special Report 301* (2014) 31, www.ustr.gov/sites/default/files/USTR%202014%20Special%20301%20Report%20to%20Congress%20FINAL.pdf.

[17] ibid 27.

[18] DP Fidler, 'Economic Cyber Espionage and International Law: Controversies Involving Acquisition of Trade Secrets through Cyber Technologies', 29 March 2013, *ASIL Insights*, www.asil.org/insights/volume/17/issue/10/economic-cyber-espionage-and-international-law-controversies-involving; J Strawbridge, 'The Big Bluff: Obama, Cyber Economic Espionage, and the Threat of WTO Litigation' (2016) 47 *Georgetown Journal of International Law* 833. Although for a different view see SS Malawer, 'Chinese Economic Cyber Espionage: U.S. Litigation in the WTO and Other Diplomatic Remedies' (2015) 16 *Georgetown Journal of International Affairs* 158.

[19] Fidler (n 18).

[20] Note that this chapter does not discuss whether cyber espionage violates the non-discrimination provisions contained within Article 2 Paris Convention and Article 3 TRIPS. These provisions would be relevant where a state *passes* trade secrets that it has stolen from a foreign company to a national company, as is often the case after economic cyber espionage has been committed. However, this monograph defines economic cyber espionage as the copying of confidential information (see chapter 1) and it assesses the application of international law to this practice – how international law applies to a state's *use* of that data after it has been appropriated is beyond the scope of this monograph.

2. Economic Cyber Espionage as a WTO 'Measure'

Articles 3.3 and 6.2 DSU make it clear that a WTO member can only challenge 'measures' undertaken by another WTO member. Thus, before we assess whether economic cyber espionage constitutes a violation of a substantive WTO rule, it is first necessary to determine whether such conduct amounts to a justiciable 'measure'.

The WTO Appellate Body has explained that, '[i]n principle, any act or omission attributable to a WTO Member can be a measure of that Member for purposes of dispute settlement proceedings',[21] where attribution is determined by the rules on state responsibility.[22] According to a consistent line of WTO jurisprudence, there are two different categories of measures that are susceptible to legal challenge.[23] First, measures undertaken by a member that actually violate WTO law and which take the form of an 'as applied' challenge and, second, measures that encompass laws or policies of a WTO member the application of which will necessarily violate WTO law and are therefore challenged 'as such'.

2.1. 'As Applied' Challenge

An 'as applied' challenge refers to 'particular acts applied only to a specific situation',[24] that is, specific measures that have been implemented by a WTO member. Where a WTO member steals data belonging to a company located within the territory of another WTO member, there is little doubt that such conduct qualifies as an 'as applied' measure and the key question is whether this type of measure violates a substantive WTO rule.

Framing an act of economic cyber espionage as an 'as applied' measure is worthwhile to the extent that it provides the DSB with the opportunity to determine whether economic cyber espionage violates WTO law and, if it decides that it does, such a determination can deter members from engaging in this type of conduct in the future.[25] Nevertheless, even if the DSB adopts a report by a Panel

[21] *United States – Sunset Review of Anti-Dumping Duties on Corrosion-Resistant Carbon Steel Flat Products from Japan*, Appellate Body Report (adopted 15 December 2003) WT/DS244/AB/R, para 81. In *Japan – Film* the Panel explained that any 'policies or actions of governments' can amount to a measure; *Japan – Measures Affecting Consumer Photographic Film and Paper*, Panel Report (adopted 31 March 1998) WT/DS44/R, para 10.52.

[22] International Law Commission, *Articles on State Responsibility for Internationally Wrongful Acts* (2001).

[23] See, for example, *United States – Countervailing Duties on Certain Corrosion-Resistant Carbon Steel Flat Products from Germany*, Appellate Body Report (adopted 28 November 2002) WT/DS213/AB/R, para 156 and *United States – Sunset Review* (n 21) para 82.

[24] *United States – Sunset Review* (n 21) para 82.

[25] While DSB reports are only binding between WTO members, there is nevertheless a discernible system of precedent within WTO jurisprudence, the impact of which is likely to deter members from engaging in conduct that has previously been determined as incompatible with WTO law.

or Appellate Body and affirms that acts of economic cyber espionage are contrary to WTO law, this is unlikely to result in a remedy for the victim member. The reason for this is that Article 19 DSU envisages that a Panel can only make recommendations in those situations 'where a violation *is* in existence'.[26] Remedies – whether requests for voluntary compensation or DSB authorised suspension of concessions – are only available where, after a reasonable period of time has passed and the offending member remains in violation of its WTO obligations, they can be used constructively to 'exercise pressure on the non-complying country to bring its measures into conformity with WTO law'.[27] In this sense, remedies available under the DSU are 'strictly forward-looking i.e. they compensate for ongoing harm once a case has succeeded on the merits, not harm that occurred in the past and gave rise to the challenge in the first place.'[28] Thus, where an 'as applied' measure has been completed and the violation of WTO law no longer exists – which would be the case with a one-off act of economic cyber espionage – it is not possible for the DSB to recommend that the offending member adjust its measures and bring them into compliance with WTO law. Indeed, the Appellate Body found that a Panel had 'erred in recommending that the DSB request the United States to bring into conformity with its WTO obligations a measure which the Panel has found no longer exists'.[29] To be clear, if there is no Panel (or Appellate Body) recommendation, there can be no access to DSU remedies.

This being said, there are indications that Panels are willing to consider awarding remedies for harm caused by past violations. For example, a Panel has explicitly stated that, at least with regard to the WTO's Agreement on Subsidies and Countervailing Measures, remedies are not limited to 'purely prospective action'.[30] However, given that the award of retroactive remedies would represent a significant departure from the adjudicative ethos that has long underpinned the DSB (that is, to ensure compliance with WTO law rather than to compensate for past violations), the likelihood of them being rolled out in the near future for successful 'as applied' challenges 'is uncertain at best'.[31]

Even if retroactive remedies do become available under the WTO's dispute settlement procedure, these are unlikely to provide effective relief to members that fall victim to a sustained campaign of economic cyber espionage. In such

[26] *India – Measures Affecting the Automotive Sector*, Panel Report (adopted 21 December 2001) WT/DS/146/R and WT/DS175/R, para 8.15.

[27] M Bronckers and N van den Broek, 'Financial Compensation in the WTO: Improving Remedies in WTO Dispute Settlement' in D Georgiev and K van der Borght (eds), *Reform and Development of the WTO Dispute Settlement System* (London, Cameron May Ltd, 2006) 43.

[28] Strawbridge (n 18) 839–40.

[29] *United States – Import Measures on Certain Products from the European Communities*, Appellate Body Report (adopted 11 December 2000) WT/DS165/AB/R, para 81.

[30] *Australia – Subsides Provided to Producers and Exporters of Automotive Leather: Recourse to Article 2.5 of the DSU by the United States*, Panel Report (21 January 2000) WT/DS126/RW, para 6.31.

[31] Strawbridge (n 18) 841. Whether monetary compensation is available for past violations of WTO law see G Vidigal, 'Re-Assessing WTO Remedies: The Prospective and the Retrospective' (2013) 16 *Journal of International Economic Law* 505.

situations, the victim member will be more concerned with challenging the underlying law or policy that sustains the economic cyber espionage campaign rather than being compensated for each individual act of espionage to which it is victim. Given this objective, it is more advantageous for the victim to mount an 'as such' challenge because, if it is successful, it will allow access to remedies (namely, trade retaliation) that can be used to induce the offending member into terminating its campaign of economic cyber espionage.

2.2. 'As Such' Challenge

In *United States – Sunset Review* the Appellate Body explained that measures consist 'not only of particular acts applied only to a specific situation, but also of acts setting forth rules or norms that are intended to have general and prospective application. In other words, instruments of a Member containing rules or norms could constitute a "measure", irrespective of how or whether those rules or norms are applied in a particular instance'.[32] Typically, then, challenges against a measure 'as such' pertain to those 'laws, regulations and administrative procedures' that have been adopted by a member and which will invariably produce future conduct that is incompatible with WTO law, even if they do not actually mandate the commission of unlawful conduct.[33] The rationale for this approach is that 'allowing claims against measures, as such, serves the purpose of preventing future disputes by allowing the root of WTO-inconsistent behaviour to be eliminated'.[34]

At this juncture, it must be noted that where a member engages in a campaign of economic cyber espionage it is unlikely that this conduct will be authorised by national law or performed according to established administrative procedures. While states have adopted laws that authorise espionage for national security purposes, these laws do not generally permit economically motivated espionage. Thus, those states that engage in economic cyber espionage often do so in a legal and administrative vacuum.

At least initially, practices, policies and methodologies were not regarded as amounting to rules or norms (that is, measures) that could give rise to an 'as such' challenge. One Panel report explained that the mere fact that 'a particular response to a particular set of circumstances has been repeated, and may be predicted or be repeated in the future, does not, in our view transform it into a measure'.[35] Another Panel report noted that even if a practice must be generally followed, '[t]he argument that expectations are created … as a result of any particular

[32] *United States – Sunset Review* (n 21) para 82 (citations omitted).

[33] ibid paras 87–88.

[34] ibid para 82.

[35] *United States – Anti-Dumping and Countervailing Measures on Steel Plate from India*, Panel Report (adopted 28 June 2002) WT/DS206/R, para 7.22.

practice that the [state] "normally" follows would not be sufficient to accord such practice an independent operational existence'.[36]

Recent jurisprudence suggests a move towards a more relaxed approach. The Appellate Body has determined that 'concerted action or practice could be susceptible to challenge in WTO dispute settlement' even if the complainant '[cannot] demonstrate the existence of a rule or norm of general and prospective application'.[37] In *United States – Countervailing Duty* the Panel noted that 'we are of the view that, in principle, even a policy or practice of an investigating authority could be a "measure" subject to WTO dispute settlement proceedings'.[38] The Panel proceeded to explain that in order to establish a policy or practice the complainant must demonstrate the measure's 'systematic application'.[39]

In *United States – Laws, Regulations and Methodology* the Appellate Body accepted that a zeroing methodology utilised by the US Department of Commerce to calculate the level of duties to be imposed on goods that are exported below their normal value constituted a measure that could be challenged 'as such'.[40] The Appellate Body satisfied itself that there had been a systematic application of the zeroing methodology on the basis that it had been embedded within computer programs used by the Department of Commerce to calculate dumping margins.[41] Note, however, that the Appellate Body cautioned that '[p]articular rigour is required on the part of a panel' to support the conclusion that a practice is systematic where it 'is *not* expressed in the form of a written document'.[42] This is important in the context of the current discussion because written documents authorising economic cyber espionage are unlikely to exist or, even if they do, it is unlikely that a complainant will be able to access them and submit them as evidence.[43] In the absence of written documents, then, an 'as such' challenge must be supported by technical evidence that implicates a member in repeated acts of economic cyber

[36] *United States – Measures Treating Exports Restraints as Subsides*, Panel Report (adopted 29 June 2001) WT/DS194/R, para 8.126.

[37] *European Communities and Certain Member States – Measures Affecting Trade in Large Civil Aircraft*, Appellate Body Report (adopted 18 May 2011) WT/DS316/AB/R, para 7.94.

[38] *United States – Countervailing Duty Measures on Certain Products from China*, Panel Report (adopted 14 July 2014) WT/DS437/R, para 7.101. Although note in *Japan – Film* the Panel noted that 'not every utterance by a governmental official or study prepared by a non-governmental body at the request of the government or with some degree of government support can be viewed as a measure of a Member government'; *Japan – Film* (n 21) para 10.43.

[39] *United States – Countervailing Duty* (n 38) para 7.109.

[40] *United States – Laws, Regulations and Methodology for Calculating Dumping Margins ('Zeroing')*, Appellate Body Report (adopted 18 April 2006) WT/DS294/AB/R, para 205.

[41] ibid paras 201–04.

[42] ibid para 198.

[43] National legal measures may bar or inhibit access to such documents. Moreover, it may be the case that a member that is accused of economic cyber espionage can invoke Article XXI of the GATT Agreement, which explains that members cannot be required 'to furnish any information the disclosure of which it considers contrary to its essential security interests'; Article XXI(a) GATT 1947 (Article 73 TRIPS repeats verbatim Article XXI GATT).

espionage to the extent that its practice can be regarded as systematic and thus its reoccurrence inevitable.

Over the last decade there have been significant improvements in the methods used to collect and assess electronic evidence. Although it is not always possible to establish attribution, nowadays a determined victim finds it easier to identify the technical source of a malicious cyber operation (including economic cyber espionage) than it did during the earlier days of the Internet. For example, in February 2013 the cyber security company Mandiant published a compelling portfolio of evidence demonstrating that China had established a secret cyber espionage unit tasked with stealing trade secrets belonging to foreign companies.[44] Similarly, in May 2014 the US concluded that there was sufficient evidence to take the unprecedented step of indicting five members of the Chinese military for their involvement in economic cyber espionage.[45] Where technical evidence can be adduced that establishes a member's responsibility for a sustained and concerted (that is, systematic) economic cyber espionage campaign, such conduct can be regarded as a measure that is challengeable 'as such'.

3. Nullification or Impairment of a Benefit

In order to challenge a measure's compatibility with WTO law before a Panel, a complainant must demonstrate that the measure resulted in the nullification or impairment of a benefit under an agreement covered by the WTO.[46] In this context, nullification or impairment of a benefit does not mean an adverse impact on 'actual trade, but rather with competitive opportunities'.[47] As it happens, Article 3.8 DSU explains that violations of a WTO rule give rise to a rebuttable presumption that a nullification or impairment of a right has been caused:

> In cases where there is an infringement of the obligations assumed under a covered agreement, the action is considered *prima facie* to constitute a case of nullification or impairment. This means that there is normally a presumption that a breach of the rules has an adverse impact on other Members parties to that covered agreement, and in such cases, it shall be up to the Member against whom the complaint has been brought to rebut the charge.

[44] Mandiant Report, *APT1: Exposing One of China's Cyber Espionage Units* (2013), www.fireeye.com/content/dam/fireeye-www/services/pdfs/mandiant-apt1-report.pdf.

[45] S Ackerman and J Kaiman, 'Chinese Military Officials Charged with Stealing US Data as Tensions Escalate', 20 May 2014, *the Guardian*, www.theguardian.com/technology/2014/may/19/us-chinese-military-officials-cyber-espionage.

[46] Article 3.8 DSU.

[47] *European Communities – Regime for the Importation, Sale and Distribution of Bananas*, Panel Report (adopted 22 May 1997) WT/DS27/R/GTM, para 7.50. For a general discussion see A Davies, 'The DSU Article 3.8 Presumption that an Infringement Constitutes a *Prima Facie* Case of Nullification or Impairment: When Does It Operate and Why?' (2010) 13 *Journal of International Economic Law* 181.

The presumption under Article 3.8 that a violation of WTO law hinders competitive opportunities means that the threshold for demonstrating a nullification or impairment of a benefit is 'set low'.[48] For others, 'as the jurisprudence [of the WTO] has developed, this presumption has become essentially *irrebuttable*'.[49] Either way, there can be no doubt that an act of economic cyber espionage – that is, stealing a company's trade secrets – inhibits competitive opportunities.[50] What is important is that we determine whether an act of economic cyber espionage represents a violation of a specific WTO rule.

4. Substantive Obligations under WTO Law

TRIPS is annexed to the WTO, meaning that all WTO members must become signatories to TRIPS. According to its Preamble, TRIPS is designed to reduce impediments to trade by ensuring that members maintain minimum standards on the protection of intellectual property rights. TRIPS does not specifically regulate economic espionage, let alone cyber-enabled economic espionage. This notwithstanding, there are a number of provisions contained within TRIPS that may be infringed where a WTO member undertakes economic cyber espionage against companies located within the territory of another WTO member: Article 10*bis* of the Paris Convention 1967 and Article 39.2 TRIPS 1994.[51]

4.1. Article 10*bis* Paris Convention 1967

Article 2.1 TRIPS explains that members 'shall comply with Articles 1 through 12, and Article 19' of the Paris Convention for the Protection of Industrial Property 1967. Articles 1 to 12 and 19 of the Paris Convention are therefore incorporated into TRIPS and WTO members must comply with these provisions.[52] This means that a WTO member can argue before a Panel that another WTO

[48] Riffel (n 1) 81.

[49] D-W Kim, *Non-Violation in WTO Law: Theory and Practice* (New York, Oxford, Verlag Peter Lang, 2006) 129.

[50] 'A company's competitiveness may depend on its capacity to protect such assets [trade secrets]'; Office of the United States Trade Representative, *2017 Special 301 Report* (2017) 18, www.ustr.gov/sites/default/files/301/2017%20Special%20301%20Report%20FINAL.PDF.

[51] Due to space limitations, this chapter does not assess TRIPS-plus agreements (sometimes referred to as free trade agreements). These are being increasingly concluded by states – either bilaterally or multilaterally – and they are designed to enhance the legal protection afforded to intellectual property rights. For example, the EU adopted Directive 2016/943 on 8 June 2016, which is concerned with protecting undisclosed business information against unlawful acquisition, use or disclosure. Given their limited scope of application – which is in contrast to the broad coverage of the WTO – this chapter focuses upon the protections offered by WTO agreements.

[52] '[B]y virtue of Article 2.1 of the *TRIPS Agreement* … specified provisions of the Paris Convention (1967) … have been incorporated into the *TRIPS Agreement* and, thus, the *WTO Agreement*.

member has violated its TRIPS obligations (specifically, Article 2.1) because it has failed to comply with Articles 1 to 12 and 19 of the Paris Convention. This is significant in the context of economic cyber espionage because Article 10*bis* of the Paris Convention provides:

1) The countries of the Union are bound to assure to nationals of such countries effective protection against unfair competition.
2) Any act of competition contrary to honest practices in industrial or commercial matters constitutes an act of unfair competition.
3) The following in particular shall be prohibited:
   (i) all acts of such a nature as to create confusion by any means whatever with the establishment, the goods, or the industrial or commercial activities, of a competitor;
   (ii) false allegations in the course of trade of such a nature as to discredit the establishment, the goods, or the industrial or commercial activities, of a competitor;
   (iii) indications or allegations the use of which in the course of trade is liable to mislead the public as to the nature, the manufacturing process, the characteristics, the suitability for their purpose, or the quantity, of the goods.

As this provision is designed to protect against unfair competition, Article 10*bis* appears to represent a useful legal tool in combating economic cyber espionage. Nonetheless, the application of Article 10*bis* to economic cyber espionage raises three tricky interpretative questions.

4.1.1. Who Qualifies as a National?

Article 2.1 of the Paris Convention stipulates that this Convention is intended to protect 'nationals' of 'any country of the Union', which is reiterated by Article 10*bis*(1). Nationals obviously include those natural persons (individuals) that are granted nationality by the domestic law of a state that is party to the Paris Convention but it can also include legal persons, that is, companies. Although the Paris Convention does not explicitly state that legal persons qualify as nationals, this is nevertheless made clear by the fact that Article 1.3 TRIPS explains that 'nationals of other Members shall be understood as those natural or legal persons that would meet the criteria for eligibility for protection provided for in the Paris Convention (1967)'. Companies are not usually granted nationality under domestic law but, where they are state-owned companies or companies that

Consequently, these obligations of countries of the Paris Union under the Paris Convention (1967) are also now obligations of all WTO Members, whether they are countries of the Paris Union or not, under the *WTO Agreement*, and, thus, are enforceable under the DSU'; *United States – Section 211 Omnibus Appropriation Act*, Appellate Body Report (adopted on 2 January 2002) WT/DS176/AB/R, para 238 (citations omitted).

have been incorporated under national law, they will be regarded as legal persons belonging to the state for the purpose of the Paris Convention.[53]

In order to broaden the scope of the protections afforded by the Paris Convention, Article 3 explains that '[n]ationals of countries outside of the Union who are domiciled or who have real and effective industrial or commercial establishments in the territory of one of the countries of the Union shall be treated in the same manner as nationals of the countries of the Union'. The Paris Convention does not define the key concepts contained within Article 3, such as when a person is 'domiciled' and what constitutes a 'real and effective' establishment. However, Article 1.3 TRIPS[54] uses these exact terms to define the concept of nationals and, usefully, WTO Panels have elaborated upon the meaning of these terms within the context of Article 1.3 TRIPS. As we saw in the preceding paragraph, given that TRIPS expressly aligns its definition of nationals to that embraced by the Paris Convention, the guidance provided by WTO Panels on the meaning of nationals within the context of TRIPS can be used to interpret this concept as it appears in the Paris Convention.

WTO Panels have interpreted domicile not to 'indicate a legal situation, but rather a more or less permanent residence of a natural person, and an actual headquarters of a legal person'.[55] The concept of 'real and effective industrial and commercial establishment' has also been defined expansively, encompassing any industrial or commercial establishment providing that it is not a 'sham or ephemeral'.[56]

4.1.2. What Amounts to Unfair Competition?

Does the theft of commercial trade secrets amount to an act of unfair competition within the meaning of Article 10*bis*? Article 10*bis* defines unfair competition as 'any act of competition contrary to honest practices in industrial or commercial matters'. The World Intellectual Property Organization (WIPO), which is a specialised agency of the UN that seeks to promote the protection of intellectual property throughout the world, defines unfair competition as:

> any act that a competitor or another market participant undertakes with the intention of directly exploiting another person's industrial or commercial achievement for his own business purposes without substantially departing from the original achievement.[57]

[53] *European Communities – Protection of Trademarks and Geographical Indications for Agricultural Products and Foodstuffs*, Panel Report (adopted 15 March 2005) WT/DS174/R, para 7.197.

[54] Article 1(3) (footnote 1) TRIPS.

[55] *European Communities – Protection of Trademarks* (n 53) para 7.198.

[56] ibid.

[57] World Intellectual Property Organization, *Protection against Unfair Competition: Analysis of the Present World Situation* (Geneva, 1994) 55.

Wadlow argues that Article 10*bis* must be interpreted narrowly.[58] After explaining that the examples of unfair competition provided by Article 10*bis* relate to activities that 'create confusion', spread 'false allegations' and 'mislead the public', he contends that the parties to the Paris Convention 'were cautious to a fault in what they were prepared to accept as binding international obligations' and, as apparent from the list they provided, they 'cannot be taken to have legislated for a restricted misrepresentation-based regime in 1925, 1934 and 1958, only to have an open-ended misappropriation-based regime foisted on them at some later date'.[59] Wadlow therefore maintains that 'Art. 10*bis* in its entirety is confined to acts of unfair competition by misrepresentation, and does not extend to acts of unfair competition by misappropriation'.[60] Such an interpretation would obviously rule out the applicability of Article 10*bis* to economic cyber espionage.

I argue for a broader reading of Article 10*bis*, namely, one that defines an act of unfair competition as including the theft of trade secrets. There are two reasons why the concept of unfair competition should be interpreted expansively. First, Article 31 of the Vienna Convention on the Law of Treaties (VCLT) 1969 explains that '[a] treaty shall be interpreted in good faith in accordance with the ordinary meaning to be given to the terms of the treaty in their context and in the light of its object and purpose'.[61] Given that Article 10*bis*(2) defines unfair competition capaciously as *any* act contrary to honest practices, the state-sponsored theft of trade secrets belonging to another company must surely fall within the scope of this provision. While it is correct that the examples of conduct contrary to honest practices identified by Article 10*bis*(3) do not include misappropriation of business information, this is an indicative list only. This is made clear by the phraseology of subsection 3, which identifies acts that are 'in particular' prohibited, that is, subsection 3 determines that these acts are specifically prohibited but at the same time accepts that this list is not exhaustive.[62] Moreover, a broad interpretation of Article 10*bis* to include misappropriation is encouraged by the fact that it meets the object and purpose of the Paris Convention, which is stated broadly as 'the protection of industrial property' and where industrial property undoubtedly includes various types of trade secret (patented technology etc).[63]

Second, Article 32 VCLT provides that supplementary means of interpretation such as the treaty's *travaux préparatoires* can be relied upon if the application of Article 31 VCLT leaves the meaning of treaty terms or provisions 'ambiguous or

[58] C Wadlow, 'Regulatory Data Protection under TRIPS Article 39(3) and Article 10bis of the Paris Convention: Is There a Doctor in the House?' (2008) 4 *Intellectual Property Quarterly* 355.

[59] ibid 370 (citations omitted).

[60] ibid 369.

[61] That WTO agreements must be interpreted consistently with the VCLT see *United States – Standard for Reformulated and Conventional Gasoline*, Appellate Body Report (adopted 29 April 1996) WT/DS2/AB/R, paras 6.7–6.8.

[62] 'The wording "in particular" of the introductory clause of paragraph 3 suggests that there are more acts of unfair competition and that the ones mentioned are exemplary'; Riffel (n 1) 66.

[63] Article 1(1) Paris Convention 1967.

obscure' or otherwise leads to a result that is 'manifestly absurd or unreasonable'. Importantly, the *travaux* of Article 10*bis* '[can] be construed to support a broader definition of "unfair competition"'.[64] Article 10*bis* dates back to 1911, when it was first codified as a substantive right under the Paris Convention. Paris Union members argued for a broad understanding of unfair competition and refused to limit its application to specific acts. For example, the UK sought to clarify the meaning of unfair competition by stating that it applied to numerals, words or marks meant to deceive the public as to the true origin of the goods. Yet, this proposal was rejected on the basis that it would limit the conduct that constitutes unfair competition, with the parties preferring a more flexible provision. Similarly, in 1934 states parties had the opportunity to list examples of unfair competition but refused to do so out of concern that it would restrict and therefore 'weaken the general principle'.[65]

Perhaps more importantly, states such as the US and international organisations such as the European Community (as it then was) concluded that the concept of unfair competition extends to the unauthorised acquisition of trade secrets.[66] Also, in 1994 WIPO explained that in addition to the examples listed in Article 10*bis* there are other acts 'which have been recognized by the courts as unfair practises' and this includes the acquisition and disclosure of trade secrets.[67]

While cyber espionage amounts to unfair competition, an important question is whether it is an 'act of competition' within the meaning of Article 10*bis*(2). This question is relevant because in the *SKF v Jordan* decision the European Economic Community (EEC) Commission explained that an act of competition can only occur between competitors and that competitors are typically regarded as those economic operators that conduct business in the same market, which is generally indicated by the fact that they have the same customer or supplier base.[68] As such, the Commission concluded that the legislative act of Jordan was not an act of competition by a competitor but instead a regulatory act of the state. The Commission explained:

> that 'acts of unfair competition' within the meaning of Article 10bis can cover only those acts carried out by competitors and, consequently, cannot include the legislative acts of a signatory State. Hence it follows that Jordan cannot be said to have failed in its duty to provide effective protection against unfair competition on the grounds that, by adopting Law 8 of 1986, it had carried out an 'act of unfair competition'.[69]

[64] Strawbridge (n 18) 850.

[65] S Ladas, *Patents, Trademarks, and Related Rights: National and International Protection* (Cambridge, Harvard University Press, 1975) 1678–83.

[66] For a discussion see J Reinbothe and A Howard, 'The State of Play in the Negotiations on TRIPS (GATT/Uruguay Round)' (1991) 13 *European Intellectual Property Review* 163.

[67] *Protection against Unfair Competition* (n 57) 48.

[68] See generally NP de Carvalho, *The TRIPS Regime of Antitrust and Undisclosed Information* (The Hague, Kluwer Law International, 2008) para 39.1.13.

[69] Commission Decision of 23 December 1988 rejecting the complaint lodged by Smith Kline and French Laboratories Limited Against Jordan under Council Regulation (EEC) No 2641/84 Decision 89/74/EEC, Official Journal L 030, 01/02/1989, para 10.

If this is the case, the state-sponsored theft of trade secrets belonging to a private company located within a foreign jurisdiction cannot be regarded as an act of competition.

The better argument is that for a violation of Article 10*bis* to be triggered, it is unnecessary to demonstrate that the act of unfair competition occurred between competitors but, instead, that 'competitive opportunities of nationals of other Members are impaired'.[70] This broader interpretation of the concept of an 'act of competition' is justified on the basis that the objective of Article 10*bis* is to eliminate unfair competition within the Paris Union generally rather than between competitors within the Union specifically. Moreover, 'a broad interpretation of the term "act of competition" accords with the modern understanding of unfair competition law as market behaviour regulation'.[71] If this broader interpretation is accepted, economic cyber espionage undertaken by a state can be an act of competition within the meaning of Article 10*bis*(2) because the stealing of trade secrets inhibits the competitiveness of the victim company and has a chilling effect upon the market.

4.1.3. *What Measures Must Members Adopt to 'Assure to Nationals' of Other Members 'Effective Protection' Against Unfair Competition?*

Strawbridge argues that Article 10*bis* only requires members to protect nationals against acts of unfair competition that occur within their own territory because 'WTO rules generally operate on a territorial basis; that is, Members are only obligated to act in accordance with WTO rules with respect to goods, services, and investments of foreign nationals that enter or take place within their territory'.[72] If this interpretation is correct, Article 10*bis* would only prohibit a member from conducting economic cyber espionage against nationals of countries of the Paris Union where they operate within its territory. This means that Article 10b*is* would not apply to those situations where a member remotely launches acts of economic cyber espionage against nationals (companies) of a Paris Union country that are located outside of its territory. At present, there is no WTO jurisprudence on the spatial scope of the obligations imposed by the Paris Convention. Yet, from a more general perspective, whether and under what circumstances treaties can apply extraterritorially has received substantial academic attention.[73]

As we saw in chapter 5, whether treaties impose obligations upon states when acting extraterritorially is not determined by a general rule of the law of

[70] Riffel (n 1) 76.

[71] ibid 77.

[72] Strawbridge (n 18) 852–53. Fidler also maintains that there is no basis for pursuing economic espionage claims under the WTO because 'WTO rules create obligations for WTO members to fulfil within their territories and do not generally impose duties that apply outside those limits'; Fidler (n 18).

[73] See M Milanovic, 'The Spatial Dimension: Treaties and Territory' in CJ Tams, A Tzanakopoulos and A Zimmermann (eds), *Research Handbook on the Law of Treaties* (Cheltenham, Edward Elgar, 2016).

treaties but, instead, it depends upon the terms of the particular treaty obligation and, more generally, the wider object and purpose of that treaty. Employing this methodology, what is required is a careful textual analysis of Article 10*bis* of the Paris Convention as well as the wider treaty. In this context, it is important to note that Article 10*bis*(1) provides that the 'countries of the Union are bound to assure to nationals of such countries effective protection against unfair competition'. Article 10*bis*(2) goes on to explain that '[a]ny act of competition contrary to honest business practices in industrial or commercial matters constitutes an act of unfair competition'. In my view, the phraseology of these subsections indicates (implicitly rather than explicitly, admittedly) that the drafters of the treaty did not intend to restrict the application of the obligation contained in Article 10*bis* to the conduct of members within their own territory. Rather, their intention was that under Article 10*bis* members must ensure that nationals of other countries of the Paris Union are protected from acts of unfair competition, regardless of whether they are located within the territory of the offending member when they are targeted.

This conclusion does not mean that Article 10*bis* can be read as imposing unreasonably burdensome obligations upon members. For example, Article 10*bis* cannot be interpreted as imposing a positive obligation upon members to undertake enforcement action within the territory of other states in order to protect nationals of other countries of the Paris Union from dishonest commercial practices. But Article 10*bis* can be read as imposing a *negative* obligation upon members to ensure that when they exercise their power and authority extraterritorially they do so in a manner that upholds their legal commitment contained in Article 10*bis* to assure to nationals of the Paris Union effective protection against 'any act of competition contrary to honest practices'. Although in the context of the extraterritorial application of the European Convention on Human Rights (ECHR), the European Court of Human Rights (ECtHR) has endorsed this distinction between positive and negative treaty obligations when it explained that human rights obligations under the ECHR can be 'divided and tailored' to the extent that a state is only required to protect those rights 'that are relevant to the situation of that individual'.[74]

Furthermore, this reading of Article 10*bis* is supported by Article XVI.4 of the Marrakesh Agreement Establishing the World Trade Organization, which explains that '[e]ach Member shall ensure the conformity of its laws, regulations and administrative procedures with its obligations as provided in the annexed Agreements [which includes TRIPS and, because TRIPS incorporates the Paris Convention into the WTO system, the Paris Convention]'. This Article suggests that any legal and administrative action undertaken by a member must comply with its WTO obligations regardless of whether it manifests within its territory or the territory of another member, unless of course the language of the treaty

[74] *Al-Skeini v United Kingdom*, Judgment, App No 55721/07, ECtHR, 7 July 2011, para 137.

obligation that is under examination indicates otherwise (which Article 10*bis* does not). All in all, given that the theft of trade secrets amounts to unfair competition, state-sponsored acts of economic cyber espionage against nationals of the Paris Union are prohibited by Article 10*bis*.

4.2. Article 39.2 TRIPS 1994

Article 39.2 TRIPS protects undisclosed information from acquisition, disclosure and use and – *ratione materiae* – can be regarded as 'a better fit for the issue of trade secret misappropriation' than Article 10*bis* of the Paris Convention.[75] Article 39 provides:

> 1. In the course of ensuring effective protection against unfair competition as provided in Article 10*bis* of the Paris Convention (1967), Members shall protect undisclosed information in accordance with paragraph 2 and data submitted to governments or governmental agencies in accordance with paragraph 3.
> 2. Natural and legal persons shall have the possibility of preventing information lawfully within their control from being disclosed to, acquired by, or used by others without their consent in a manner contrary to honest commercial practices so long as such information:
>   a) is secret in the sense that it is not, as a body or in the precise configuration and assembly of its components, generally known among or readily accessible to persons within the circles that normally deal with the kind of information in question;
>   b) has commercial value because it is secret; and
>   c) has been subject to reasonable steps under the circumstances, by the person lawfully in control of the information, to keep it secret.

Whether and to what extent Article 39.2 TRIPS can be used to suppress economic cyber espionage depends upon four issues: 1) whether the company targeted qualifies as a national under TRIPS; 2) whether Article 39.2 protects trade secrets; 3) the nature of the obligation imposed by Article 39.2; and 4) whether Article 39.2 applies extraterritorially. These issues will be now addressed in turn.

4.2.1. *Who Qualifies as a National?*

Article 1.3 TRIPS explains that 'Members shall accord the treatment provided for in this Agreement to the nationals of other Members' and, as we have already seen, Article 1.3 further provides that 'the nationals of other Members shall be understood as those natural or legal persons that would meet the criteria for eligibility for protection provided for in the Paris Convention (1967)'. The analysis

[75] Strawbridge (n 18) 855.

undertaken above in relation to who qualifies as a national for the purpose of the Paris Convention can be therefore used to determine nationality under TRIPS. Crucially, both Article 1.3 TRIPS and Article 39.2 TRIPS make it clear that nationals include natural as well as 'legal' persons, that is, companies.

4.2.2. Article 39.2 and Trade Secrets

Article 39.2 TRIPS is designed to prevent unfair competition by protecting the confidentiality of undisclosed information. In the context of this chapter, the relevant question is whether confidential business information can be classified as undisclosed information. Article 39.2 provides three criteria for determining whether information is undisclosed.

First, information must be secret in the sense that it is not generally known within the setting of that particular industry. Whether information is secret is therefore highly contextual. This being said, this criterion poses few problems in relation to economic cyber espionage because, by definition, this practice describes the theft of information that is *secret*.

Second, for Article 39.2 to bite, the secret information appropriated must have 'commercial value'. Again, this criterion is readily met in the context of economic cyber espionage because trade secrets enable companies to develop new products and services and thus retain existing customers and attract new ones. Indeed, some commentators argue that because a competitor steals or attempts to steal confidential information, this is a prima facie indicator that it is of commercial value.[76]

Third, undisclosed information must be subject 'to reasonable steps under the circumstances, by the person lawfully in control of the information, to keep it secret'. Companies adopt a variety of different strategies that can indicate that they have taken reasonable steps to keep information secret, such as keeping information under lock and key, restricting access to information to certain individuals and requiring those individuals that do have access to confidential information to sign contracts requiring them by law to maintain that information's confidentiality. In the cyber setting, where information is hidden behind a password-protected firewall or where it is encrypted, it can be concluded that the owner of that information has taken reasonable steps to keep it secret.

The protection afforded by Article 39.2 TRIPS is only available where the unauthorised disclosure, acquisition or use of undisclosed information occurs 'in a manner contrary to honest commercial practices'. Footnote 10 to Article 39.2 TRIPS explains that '"a manner contrary to honest commercial practices" shall mean at least practices such as breach of contract, breach of confidence and inducement to breach'. The use of the term 'at least' in this footnote indicates that the examples of dishonest commercial practices that it provides are not exhaustive;

[76] D Gervais, *The TRIPS Agreement: Drafting History and Analysis* (London, Sweet and Maxwell, 1998) 425; Strawbridge (n 18) 856.

in other words, it leaves open the possibility that other types of conduct can amount to dishonest commercial practices, such as espionage.

There can be no doubt that the theft of trade secrets is contrary to honest commercial practices, not least because the negotiating history of Article 39 demonstrates that the US[77] and the European Community[78] (as it then was) were in agreement that the theft of trade secrets amounted to a dishonest business practice. In fact, the US proposed that the footnote to Article 39.2 – which provides examples of dishonest business practices – include 'electronic and other forms of commercial espionage'.[79] Reportedly, these examples were not included in the final text only because the negotiators were of the view that 'there was consensus that these practices constitute a manner contrary to honest commercial practices' and it was therefore superfluous to expressly include them.[80]

4.2.3. The Nature of the Obligation Imposed by Article 39.2 TRIPS

Under Article 39.2 TRIPS, members must afford nationals of other TRIPS members the 'possibility of preventing' the unauthorised acquisition, disclosure or use of confidential information that is within their control. Article 39.2 does not prohibit members from engaging in conduct that deprives undisclosed information of its confidentiality and thus does not enable victim members to directly challenge the legality of a member's involvement in economic cyber espionage before a Panel. Rather, and this is a crucial point, Article 39.2 imposes an obligation upon members to establish national laws (injunctions, for example) and procedures (such as independent judicial processes) that allow for information to be protected where its confidentiality is threatened.[81] That Article 39.2 only

[77] During the negotiation of TRIPS, the US made it clear that it regarded the unauthorised acquisition of trade secrets as being a dishonest commercial practice that must be prohibited: 'Trade Secrets should be broadly defined to include undisclosed valuable business, commercial, technical or other proprietary data as well as technical information. Misappropriation, including the unauthorized acquisition, use or disclosure of a trade secret, must be prevented'; *Suggestion by the United States for Achieving Negotiating Objective* (MTN.GNG/NG11/W/14), 20 October 1987, 20.

[78] During the negotiation of TRIPS, the European Community was clear in its view that the unauthorised acquisition of trade secrets is contrary to honest commercial practices: 'Trade secrets and business secrets shall be protected by law at least by providing their proprietor the right to prevent these secrets from becoming available to, or being used by, others in a manner contrary to honest commercial practices'; *Guidelines and Objectives by the European Community for the Negotiations on Trade-Related Aspects of Substantive Standards of Intellectual Property Rights* (MTN.GNG/NG11/W/26), 7 July 1988, 11.

[79] Quoted in Strawbridge (n 18) 857 footnote 92.

[80] M Peter and M Michaelis, 'The Law of Unfair Competition with Regards to Undisclosed Information' in P-T Stoll, J Busche and K Arend (eds), *WTO: Trade-Related Aspects of Intellectual Property Rights* (Leiden and Boston, Martinus Nijhoff, 2009) 644.

[81] 'TRIPS Article 39.2 requires Members to provide those persons who lawfully control undisclosed information with the right to initiate an action against those who exploit the information without consent in a manner contrary to honest commercial practices'; GL Skillington and EM Solovy, 'The Protection of Test and Other Data Required by Article 39.3 of the TRIPS Agreement' (2003) 24 *Northwestern Journal of International Law and Business* 1, 22.

requires members to implement causes of action is indicated not just by the terminology employed by this provision ('the possibility of preventing') but also the broader context of Article 39. For example, Article 39.3 TRIPS imposes a direct obligation upon members insofar as it requires that they 'shall protect' undisclosed test data relating to pharmaceutical or agricultural chemical products, which can be juxtaposed with the 'possibility of preventing' language used to frame the obligation contained within Article 39.2.[82]

Most members possess laws and judicial processes that can be used to protect undisclosed information from unauthorised acquisition, disclosure or use, rendering Article 39.2 TRIPS 'of limited usefulness' in combating economic cyber espionage.[83] But Article 39.2 is useful to the extent that it can be relied upon to compel recalcitrant members to adopt national laws and procedures that enable trade secrets to be protected, and therefore promotes the harmonisation of standards for the protection of undisclosed information across WTO members.

The argument could perhaps be made that, while a member may have in place causes of action that technically allow actors to protect the confidentiality of undisclosed information, the reality is that the particular features of the national legal system make it *impossible* for a cause of action to be successfully invoked; for example, because the judicial system does not possess the resources necessary to enable it to carry out its work effectively, or where bias within the judicial system renders any attempt to utilise national legal processes pointless.[84] The fact of the matter, however, is that, upon a textual interpretation of Article 39.2 TRIPS, all members are required to do is to establish causes of action that afford the possibility of protecting undisclosed information from acquisition. The text of Article 39.2 does not enable a Panel to scrutinise the effectiveness of national laws and procedures implemented by members and, in fact, appears to expressly rule out this possibility.

4.2.4. *Extraterritoriality*

A number of commentators argue that, as with Article 10*bis* of the Paris Convention, the scope of the obligation contained within Article 39.2 TRIPS is territorially limited in the sense that it only requires members to implement national laws and procedures that afford those persons that are located within their territory the possibility of preventing the acquisition, disclosure or use of undisclosed information: 'Once again, the language of TRIPS Article 39.2 appears to imply a jurisdictional limitation – i.e., WTO Members must afford this "possibility" only

[82] 'From a review of these Articles [Articles 39.2 and 39.3], it is clear that the drafters of the TRIPS Agreement understood the difference between requiring the creation of a private right of action, and requiring a Member to fulfill an obligation directly'; ibid.

[83] Strawbridge (n 18) 859.

[84] As the US identifies, '[i]n practice, effective remedies appear to be difficult to obtain in a number of countries, including China and India'; *2017 Special 301 Report* (n 50) 18.

to natural and legal persons who are operating within their territory'.[85] If this interpretation of Article 39.2 is correct, it further limits the utility of this provision in compelling members to develop national laws and procedures that can be used to confront economic cyber espionage because economic cyber espionage usually involves states stealing trade secrets from companies located within foreign jurisdictions.

As we have seen, the law of treaties does not presume one way or the other as to whether states owe their treaty obligations to persons located outside of their territory. Instead, it is the terms of the treaty obligation in conjunction with the aims and objectives of the treaty that provide the clues as to whether it is owed extraterritorially. Turning to an examination of Article 39.2 TRIPS, the text of this provision instructs TRIPS members to implement causes of action that afford nationals of other TRIPS members the possibility of protecting undisclosed information that is under their control. Clearly, Article 39.2 TRIPS does not impose any restriction as to where nationals of other TRIPS members must be geographically located in order for them to invoke these causes of action. This broader reading of Article 39.2 TRIPS is further supported by the Preamble to TRIPS, which explains that the objective of this agreement is 'to reduce distortions and impediments to international trade', 'to promote effective and adequate protection of intellectual property rights' and 'to ensure that measures and procedures to enforce intellectual property rights do not themselves become barriers to legitimate trade'. If these objectives are to be achieved across the TRIPS union, nationals of TRIPS members must be able to utilise the laws and procedures of other TRIPS members and challenge dishonest commercial practices that threaten the integrity of their undisclosed information, regardless of where they are based geographically.

5. Non-Violation Complaints

Where a WTO member adopts a measure but it cannot be established that a WTO rule has been directly infringed, Article 26.1 DSU nevertheless enables a complainant to mount what is known as a non-violation complaint, which challenges a measure that has been applied by a WTO member on the basis that it 'nullif[ies] or impair[s] benefits under, or impede[s] the attainment of objectives, of the relevant covered agreement'.

Article 64.1 TRIPS permits the use of non-violation complaints within the context of TRIPS.[86] On the face of it, members may find this type of complaint

[85] Strawbridge (n 18) 858. For a similar view see Fidler (n 18).

[86] See generally M Kennedy, *WTO Dispute Settlement and the TRIPS Agreement: Applying Intellectual Property Standards in a Trade Law Framework* (Cambridge, Cambridge University Press, 2016) chapter 7.

useful in challenging economic cyber espionage before a WTO Panel. There can be little doubt that economic cyber espionage impedes the objectives of TRIPS, which are to 'reduce distortions and impediments to international trade' and 'to promote effective and adequate protection of intellectual property rights'.

Notwithstanding the apparent utility of non-violation complaints, there are two significant hurdles preventing their use. First, given that non-violation complaints do not require a breach of a WTO rule to be established, the Appellate Body has maintained that they 'should be approached with caution and should remain an exceptional remedy'.[87] Indeed, with specific regard to TRIPS, when this agreement was concluded Article 64.2 TRIPS explained that the non-violation complaints procedure would not be available for the first five years subsequent to TRIPS coming into force. Article 64.3 TRIPS further provides that, once this five-year period has expired and where there is consensus within the TRIPS Ministerial Council, suspension of the non-violation complaints procedure can be periodically extended. The Article 64.2 suspension expired on 1 January 2000 but, since November 2001, the Council has concluded a series of moratoriums on the use of non-violation complaints under Article 64.3,[88] with members expressing their concern about the 'debilitating impact' that this type of complaint 'can have on the regulatory policy space of Members, on TRIPS flexibilities, as well as on increasing the complexity of interpreting the TRIPS provisions'.[89] While members such as the US and Switzerland have argued that the moratorium on the use of non-violation complaints should be lifted,[90] in December 2017 the TRIPS Ministerial Council agreed that 'Members will not initiate such complaints under the TRIPS Agreement', although it explained that this decision will be reviewed at 'our next session in 2019'.[91]

Second, even if this moratorium is lifted at the 2019 meeting and a Panel upholds a non-violation complaint concerning economic cyber espionage, the available remedies are weak and are unlikely to provide the victim member with effective redress. For example, a Panel cannot recommend – under threat of suspension

[87] *Japan – Film* (n 21) para 10.37; *European Communities – Measures Affecting Asbestos and Asbestos-Containing Products*, Appellate Body Report (adopted 12 March 2001) WT/DS135/AB/R, para 186.

[88] Doha Declaration on Implementation-Related Issues and Concerns of 14 November 2001, WT/MIN(01)/17, para 11.1; General Council Decision of 1 August 2004, WLT/L/579, para 1(h); Hong Kong Ministerial Declaration, WT/MIN(05)/DEC, para 45; Decision of the Ministerial Conference on TRIPS Non-Violation and Situation Complaints of 2 December 2009, WT/L/783; Decision of the Ministerial Conference on TRIPS Non-Violation and Situation Complaints of 17 September 2011, WT/L/842; Decision of the Ministerial Conference on TRIPS Non-Violation and Situation Complaints of 7 December 2013, WT/L/906.

[89] India, *Minutes of Meeting for the Council for Trade-related Aspects of Intellectual Property Rights* (IP/C/M/86/Add.1) 12 September 2017, para 94.

[90] WTO 2015 News Item, *Draft Decision Agreed on 'Non-Violation' Cases in Intellectual Property*, 23 November 2015, www.wto.org/english/news_e/news15_e/trip_ss_23nov15_e.htm.

[91] Decision of the Ministerial Conference on TRIPS Non-Violation and Situation Complaints of 13 December 2017, WT/L/1033.

of concessions – that the offending member bring its measures into conformity with WTO law. As Article 26.1(b) DSU explains, at most a Panel can 'recommend that the member concerned make a mutually satisfactory adjustment', which it can refuse to do. In this sense, non-violation complaints do not give rise to legally enforceable remedies. This being said, a Panel report that upholds a non-violation complaint is not without utility and significance because, at a minimum, it allows the victim member to 'ratchet up political pressure on the offending Member by giving voice to the opinion of the international legal community'.[92]

6. Conclusion

In recent years, policymakers have suggested that the WTO can be invoked to confront the growing threat posed by economic cyber espionage. International lawyers have rejected this contention, concluding that, 'as a legal matter, it would be difficult to challenge cyber economic espionage as a violation (or non-violation) of WTO rules'.[93]

This chapter has examined whether WTO law can be used to dampen and suppress economic cyber espionage, with particular attention being paid to Article 10*bis* of the Paris Convention and Article 39.2 TRIPS. Both of these provisions are applicable to economic cyber espionage insofar as Article 10*bis* prohibits acts that constitute unfair competition and Article 39.2 protects confidential information from unauthorised acquisition, disclosure or use. This being said, there are several sticking points when it comes to applying these provisions to economic cyber espionage. With regard to Article 10*bis*, the principal difficulty is whether this provision protects nationals of the countries of the Paris Union from acts of unfair competition where they are located outside of the territory of the offending member, as would be the case with economic cyber espionage given its transboundary dimension. I have argued that there is nothing within Article 10*bis* specifically or the Paris Convention generally to indicate that the scope of protection afforded by this provision only applies to acts of unfair competition that occur within a member's territory. In fact, the wording of Article 10*bis* encourages a broad reading of this provision. Consequently, under Article 10*bis*, members are subject to a negative obligation to abstain from committing acts of economic cyber espionage (acts of unfair competition) against nationals of the Paris Union regardless of where they are geographically located. With regard to Article 39.2 TRIPS, the main limitation is that it does not directly prohibit members from acquiring, disclosing or using undisclosed information that is

[92] Strawbridge (n 18) 863.
[93] ibid.

within the control of a national of another TRIPS member. At most, Article 39.2 TRIPS requires that members implement national laws and procedures that provide nationals of other TRIPS members with the possibility of preventing the acquisition, disclosure or use of undisclosed information under their control. Nonetheless, Article 39.2 TRIPS contributes towards the suppression of economic cyber espionage insofar as it requires members to implement minimum legal standards for the protection of confidential information.

7

Cyber Espionage and the Existence of Customary International Law Exceptions

1. Introduction

Claims that different types of espionage violate different primary rules of international law are usually undercut by assertions that such conduct is nevertheless lawful on the basis that customary international law contains a permissive and all-encompassing espionage exception.[1] State practice can engender developments in customary law that modify the scope of primary rules of international law. However, the claim that there is a general customary exception in favour of espionage is misplaced because different types of espionage engage different international legal rules. When determining whether customary international law permits espionage, what is required is that, first, we identify which primary rules of international law are violated by different types of espionage and, second, we examine whether state practice in relation to each type of espionage gives rise to a permissive exception to that primary rule under customary law.[2]

Adopting this methodology, international legal scholars argue that, while territorially intrusive acts of political espionage violate the rule of territorial

[1] '[B]ecause espionage is such a fixture in international affairs, it is fair to say that the practice of states recognizes espionage as a legitimate function of the state, and therefore it is legal as a matter of customary international law'; JH Smith, 'Keynote Address: State Intelligence Gathering and International Law' (2007) 28 *Michigan Journal of International Law* 543, 544. 'No serious proposal ever has been made within the international community to prohibit intelligence collection as a violation of international law because of the tacit acknowledgment by nations that it is important to all, and practiced by each'; WH Parks, 'The International Law of Intelligence Collection' in JN Moore, FS Tipson and RF Turner (eds), *National Security Law* (Durham, North Carolina, Carolina Academic Press, 1990) 433–34.

[2] As Wrange observes, 'the various acts of espionage have to be subsumed under established heads of legal terminology, to be assessed, each on its own merits'; P Wrange, 'Intervention in National and Private Cyberspace and International Law' in J Ebbesson, M Jacobsson, M Klamberg, D Langlet and P Wrange (eds), *International Law and Changing Perceptions of Security: Liber Amicorum Said Mahmoudi* (Leiden, Brill, Nijhoff, 2014) 321.

sovereignty, this conduct is nevertheless lawful due to developments in customary international law.[3] In the words of Deeks:

> [I]deas such as non-intervention and sovereignty developed against a background understanding that states do and will spy on each other, thus establishing a carve-out for espionage within those very concepts.[4]

As I argued in chapter 3, acts of cyber espionage that penetrate computer networks and systems supported by cyber infrastructure located within the territory of another state are intrusive in a manner analogous to sending spies into the physical territory of another state. Recognising this analogy, commentators argue that acts of political *cyber* espionage that run into conflict with the rule of territorial sovereignty benefit from the same customary exception as territorially intrusive acts of political espionage. For Brown and Poellet:

> Years of state practice accepting violations of territorial sovereignty for the purpose of espionage have apparently led to the establishment of an exception to traditional

[3] As far as I am aware, there is no claim within academic literature that economically motivated espionage that is otherwise violative of the rule of territorial sovereignty benefits from a customary exception. This may be surprising given that instances of economic espionage have increased in recent years. This being said, various states have expressly declared that they do not participate in economic espionage. For example, the members of the G20 have determined that 'no country should conduct or support ICT-enabled theft of intellectual property, including trade secrets or other confidential business information, with the intent of providing competitive advantages to companies or commercial sectors'; *G20 Leaders' Communiqué Antalya Summit*, 15–16 November 2015, www.consilium.europa.eu/en/press/press-releases/2015/11/16/g20-summit-antalya-communique/. In addition, the US, the UK, Australia and Canada have signed non-legally binding bilateral agreements with China, which require the signatory states to abstain from stealing intellectual property belonging to companies located in foreign jurisdictions; see M Dahl, 'Agreements on Commercial Cyber Espionage: An Emerging Norm?', 4 December 2015, *Lawfare*, www.lawfareblog.com/agreements-commercial-cyber-espionage-emerging-norm. Initial reports indicate that instances of economic espionage have declined significantly since the signing of these agreements: 'Chinese Economic Cyber-Espionage Plummets in U.S.', 21 June 2016, *Fortune*, www.fortune.com/2016/06/20/chinese-economic-cyber-espionage/. In light of these developments, it cannot be seriously argued that a customary practice has emerged that recognises economic espionage – and by extension cyber-enabled economic espionage – as constituting a permissive exception to the rule of territorial sovereignty.

[4] A Deeks, 'An International Legal Framework for Surveillance' (2015) 55 *Virginia Journal of International Law* 291, 302. In the same article, Deeks further explains that 'the widespread and longstanding practice of spying – committed by many states in different regions of the world during time periods that both precede and post-date the UN Charter – undercuts arguments that these customary principles either were intended to prohibit espionage at the time they developed or should be deemed to do so today'; ibid 305. '[C]ustomary international law has evolved such that spying has become the long-standing practice of nations. Indeed, while the surreptitious penetration of another nation's territory to collect intelligence in peacetime potentially conflicts with the customary principle of territorial integrity, international law does not specifically prohibit espionage'; RD Scott, 'Territorially Intrusive Intelligence Collection and International Law' (1999) 46 *Air Force Law Review* 217, 217. 'Although some may assert that the act of espionage violates the longstanding principle of refraining from violations of another nation-state's territorial integrity, there remains the reality of long-accepted practice'; G Sulmasy and J Yoo, 'Counterintuitive: Intelligence Operations and International Law' (2007) 28 *Michigan Journal of International Law* 625, 629 (citations omitted). 'A few of the Experts were of the view that the extensive State practice of conducting espionage on the target State's territory has created an exception to the generally accepted premise that non-consensual activities attributable to a State while physically present on another's territory violate sovereignty'; MN Schmitt, *Tallinn Manual 2.0 on the International Law Applicable to Cyber Operations* (Cambridge, Cambridge University Press, 2017) 19.

> rules of sovereignty – a new norm seems to have been created. As cyber activities are frequently akin to espionage, even if conducted for another purpose, perhaps it is not too much of a leap to assert that most cyber activities can also occur without violating territorial sovereignty.[5]

A separate claim among international legal scholars is that acts of political espionage against and from within diplomatic and consular premises is so widespread within international relations that customary international law has carved out permissive exceptions to those provisions of the Vienna Convention on Diplomatic Relations (VCDR) 1961 and the Vienna Convention on Consular Relations (VCCR) 1963 that otherwise prohibit espionage.[6] According to Reisman and Freedman:

> [S]tate practice now appears to tolerate – perforce – much, if not widespread, listening to communications to, from, and within premises, inconsistent with the letter of the 1961 Vienna Convention.[7]

By extension, commentators argue that acts of political cyber espionage committed against and from within diplomatic missions and consular posts in contravention of diplomatic and consular law are also acceptable under customary international law. For example, 'a few' of the Experts that drafted the *Tallinn Manual 2.0* considered that diplomatic missions and consular posts can be used to engage in

[5] G Brown and K Poellet, 'The Customary International Law of Cyberspace' (2012) 6 *Strategic Studies Quarterly* 126, 134. 'By extension, cyber espionage in line with the same objectives of traditional espionage may be seen as acceptable state practice under international law as long as such activities stay within the bounds of acceptable limits analogous to those rules of traditional espionage that have been accepted by states'; C Lotrionte, 'Countering State-Sponsored Cyber Economic Espionage under International Law' (2015) 40 *North Carolina Journal of International Law and Commercial Regulation* 443, 477. 'Since all States engage in espionage, including via cyberspace, mere intrusions into foreign computers or networks are not covered by the prohibition [that protects territorial sovereignty]'; WH von Heinegg, 'Territorial Sovereignty and Neutrality in Cyberspace' (2013) 89 *International Law Studies* 123, 136. 'The State practice regarding exfiltration appears so thick, and the condemnation on the basis of international law so muted, that I find it implausible to argue that sovereignty is violated by these commonplace cyber operations'; MN Schmitt, 'Cyber Responses "By The Numbers" in International Law', 4 August 2015, EJIL: *Talk!*, www.ejiltalk.org/cyber-responses-by-the-numbers-in-international-law/. 'Momentum is building behind a view that mere compromises or thefts of data are not violations of sovereignty, but rather routine facets of espionage and competition among States'; S Watts, 'International Law and Proposed U.S. Responses to the D.N.C. Hack', 14 October 2016, *Just Security*, www.justsecurity.org/33558/international-law-proposed-u-s-responses-d-n-c-hack/.

[6] As far as I am aware, there are no claims within academic literature that the use of diplomatic and consular premises to conduct *economic* espionage is acceptable under customary law and, presumably, this is because there is no evidence to suggest that diplomatic missions or consular posts engage (at least regularly) in economic espionage.

[7] WM Reisman and EE Freedman, 'The Plaintiff's Dilemma: Illegally Obtained Evidence and Admissibility in International Adjudication' (1982) 76 *AJIL* 737, 751–52. Reisman and Freedman go on to explain that 'states that engage in such conduct must conclude, and presumably have concluded, that the need for and value of intelligence gained by electronic surveillance outweighs the incremental erosion of the norm upholding the inviolability of diplomatic premises and their communications'; ibid 752, footnote 71. For Deeks, given that espionage in violation of diplomatic and consular law was widespread before the signing of the Vienna conventions, 'it would be a notable change to interpret the VCDR to prohibit such activities'; AS Deeks, 'Confronting and Adapting: Intelligence Agencies and International Law' (2016) 102 *Virginia Law Review* 599, 643.

cyber espionage against third party states because the 'long-standing allegations of State practice' point to the permissibility of this practice.[8]

This chapter responds to these claims and in doing so assesses the customary status of political cyber espionage vis-a-vis the rule of territorial sovereignty and diplomatic and consular law. This chapter is structured accordingly. Section 2 examines the doctrine of customary international law and in particular identifies the criteria that must be used to determine whether customary law has crystallised. As we shall see, customary law develops on the back of state practice coupled with *opinio juris*. Section 3 assesses whether state practice in support of political espionage is of sufficient quantity and quality to create customary exceptions to the rule of territorial sovereignty and the inviolability provisions of diplomatic and consular law. Assuming that there is sufficient evidence of state practice, section 4 considers whether this practice is accompanied by the requisite *opinio juris*. Section 5 provides concluding remarks.

2. Customary International Law

According to Article 38(1)(b) of the Statute of the International Court of Justice 1945, customary international law emerges on the basis of 'a general practice accepted as law'. Customary international law therefore possesses two elements: first, state practice of the rule in question; and second, the belief that this practice is required or permitted by customary international law (*opinio juris sive necessitatis*). This 'two-element approach'[9] is often referred to as the inductive method for establishing the existence of customary rules – state practice in combination with *opinio juris* induces the formation of custom.

The inductive method imposes a stringent standard for identifying the existence of customary international law.[10] With the objective of lowering this threshold and thus providing a more productive source of law, Kirgis has pioneered an interpretation of Article 38(1)(b) that induces the formation of customary law on the basis of either state practice or *opinio juris*.[11] For Kirgis, custom emerges on a 'sliding scale' between these two elements insofar as where there is substantial evidence of state practice there is no need to demonstrate the separate existence of *opinio juris*. 'At the other end of the scale, a clearly demonstrated *opinio juris* establishes a customary rule without much (or any) affirmative showing that governments are consistently behaving in accordance with the asserted rule.'[12]

[8] *Tallinn Manual 2.0* (n 4) 229.

[9] International Law Commission, *Second Report on Identification of Customary International Law*, UN Doc A/CN.4/672, 22 May 2014, para 21.

[10] S Talmon, 'Determining Customary International Law: The ICJ's Methodology between Induction, Deduction and Assertion' (2015) 26 *EJIL* 417, 429; AE Roberts, 'Traditional and Modern Approaches to Customary International Law: A Reconciliation' (2001) 95 *AJIL* 757, 759.

[11] FL Kirgis, 'Custom on a Sliding Scale' (1987) 81 *AJIL* 146.

[12] ibid 149.

Kirgis cites the decision of the International Court of Justice (ICJ) in *Nicaragua* to support his approach.[13] According to Kirgis, the ICJ recognised the customary status of the non-use of force and non-intervention rules without an assessment of state practice. Instead, he argues, the ICJ confirmed their customary nature on the basis that states had voted overwhelmingly in favour of a UN General Assembly declaration – the 'Declaration on Principles of International Law Concerning Friendly Relations and Co-Operation among States in accordance with the Charter of the United Nations' – which could be regarded as evidence of their belief that the principles contained within the declaration were reflective of international law.

Putting aside the normative desirability of Kirgis's approach and the fact that it has attracted support among academics,[14] extensive jurisprudence of international tribunals[15] and the work of the International Law Commission[16] (ILC) concludes that, for custom to emerge, the rule in question must be supported by state practice and *opinio juris*, thereby rejecting Kirgis's sliding scale thesis. Indeed, as Talmon notes, the novelty of the ICJ's approach in *Nicaragua* was not that it introduced a sliding scale for identifying customary law but that it was prepared to rely upon General Assembly declarations as evidence of state practice and *opinio juris*.[17] In fact, in *Nicaragua* the ICJ expressly affirmed that both elements of state practice and *opinio juris* must be present for customary law to crystallise.[18]

3. State Practice

State practice is the objective or material element of customary international law. State practice can take the form of acts or omissions and comprises both physical

[13] *Military and Paramilitary Activities in and against Nicaragua (Nicaragua v United States of America)*, Judgment (Merits) [1986] ICJ Rep 14.

[14] J Tasioulas, 'In Defence of Relative Normativity: Communitarian Values and the Nicaragua Case' (1996) 16 *Oxford Journal of Legal Studies* 85; BD Lepard, *Customary International Law: A New Theory with Practical Applications* (Cambridge, Cambridge University Press, 2010).

[15] 'Not only must the acts concerned amount to a settled practice, but they must also be such, or be carried out in such a way, as to be evidence of a belief that this practice is rendered obligatory by the existence of a rule of law requiring it'; *North Sea Continental Shelf Cases*, Judgment [1969] ICJ Rep 3, para 77. 'It is of course axiomatic that the material of customary international law is to be looked for primarily in the actual practice and *opinio juris* of States'; *Continental Shelf (Libya Arab Jamahiriya/Malta)*, Judgment [1985] ICJ Rep 13, para 27. See also *Legality of the Threat or Use of Nuclear Weapons* (Advisory Opinion) [1996] ICJ Rep 226, para 70.

[16] See, for example, International Law Commission, *Third Report on Identification of Customary International Law*, UN Doc A/CN.4/682, 27 March 2015, para 7 ('Delegations fully supported the two-element approach, with several adding that the view according to which, in some fields, one constituent element alone would be sufficient to establish a rule of customary international law was not supported by international practice and in the jurisprudence').

[17] 'In the *Nicaragua* case, the Court did not abandon the traditional two-element test of customary international law but, with 'the attitude of states towards certain General Assembly resolutions', introduced a new piece of evidence of *opinio juris*'; Talmon (n 10) 432 (quoting the ICJ's *Nicaragua* decision (citations omitted)).

[18] '[F]or a new customary rule to be formed, not only must the acts concerned "amount to a settled practice", but they must be accompanied by the *opinio juris sive necessitatis*'; *Nicaragua* (n 13) para 207.

and verbal conduct committed by the legislature, executive and judiciary, including diplomatic correspondence, policy statements, the opinions of legal advisers, military manuals, legislation, international and national decisions and resolutions of international organisations.[19]

State practice must be of a certain duration, generality and uniformity in order to establish this element of customary international law:

> Although the passage of only a short period of time is not necessarily, or of itself, a bar to the formation of a new rule of customary international law on the basis of what was originally a purely conventional rule, an indispensable requirement would be that within the period in question, short though it might be, State practice, including that of States whose interests are specially affected, should have been both extensive and virtually uniform in the sense of the provision invoked.[20]

This chapter identifies a fourth element that must be present for customary international law to form: states must *publicly acknowledge* their responsibility for their practice. This section explores the meaning of these features of customary international law and then assesses their application to acts of political espionage that are in violation of the rule of territorial sovereignty and diplomatic and consular law.

3.1. Duration

For Hart, customary law develops according to a 'slow process of growth, whereby courses of conduct once thought optional become first habitual or usual, and then obligatory'.[21] However, state practice does not need to extend over a long period of time in order for a norm to transition into a binding rule of customary law. In fact, custom can develop instantaneously – such as where states vote overwhelmingly in favour of a General Assembly declaration – providing that state practice is accompanied by the belief that such conduct is required by law.[22] As a result, duration is less important to the determination of state practice than the requirements of generality, uniformity and public acknowledgement.

3.2. Generality

The requirement of generality comprises two constituent elements. First, for customary law to form state practice must be 'widespread'[23] within the

[19] J Crawford, *Brownlie's Principles of Public International Law* (Oxford, Oxford University Press, 2012) 24.

[20] *North Sea* (n 15) para 74.

[21] HLA Hart, *The Concept of Law* (Oxford, Oxford University Press, 1961) 90.

[22] B Cheng, *Studies in International Space Law* (Oxford, Clarendon Press, 1997) chapter 7.

[23] *Maritime Delimitation and Territorial Questions between Qatar and Bahrain (Qatar v Bahrain)*, Judgment (Merits) [2001] ICJ Rep 40, para 205.

international society. It is not possible to identify numerically the number of states that must engage in a particular practice for it to be regarded as widespread, but it is clear that the putative rule 'need not pass the test of universal acceptance'.[24] What is important is that '[t]he practice must have been applied by the overwhelming majority of states which hitherto had an opportunity of applying it'[25] and that '[t]he available practice … [is] so widespread that any remaining inconsistent practice will be marginal and without direct legal effect'.[26] Thus, in the *North Sea* case the ICJ noted that 15 examples of state practice represented only 'a very small proportion … [of] the world as a whole' and thus could not form the basis of a customary rule.[27]

Second, even where state practice is widespread within the international society, for customary law to crystallise this practice must be 'representative'[28] of its members; 'namely that States with different political, economic and legal systems, [and] States of all continents, [must] participate in the process'.[29] Note that when determining whether state practice in favour of a customary rule is sufficiently widespread and representative, due regard must be accorded to the practice of those states whose interests are specially affected by the rule in question.[30]

3.3. Uniformity

With regard to the requirement of uniformity, '[i]t is not to be expected that in the practice of States the application of the rules in question should have been perfect'.[31] In the *Fisheries Jurisdiction* case, the ICJ stressed that 'too much importance need not be attached to the few uncertainties or contradictions' in state practice.[32] Rather, what is required is that 'State practice must be common, consistent and concordant'[33] with the putative rule. In the *Newfoundland Continental Shelf* case, the Supreme Court of Canada had to consider whether the right to explore and exploit the continental shelf was a matter of customary law by 1949 and, if so, how far and how deep a state's claim to the continental

[24] *North Sea* (n 15) 229 (Dissenting Opinion of Judge Lachs).

[25] JL Kunz, 'The Nature of Customary International Law' (1953) 47 *AJIL* 662, 666.

[26] ME Villiger, *Customary International Law and Treaties: A Manual on the Theory and Practice of the Interrelation of Sources* (The Hague, Kluwer International Law, 1997) 30.

[27] *North Sea* (n 15) para 75.

[28] ibid para 73.

[29] ibid 227 (Dissenting Opinion of Judge Lachs).

[30] *Fisheries Jurisdiction (United Kingdom v Iceland)*, Judgment (Merits) [1974] ICJ Rep 3, para 69.

[31] *Nicaragua* (n 13) para 186. 'The Court does not consider that, for a rule to be established as customary, the corresponding practice must be in absolutely rigorous conformity with the rule. In order to deduce the existence of customary rules, the Court deems it sufficient that the conduct of States should, in general, be consistent with such rules'; ibid.

[32] *Fisheries Case (UK v Norway)*, Judgment [1951] ICJ Rep 116, 138.

[33] *Fisheries Jurisdiction (United Kingdom v Iceland)* (n 30) para 16 (Joint Separate Opinions of Judges Forster, Bengzon, Jiménez de Aréchaga, Nagendra Singh and Ruda).

shelf extended. In looking for generality and uniformity of practice, the Court identified approximately 15 decrees issued by states that it regarded as constituting claims to the continental shelf. Yet, the Court concluded that such a right did not exist because, first, the number of claims was not large and, second, that the terms of the claims made by these 15 states 'were far from uniform'.[34] While these 15 states considered the shelf as forming part of their territory, some of them claimed the continental shelf as well as superjacent waters, others claimed the geographic shelf to a limited depth, and others claimed the shelf to a limit of 200 miles from the coast, whatever the depth.

3.4. Public Acknowledgment

That state conduct must be of a certain character to qualify as state practice was recognised by the International Criminal Tribunal for the Former Yugoslavia (ICTY) in the *Tadić* case when it expressed concern regarding the identification of customary international law in the context of armed conflict. The ICTY explained that on the battlefield 'it is difficult, if not impossible,' to pinpoint the actual practice of states with a view to establishing the existence of a customary rule because 'access to the theatre of military operations [is] normally refused to independent observers'.[35] In light of this, the ICTY determined that when ascertaining customary international humanitarian law obligations recourse should be had to more reliable forms of state practice such as publicly available military documents.[36]

It is widely accepted that secret state practice is methodologically irrelevant to the development of customary international law:[37] Principle 5 of the International Law Association's (ILA) Report into the formation of customary law explains that '[a]cts do not count as practice if they are not public'.[38] The reason for this is that

[34] *Reference Re Newfoundland Continental Shelf* [1984] 1 SCR 86, 119.

[35] *Prosecutor v Tadić*, Case No IT-94-AR72, Decision on the Defence Motion for Interlocutory Appeal on Jurisdiction, 2 October 1995, para 99.

[36] ibid.

[37] To be clear, I am not arguing that secret state practice is per se unlawful under international law. State practice – whether committed openly or secretly – may or may not be internationally wrongful depending upon the primary norms of international law that are applicable to such conduct. Instead, my argument is that secret state practice is inadmissible when it comes to determining the content of customary international law.

[38] International Law Association, *Committee on the Formation of Customary (General) International Law* (2000). The ILA Report goes on to explain that '[i]nternal memoranda are therefore not, as such, forms of State practice, and the confidential opinions of Government legal advisers, for instance, are not examples of the objective element in custom'; ibid para 5(a). Similarly, Perina argues that 'evidence of the [state] practice and the status of acceptance must be public'; AH Perina, 'Black Holes and Open Secrets: The Impact of Covert Action on International Law' (2015) 53 *Columbia Journal of Transnational Law* 507, 567. For Schmitt and Vihul, '[u]ndisclosed acts cannot, as a practical matter, amount to state practice contributing to the emergence of customary international law'; MN Schmitt and L Vihul, 'The Nature of International Law Cyber Norms' in A-M Osula and H Rõigas (eds), *International Cyber Norms: Legal, Policy and Industry Perspectives* (CCDCOE, 2016) 43. Treves explains that

customary rules are the product of an 'iterative process of claim and response'[39] between sovereign states. In order for a norm to crystallise as customary international law, a state must present a claim to other members of the international society that such conduct is a permissible feature of international relations. Other states are then provided with the opportunity to express their sovereignty and accept or reject that claim or, instead, to identify themselves as persistent objectors to the binding character of that customary rule.

Evidently, this process can only occur where state practice is conspicuous,[40] 'detectable'[41] or, in other words, public, because it is only in these circumstances that members of the international society can 'respond to it positively or negatively'.[42] Secret state practice cannot therefore influence the development of customary international law because it excludes other states from participating in the law formation process and by doing so undermines their sovereignty.

State practice committed in secret can contribute to the formation of customary international law once 'it has been disclosed publicly'.[43] According to Worster,

'[u]npublished practice, while it may have an impact on the incident it concerns, has reduced influence on the customary process as it remains unknown to most States'; T Treves, 'Customary International Law' (2006) *Max Planck Encyclopedia of Public International Law*, para 79. Bethlehem asks '[d]oes conduct need to be public in order to inform the law?' He answers this question by saying that '[i]t clearly must be public, at one level, for reasons of predictability, for reasons of accountability, for reasons of opposability, and for reasons of objection. So, at one level conduct must be public in order to be appreciable for reasons of the law'; D Bethlehem, 'The Secret Life of International Law' (2012) 1 *Cambridge Journal of International and Comparative Law* 23, 35–36.

[39] Perina (n 38) 567. For Shaw, customary international law develops according to 'the process of claims and counter-claims'; M Shaw, *International Law* (Cambridge, Cambridge University Press, 2017) 62. The ILA explains that '[i]t is often helpful to think of customary rules as emerging, in the typical case, from a process of express or implied claim and response'; ILA Report (n 38) para 1(c).

[40] 'This factor of conspicuousness emphasises both the importance of the context within which the usage operates and the more significant elements of the overt act which affirms the existence of a custom'; Shaw (n 39) 59.

[41] F Gény, *Méthode d'interprétation et Sources en Droit Privé Positif* (1899) section 110, quoted in A D'Amato, *The Concept of Custom in International Law* (Ithaca and London, Cornell University Press, 1971) 49.

[42] 'Another condition for State conduct – if it is to count in assessing the formation of custom – is that it must be transparent, so as to enable other States to respond to it positively or negatively'; Y Dinstein, 'The Interaction between Customary Law and Treaties' (2006) 322 *Recueil des Cours* 243, 275. 'States concur in the creation of law by not protesting, that is to say, by not reacting. If that is so, the states concerned must get an opportunity to react. From this there flow two further requirements for the formation of law: it must be possible to indicate at least one express manifestation of the will to create a law, and this express manifestation of will must be cognoscible for all states which will be considered as wishing to concur in the creation of the new rule if they do not protest'; H Meijers, 'How is International Law Made? – The Stages of Growth of International Law and the Use of its Customary Rules' (1978) 9 *Netherlands Yearbook of International Law* 3, 19.

[43] 'It is difficult to see how [non-publicly available] practice can contribute to the formation or identification of general customary international law unless and until it has been disclosed publicly'; ILC Second Report (n 9) para 47. In a similar vein, the ICRC's Customary International Humanitarian Law Study concludes that actions of states 'do not contribute to the formation of customary international law if they are never disclosed … In order to count, practice has to be public or communicated to some extent'; J-M Henckaerts and L Doswald-Beck, *Customary International Humanitarian Law: Volume I: Rules* (Cambridge, Cambridge University Press, 2005) xxxiv.

all that is required is that secret state practice is made available to the international society in a factual sense. For Worster, publication of state practice can occur where a state publicly acknowledges that it was or is engaged in particular conduct or, providing that there is credible evidence attributing conduct to a state, through leaks and revelations by whistleblowers or allegations by other state or non-state actors that a state has participated in certain conduct, even if that state refuses to acknowledge responsibility for it.[44] To be clear, the argument is that the provenance of the disclosure is irrelevant because if the critical issue is that members of the international society are provided with an opportunity to react positively or negatively to a putative rule, what is important is that states are, from an ontological perspective, aware that a certain type of activity is being conducted within the international society.[45]

I reject this view. For me, the better approach is that where conduct is performed in secret but is subsequently disclosed to the international society, state practice in the sense required for customary international law formation only crystallises where the responsible state publicly acknowledges that conduct as its own. The reason that public acknowledgement is necessary is because, as noted above, customary law develops where states present a claim to the international society that certain conduct is reflective of customary international law and this claim is subsequently accepted by the society. It goes without saying that in order for this type of claim to be submitted to the international society, the responsible state must publicly acknowledge its participation in that conduct. As Perina observes:

> [E]ven if the covert conduct is an open secret – the facts of an event widely and credibly reported, and a putatively responsible state has articulated a legal position that could justify it – non-acknowledgement precludes the responsible state from relying on that conduct as evidence that defines or shapes the law. Unless and until a state acknowledges its conduct, there is, in the process of custom, no 'claim'.[46]

This being said, unacknowledged leaks/allegations/rumours that states engage in certain conduct can stimulate a discussion of that practice within the international society. These discussions can then lead to states declaring that they do or do not engage in that conduct – or that they are or are not prepared to engage in that conduct in the future – and this type of public reaction can amount to verbal

[44] 'A highly visible, public act that was described in a confidential memorandum that was subsequently leaked should be admissible as evidence of the public practice … There is no justifiable reason for distinguishing between information made public through official or inadvertent release and leaked, other than the usual concerns about reliability that would be applied to an evidentiary matter'; WT Worster, 'The Effect of Leaked Information on the Rules of International Law' (2013) 28 *American University International Law Review* 443, 477–78.

[45] '[L]eaked acts should qualify as public. In any event, once leaked, the information becomes public, and states have ample opportunity to complain'; ibid 478.

[46] Perina (n 38) 568 (citations omitted).

state practice.[47] But to be clear, secret state conduct that is unacknowledged by the responsible state cannot (in and by itself) count as state practice when it comes to determining the existence of customary international law.

3.5. Assessment

Political espionage is nearly always committed in secret.[48] Critically, and as mentioned above, state conduct committed in secret cannot be classified as state practice for the purpose of customary law formation. In the words of the ILA, 'a secret physical act (e.g. secretly "bugging" diplomatic premises) is probably not an example of the objective element [of state practice]'.[49] For Ratner:

> With intelligence gathering ... all the evidence of law is secret. How can we possibly even know how states are interpreting a treaty, or what they regard as a norm of custom, if they will not acknowledge what they are doing or whether and how they believe it is legal? Even if a state has an interest in acting according to law, it will not publicly reveal its interpretation and in many cases will have reasons to avoid public protest of claims by other states that it rejects.[50]

While espionage is usually conducted in secret, there are nevertheless various claims, reports and leaks that suggest that there is extensive evidence of state practice of political espionage in violation of the rule of territorial sovereignty and diplomatic and consular law. For example, in relation to political espionage in violation of the rule of territorial sovereignty, Poland claimed during a Security Council meeting that was convened to discuss the legality of the US's use of spy planes within the territorial airspace of the USSR that 'such activities are unfortunately the normal practice. Is there any country which is not involved and which would be entitled to cast the first stone?'[51] At the same meeting, China observed that '[e]spionage is not a new phenomenon; nor is it a rare phenomenon'.[52]

[47] ILC Second Report (n 9) para 41(b).

[48] As US President Dwight Eisenhower explained, '[m]y second point [relates to] the nature of intelligence-gathering activities. These have a special and secret character. They are, so to speak, "below the surface" activities. They are secret because they must circumvent measures designed by other countries to protect secrecy of military preparations'; Central Intelligence Agency: Office of Training, *Presidents of the United States on Intelligence* (1969) 16.

[49] ILA Report (n 38) para 5(b).

[50] S Ratner, 'Introduction: State Intelligence Gathering and International Law' (2007) 28 *Michigan Journal of International Law* 539, 539. Similarly, Khalil contends that '[acts of states] do not contribute [to the formation of international law] if they are conducted in secrecy and not communicated to other states, as is the case with spying'; C Khalil, 'Thinking Intelligently About Intelligence: A Model Global Framework Protecting Privacy' (2015) 47 *George Washington International Law Review* 919, 939.

[51] 858th Meeting of the Security Council, UN Doc S/PV.858, 24 May 1960, para 9.

[52] ibid para 64.

More recently, when responding to the Snowden disclosures, US President Barack Obama explained that 'the intelligence services of every other nation' collects non-publicly available information from 'all around the world'.[53]

With regard to political espionage in violation of diplomatic and consular law, in 1975 Antonin Scalia (while working at the US Department of Justice's Office of Legal Counsel) drafted a memorandum explaining that espionage against (and presumably from within) diplomatic missions was an endemic feature of diplomatic and consular relations.[54] As another illustration, in 1978 the US Congress expressed concern that those provisions of the Foreign Intelligence Surveillance Bill that would authorise US intelligence agencies to conduct espionage against diplomatic missions and consular posts were in violation of diplomatic and consular law. To assuage the concerns of Congress, the US Administration 'prepared a list of states that had targeted U.S diplomatic installations overseas either with electronic surveillance or physical intrusion. As you might imagine that list was very long. But it satisfied Congress that this was such a widely accepted practice of states that, although not specifically authorized by the Vienna Convention, one could hardly argue violated the Convention, since everybody was doing it.'[55] Furthermore, and as we saw in chapter 4, the Snowden leaks revealed that the US and a number of other states had conducted cyber espionage against and from within diplomatic missions and consular posts. All in all, '[r]ecent news reports are rife with descriptions of spying conducted from within diplomatic posts'.[56]

As we have seen, allegations and rumours that states are involved in a particular activity do not constitute state practice for the purpose of customary international law formation unless and until the responsible state publicly acknowledges that conduct as its own, regardless of how credible those allegations and rumours may be. Crucially, when states are implicated in political espionage, their standard response is to remain silent and refuse to acknowledge their participation in this practice. Even where states have been pressurised into responding publicly to allegations of political espionage, they have 'sought to deny, with rare exceptions, any systematic involvement in espionage'.[57] Consequently, even though it may be 'an

[53] President Barack Obama, *Remarks on Review of Signals Intelligence*, 17 January 2014, www.obamawhitehouse.archives.gov/the-press-office/2014/01/17/remarks-president-review-signals-intelligence. President Obama further noted that '[w]e know that the intelligence services of other countries – including some who feign surprise over the Snowden disclosures – are constantly probing our government and private sector networks, and accelerating programs to listen to our conversations, and intercept our emails, and compromise our systems'; ibid.

[54] A Scalia, Assistant Attorney General, Office of Legal Counsel, *Memorandum for the Attorney General on the Vienna Convention* (24 December 1975).

[55] Smith (n 1) 545.

[56] Deeks (n 4) 312. Chesterman explains that '[d]iplomacy and intelligence gathering have always gone hand in hand'; S Chesterman, 'The Spy Who Came in from the Cold War: Intelligence and International Law' (2006) 27 *Michigan Journal of International Law* 1071, 1087.

[57] Lotrionte (n 5) 474. Edmondson notes that when states are accused of espionage denial is 'the most accepted ritual'; LS Edmondson, 'Espionage in Transnational Law' (1972) 5 *Vanderbilt Journal of Transnational Law* 434, 445. Edmondson goes on to explain that '[t]he law of peace seems to be settled in only one situation: a secret agent captured within the interior of another state, under circumstances

open secret that countries spy on friends and foes alike',[58] non-acknowledgment of their participation in this activity precludes the formation of state practice of the requisite quality to influence the shape and content of customary law.

Yet, exceptionally, states have publicly acknowledged their involvement in espionage. For example, although initially refusing to admit that the US had used spy planes within the territorial airspace of the Soviet Union, US President Dwight Eisenhower eventually acknowledged that a US aircraft shot down while in USSR airspace on 1 May 1960 was in fact a spy plane.[59] Similarly, in 1982 the US Ambassador to the UN admitted before the Security Council that the US had regularly conducted reconnaissance flights over Nicaraguan territory.[60] More recently, when discussing the revelations that the NSA had been involved in cyber espionage activities, President Obama explained that 'our intelligence agencies will continue to gather information about the intentions of governments – as opposed to ordinary citizens – around the world'.[61] Indeed, President Obama was clear that US intelligence agencies would undertake espionage (as opposed to collecting open source information only) when he underscored that 'the whole point of intelligence is to obtain information that is not publicly available'.[62]

These types of public acknowledgment of espionage constitute verbal acts of state practice that can satisfy the material or objective element of customary law. This being said, examples of states publicly acknowledging their political espionage activities are incredibly rare, and this only occurs where the evidence implicating a state's involvement in espionage is so overwhelming that it cannot be plausibly denied. While the *character* of this verbal state practice is admissible to the formation of customary law, it is not of sufficient *quantity* for customary espionage exceptions to emerge.

There is, however, another potential source of publicly acknowledged state practice on political espionage. One of the ways in which states have sought to address the threat posed by international terrorism has been to expand their

uncomplicated by a separate violation of international law, gives rise to an exchange of notes, a protest and a denial'; ibid 445–46. 'Plausible denial was the universal international posture regarding spies; intelligence overflights seemed to merit the same response'; GB Demarest, 'Espionage in International Law' (1996) 24 *Denver Journal of International Law and Policy* 321, 340. Terry explains that when confronted with accusations of espionage states have 'flatly denied the charge'; PCR Terry, '"Absolute Friends": United States Espionage Against Germany and Public International Law' (2015) 28 *Revue Québécoise de Droit International* 173, 184. 'The sending state normally disavows all knowledge of the mission of a spy'; I Delupis, 'Foreign Warships and Immunity for Espionage' (1984) 78 *AJIL* 53, 66. With regard to diplomatic and consular espionage, Seyersted observes that '[w]hen microphones have been found in embassies, protests have of course been made, but the receiving State has never, so far as one knows, admitted that it has installed them'; F Seyersted, 'Diplomatic Freedom of Communication' (1970) 14 *Scandinavian Studies in Law* 193, 220.

58 Brown and Poellet (n 5) 133.

59 F Belair Jr, 'President Asserts Secrecy of Soviet Justifies Spying', 12 May 1960, *New York Times*, www.nytimes.com/1960/05/12/archives/president-asserts-secrecy-of-soviet-justifies-spying-stresses.html.

60 2335th Meeting of the Security Council, UN Doc S/PV.2335, 25 March 1982, para 132.

61 *Review of Signals Intelligence* (n 53).

62 ibid.

intelligence operations. But the intensity of these activities, as revealed by various high profile leaks and disclosures such as those by Edward Snowden, has given the impression that state-sponsored spying is 'out of control'.[63] This has led to a 'media firestorm'[64] and 'public outcry about surveillance'[65] which has, in turn, placed considerable pressure upon states to ensure that their intelligence agencies operate according to the rule of law.[66] In response, states have adopted various measures that are designed to enhance the accountability of their intelligence agencies, including the adoption of national laws that provide their agencies with express legal authority to conduct espionage abroad. This is a significant development because, as the ICJ has noted, '[l]egislation is an important aspect of State practice' and, in particular, *public* state practice.[67] Indeed, a number of scholars have argued that, due to their adoption of national espionage laws, states have publicly acknowledged their espionage activities. For example, Lotrionte explains that, '[t]oday, many states have open laws that provide explicit details about the authorities and limitations that have been granted to intelligence organizations within the state';[68] the Experts that drafted the *Tallinn Manual 2.0* also noted that 'a number of States have by domestic law authorised their security services to engage in espionage, including cyber espionage'.[69]

Canada provides an interesting example of states adopting clear, express and public national laws authorising espionage abroad. As we saw in chapter 3, in 2008 the Federal Court of Canada concluded that the Canadian Security Intelligence Service (CSIS) could not conduct espionage within foreign territory on the basis that it was unlawful under international law and that the authorising legislation did not expressly overrule Canada's international legal obligations.[70] Partly in response to this decision, in 2015 Canada adopted a number of amendments to the

[63] J Moran and C Walker, 'Intelligence Powers and Accountability in the UK' in ZK Goldman and SJ Rascoff (eds), *Global Intelligence Oversight: Governing Security in the Twenty-First Century* (New York, Oxford University Press, 2016) 289.

[64] D Severson, 'American Surveillance of Non-U.S. Persons: Why New Privacy Protections Offer Only Cosmetic Change' (2015) 56 *Harvard International Law Journal* 465, 465.

[65] Deeks (n 4) 319.

[66] That 'the oversight of intelligence agencies is undergoing major transformation' see ZK Goldman and SJ Rascoff, 'Introduction' in Goldman and Rascoff (n 63) xvii. See A Travis, 'Snowden Leak: Governments' Hostile Reaction Fuelled Public's Distrust of Spies', 15 June 2015, *the Guardian*, www.theguardian.com/world/2015/jun/15/snowden-files-us-uk-government-hostile-reaction-distrust-spies.

[67] *Jurisdictional Immunities of the State (Germany v Italy: Greece intervening)*, Judgment [2012] ICJ Rep 99, para 3 (Dissenting Opinion of Judge ad hoc Gaja). According to the ILC, '[t]he term legislation is here employed in a comprehensive sense; it embraces the constitutions of States, the enactments of their legislative organs, and the regulations and declarations promulgated by executive and administrative bodies'; International Law Commission Yearbook, 1950, vol II, Part II, 370.

[68] Lotrionte (n 5) 478. 'Most domestic legal systems … seek to prohibit intelligence gathering by foreign agents while protecting the state's own capacity to conduct such activities abroad'; Chesterman (n 56) 1072.

[69] *Tallinn Manual 2.0* (n 4) 169.

[70] *Re Canadian Security Intelligence Service Act* [2008] FC 301, [2008] 4 FCR 230.

Canadian Security Intelligence Service Act 1984. In particular, Section 12(2) was added to this Act in order to provide intelligence agencies with the express legal authority to collect information relating to national security 'within or outside Canada.'[71]

Other states have also implemented laws that permit the collection of information abroad.[72] As the UN Special Rapporteur on Privacy has observed, 'a number of States have begun to adopt laws that purport to authorize them to conduct extra-territorial surveillance or to intercept communications in foreign jurisdictions'.[73] The Special Rapporteur went on to explain that '[t]hese developments suggest an alarming trend towards the extension of surveillance powers beyond territorial borders'.[74]

What is important to note from the Special Rapporteur's remarks is that, at present, there is only a 'trend' being set by 'a number of States' towards the adoption of national laws that authorise their intelligence agencies to collect confidential information abroad. As Deeks explains, the reality is that '[v]ery few laws around the globe regulate purely extraterritorial collection [of information]'.[75] Moreover, the states that have adopted these laws are politically homogenous in the sense that the overwhelming majority of them are liberal democracies, meaning that existing state practice is far from representative of the international society as whole. Indeed, it is revealing that when the *Tallinn Manual 2.0* notes that 'a number of States' have adopted national laws authorising foreign espionage, the Experts cite only six states to support this contention and all of these are liberal democracies within Europe (Sweden, Germany, Switzerland, Austria, The Netherlands and the UK).[76] While these trends may catalyse other states into adopting national laws that authorise foreign espionage, which may in the future snowball into widespread and representative state practice that can support the existence of customary law, at present this point has yet to be reached. In short, mere trends do not produce customary rules.

[71] For an overview of these legislative developments see C Forcese, 'A Longer Arm for CSIS: Assessing the Extraterritorial Spying Provisions', 28 October 2014, *National Security Law*, www.craigforcese.squarespace.com/national-security-law-blog/2014/10/28/a-longer-arm-for-csis-assessing-the-extra-territorial-spying.html/.

[72] See, for example, Sections 702–704 FISA Amendments Act 2008 (USA); Article 4A, Security Intelligence Service Act 1969 (New Zealand); Sections 6 and 7, Intelligence Services Act 2001 (Australia); Section 7(1)(1), Security Authorities Act 2000 (Estonia); Section 2(a), Act 11/2002 (2002) (Spain); Section 3(2), Denmark Act, No 602 (2003) (Denmark); Section 6(2), Law No. 124 (2007) (Italy).

[73] *Report of the Special Rapporteur on the Promotion and Protection of the Right to Freedom of Opinion and Expression*, UN Doc A/HRC/23/40, 17 April 2013, para 64.

[74] ibid.

[75] Deeks (n 4) 345. 'There is no question that there are far fewer countries that have actually regulated their foreign surveillance activities through primary legislation, as opposed to regulation by means of secret executive orders'; A Lubin, '"We Only Spy on Foreigners": The Myth of a Universal Right to Privacy and the Practice of Foreign Mass Surveillance' (2018) 18 *Chicago Journal of International Law* 502, 542.

[76] *Tallinn Manual 2.0* (n 4) 169.

4. *Opinio Juris*

Even if we assume *arguendo* that there is extensive state practice of political espionage not in conformity with the rule of territorial sovereignty and diplomatic and consular law, this does not on its own give rise to customary exceptions. Rather, state practice must be accompanied by *opinio juris*,[77] that is, 'evidence of a belief that this practice is rendered obligatory by the existence of a rule of [customary] law requiring it'.[78] Establishing this subjective element is crucial in order to distinguish between state practice that does not create legal duties – such as state conduct that is motivated by 'considerations of courtesy, good neighbourliness and political expediency'[79] – and state practice that flows from a sense of legal obligation.[80] In the *Nicaragua* case, for example, the ICJ concluded that while there was evidence that states such as the US had intervened in the internal affairs of other states in support of dissident groups, this form of intervention had not emerged as a customary right because these states had failed to claim that this conduct was permissible under customary international law:

> The United States authorities have on some occasions clearly stated their grounds for intervening in the affairs of a foreign State for reasons connected with, for example, the domestic policies of that country, its ideology, the level of its armaments, or the direction of its foreign policy. But these were statements of international policy, and not an assertion of rules of existing international law … In particular, as regards the conduct towards Nicaragua which is the subject of the present case, the United States has not claimed that its intervention, which it justified in this way on the political level, was also justified on the legal level, alleging the exercise of a new right of intervention.[81]

The ICJ's decision in *Nicaragua* is important in the context of espionage because the Court had to consider under what circumstances customary international law can modify the scope of a primary rule of international law, namely, when can a customary exception to a primary rule emerge. As a general rule, the ICJ was of the view that where 'a State acts in a way prima facie incompatible with a recognized rule, but defends its conduct by appealing to exceptions or justifications contained within the rule itself, then whether or not the State's conduct is in fact justifiable on that basis, the significance of that attitude is to confirm rather than to weaken the rule'.[82] Recognising, however, that strict adherence to this rule precludes

[77] '[E]ven if these instances of action … were much more numerous than they in fact are, they would not, even in the aggregate, suffice in themselves to constitute the *opinio juris* … The frequency, or even habitual character of the acts is not in itself enough'; *North Sea* (n 15) para 77.

[78] ibid.

[79] *Colombian-Peruvian Asylum Case*, Judgment [1950] ICJ Rep 266, 285.

[80] In the polemic words of Thirlway, *opinio juris* is the 'philosopher's stone which transmutes the inert mass of accumulated usage into the gold of binding legal rules'; HWA Thirlway, *International Customary Law and Codification: An Examination of the Continuing Role of Custom in the Present Period of Codification of International Law* (Leiden, AW Sijthoff, 1972) 47.

[81] *Nicaragua* (n 13) paras 207–08.

[82] ibid para 186.

developments in customary law, the ICJ accepted that customary exceptions to primary rules can form 'if shared in principle by other States'.[83] In short, what the ICJ is saying is that customary exceptions to primary rules of international law can develop but only where states expressly claim these exceptions under customary law and, in addition, where there is a strong showing of *opinio juris* within the international society in their favour.

That state practice must be accompanied with a clear and determined expression of *opinio juris* is problematic in the context of espionage because states do not assert that such conduct is permissible under customary international law.[84] In fact, it is a corollary of their failure (or refusal) to acknowledge their involvement in spying that states adopt what one commentator has referred to as a 'policy of silence' when it comes to their espionage operations.[85] This reticence is captured by the statement of the Australian Prime Minister to the Australian Parliament in 2013 when he explained that 'the Australian government never comments on specific intelligence matters. This has been the long tradition of governments of both political persuasions and I don't intend to change that today.'[86] Evidently, silence is the antithesis of *opinio juris* and under these conditions state practice cannot mature into binding rules of customary law; even where there is a significant accretion of state practice, when it is accompanied by silence the process of customary law formation is terminated.[87]

[83] ibid para 207.

[84] As Forcese explains, 'spying is a poor candidate for a customary international law exception to sovereignty – whatever state practice exists in the area is hardly accompanied by *opinio juris*'; C Forcese, 'Spies Without Borders: International Law and Intelligence Collection' (2011) 5 *Journal of National Security Law and Policy* 179, 202. 'There is little chance that *opinio juris* is constituted in the conduct of espionage'; N Jupillat, 'From the Cuckoo's Egg to Global Surveillance: Cyber Espionage that Becomes Prohibited Intervention' (2017) 42 *North Carolina Journal of International Law and Commercial Regulation* 933, 956. 'In the case of espionage, the *opinio juris* element is completely lacking'; Terry (n 57) 183. Chesterman argues that in the context of espionage 'state practice and *opinio juris* appear to run in opposite directions'; Chesterman (n 56) 1072. 'Even if there is [state] practice [of espionage], the *opinio juris* is lacking. States do spy, but they are not opining that this is lawful under international law. Quite to the contrary, they are conscious that they are breaching international law'; A Peters, 'Surveillance Without Borders? The Unlawfulness of the NSA-Panoptican, Part I', 1 November 2013, EJIL: *Talk!*, www.ejiltalk.org/surveillance-without-borders-the-unlawfulness-of-the-nsa-panopticon-part-i/. Ziolkowski explains that espionage 'is not accompanied by government statements which could allow any inference as to the assessment of the legality or illegality of such activities (*opinio juris*)'; K Ziolkowski, 'Peacetime Cyber Espionage – New Tendencies in Public International Law' in K Ziolkowski (ed), *Peacetime Regime for State Activities in Cyberspace: International Law, International Relations and Diplomacy* (CCDCOE, 2013) 438. 'The weakness in this rationale [that espionage is lawful on the basis of developments in customary international law] is the limited amount of *opinio juris* on point, for a new customary international law rule must be grounded in both State practice and *opinio juris*'; MN Schmitt and L Vihul, 'Respect for Sovereignty in Cyberspace' (2017) 95 *Texas Law Review* 1639, 1645.

[85] I Navarrete, 'L'Espionnage en Temps de Paix en Droit International Public' (2016) 53 *Canadian Yearbook of International Law* 1, 7. 'States have remained silent in the face of such accusations [that they have committed espionage]'; Terry (n 57) 184.

[86] Quoted in 'Indonesia Voices Anger at Australia Alleged Spying', 18 November 2013, *CNN*, www.edition.cnn.com/2013/11/18/world/asia/indonesia-australia-spy-allegations/index.html.

[87] The inability of state practice to contribute to the development of customary international law in the absence of *opinio juris* is well put by Denza in relation to acts of political espionage committed

Interestingly, commentators argue that, while states refuse to acknowledge their espionage activities and justify them as legal, this does not necessarily mean that they do not regard this conduct as lawful. Instead, these commentators maintain that states adopt a policy of silence towards espionage because they are concerned that if they admit to engaging in this type of activity it will cause friction between members of the international society and disrupt international cooperation. As Lotrionte explains, '[i]n not acknowledging the spy, the sending state is not doing so necessarily because of a sense that its actions are illegal, but rather in order to put off what would be a very tense diplomatic conversation, but not necessarily a violation of international law'.[88]

Respectfully, the reasons why states fail (or refuse) to justify their espionage activities as lawful are irrelevant. The crux of the matter is that customary international law *only* forms where states claim before the international society that they are engaging in a practice that is permissible under customary international law. The requirement that state practice is coupled with *opinio juris* is essential because it is only where states advocate for the existence of a customary rule that other members of the international society are able to comprehend the legal nature of the claim being made and thus decide whether to accept or reject that norm as a binding rule.

Finally, and as mentioned in the previous section, on rare occasions states have publicly acknowledged their espionage activities and, in doing so, have sought to provide justifications for this conduct. Crucially, however, these states have steadfastly refused to justify their conduct on the basis that it is lawful under customary international law. For example, on several occasions during the Cold War the US invoked the doctrine of self-defence – which is contained in Article 51 UN Charter and also customary international law – to justify its espionage activities against states such as the Soviet Union[89] and Nicaragua.[90] More recently, in response to

against diplomatic missions. She explains that while state practice in this area is seemingly widespread, '[t]here is, however, no indication whatsoever from public diplomatic exchanges of any attempt to justify any forms of surveillance of diplomatic communications on any legal basis, whether by reference to relations with the State or international organizations whose communications are intercepted or by reference to the purpose of the particular interception … [There is] no *opinio juris* suggesting that the law prohibiting violation of the right to free and secret diplomatic communication as set out in Article 27 has changed'; E Denza, *Diplomatic Law: Commentary on the Vienna Convention on Diplomatic Relations* (Oxford, Oxford University Press, 2016) 187–88.

[88] Lotrionte (n 5) 487. For Stone, the reluctance of states to openly discuss their spying activities is 'like some situations that occasionally arise between friends and even, I understand, between husband and wife, when one of them does the sort of thing about which it isn't really any use for them to talk'. Thus, the failure of states to acknowledge their espionage activities has 'no particular significance at all in determining what the law is'; J Stone, 'Legal Problems of Espionage in Conditions of Modern Conflict' in RJ Stanger (ed), *Essays on Espionage and International Law* (Columbus, Ohio State University Press, 1962) 39.

[89] '[E]ver since the beginning of my administration I have issued directives to gather, in every feasible way, the information required to protect the United States and the free world against surprise attack and to enable them to make effective preparations for defense'; Statement of President Dwight Eisenhower, 42 Department of State Bulletin 1091, 11 May 1960, 851–52.

[90] '[T]he United States Government undertook overflights to safeguard our own security and that of other States which are threatened by the Sandinista Government [in Nicaragua]'; US Representative to the UN, UNSC, 2335th Meeting, UN Doc S/PV.2335, 25 March 1982, para 132.

the Snowden revelations, President Obama explained that the NSA only engages in espionage where there is a 'compelling national security purpose' to do so,[91] appearing to invoke the customary international law doctrine of necessity to preclude responsibility for this internationally wrongful conduct. It goes without saying that where states justify espionage on the grounds of self-defence and necessity they are not asserting a legal right to spy under *customary* international law and, consequently, there is no *opinio juris* detectable to support the existence of a customary exception.[92]

4.1. Acquiescence and Protest

Where state practice is widespread within the international society and other states fail to protest against the legality of that conduct, their silence can be regarded as toleration of or acquiescence to that norm which, in turn, amounts to 'acceptance as law' within the meaning of Article 38(1)(b) of the Statute of the International Court of Justice.[93] In the *Gulf of Maine* case, for example, the ICJ explained that '[state] acquiescence is equivalent to tacit recognition manifested by unilateral conduct which the other party may interpret as consent'.[94]

A number of scholars rely upon this 'acquiescence as acceptance' approach to support their conclusion that political espionage is permissible under customary international law. McDougal, Laswell and Reisman argue that '[i]n terms of the actual volume of this activity [espionage] … the number of formal protests which have been lodged have been relatively insignificant' and this therefore indicates 'a deep but reluctant admission of the lawfulness of such intelligence gathering, when conducted within customary normative limits'.[95] Colby makes a similar observation in relation to spying from within diplomatic premises, noting that '[t]here is also growing recognition and tolerance for the performance of the

[91] *Review of Signals Intelligence* (n 53).

[92] Whether the doctrines of self-defence and necessity can be relied upon to justify cyber espionage is considered in chapter 8.

[93] '[T]oleration of a practice by other States, considering all relevant circumstances, justifies the presumption of its acceptance as law'; K Wolfke, *Custom in Present International Law* (Wroclaw, Prace Wrocławskiego Towarzystwa Naukowego, 1964) 48.

[94] *Delimitation of the Maritime Boundary in the Gulf of Maine Area*, Judgment [1984] ICJ Rep 246, para 130.

[95] MS McDougal, HD Lasswell and WM Reisman, 'The Intelligence Function and World Public Order' (1973) 46 *Temple Law Quarterly* 365, 394. For Kraska, 'the activity of espionage may not be inconsistent with international law, as spying has been tolerated by the community of states'; J Kraska, 'Putting Your Head in the Tiger's Mouth: Submarine Espionage in Territorial Waters' (2015) 54 *Columbia Journal of Transnational Law* 164, 246. 'States freely engage in espionage and generally accept it from other states'; G Brown, 'Spying and Fighting in Cyberspace: What is Which?' (2016) 8 *Journal of National Security Law and Policy* 621, 622. 'In the face of the longstanding practice by states of spying on each other and attempting to influence each other's policies with limited legal restraint, one can argue that states and their officials are on notice that they are subject to foreign intelligence activity and, where they have not objected to it, have tacitly consented to being the targets of that activity'; Deeks (n 7) 646.

security intelligence function by diplomatic representatives stationed in foreign states'.[96] Two points must be recorded.

First, this 'acquiescence as acceptance' methodology for identifying *opinio juris* must be employed cautiously. As Fitzmaurice explains, 'absence of opposition is relevant only in so far as it implies consent, acquiescence or toleration on the part of the States concerned; but absence of opposition per se will not necessarily or always imply this. It depends on whether the circumstances are such that opposition is called for because the absence of it will cause consent or acquiescence to be presumed'.[97] Stated succinctly, silence can only be regarded as acquiescence (and so acceptance) where 'the conduct of the other State calls for a response'.[98]

It goes without saying that, in order for interested states to have the opportunity to oppose a putative customary rule during its process of development, the state practice supporting that rule must be observable/discernible. This is important in the context of espionage because, as already noted, this is a practice that is invariably committed in secret. States are therefore often unaware that espionage is occurring or has occurred and this is particularly the case with cyber espionage given that the characteristics of cyberspace make it more likely that malicious conduct will go undetected. Where victim states and the broader international society are unaware of espionage, they are not afforded the opportunity to protest and, as a result, little legal significance can be attached to their failure to protest against the legality of this conduct.

Second, it appears that a considerable number of states have actually protested against the legality of espionage under international law. For example, after the USSR discovered that the US had been using reconnaissance aircraft within its airspace in 1960, it requested that the Security Council be convened 'to consider the question of aggressive acts by the United States Air Force against the Soviet Union'.[99] Before the Security Council, the Soviet Union claimed that the US's conduct 'quite unceremoniously encroached on the sovereignty of other States,

[96] JE Colby, 'The Developing Law on Gathering and Sharing Security Intelligence' (1974) 1 *Yale Journal of International Law* 49, 88 (citations omitted).

[97] G Fitzmaurice, 'The Law and Procedures of the International Court of Justice, 1951–1954: General Principles and Sources of Law' (1953) 30 *BYIL* 1, 33. Similarly, Danilenko maintains that, '[u]nder existing international law, absence of protests implies acquiescence only if practice affects interests and rights of an inactive state'; GM Danilenko, *Law-Making in the International Community* (Dordrecht, Nijhoff, 1993) 108.

[98] 'The absence of reaction may well amount to acquiescence … That is to say, silence may also speak, but only if the conduct of the other State calls for a response'; *Sovereignty over Pedra Branca/Pulau Batu Puteh, Middle Rocks and South Ledge (Malaysia/Singapore)*, Judgment (2008) ICJ Reports 12, para 121. 'Failure to react over time to a practice may serve as evidence of acceptance as law (*opinio juris*), provided that States were in a position to react and the circumstances called for some reaction'; International Law Commission, *Identification of Customary International Law: Text of the Draft Conclusions Provisionally Adopted by the Drafting Committee*, UN Doc A/CN.4/L.872, 30 May 2016, Draft Conclusion 10(3).

[99] UN Doc S/4314, 19 May 1960, 157.

intruding upon their territory without asking permission'.[100] Similarly, Poland determined that the US's espionage activities were unlawful:

> There is no doubt ... that the way in which the United States acted in this case constitutes a violation of international law which recognizes complete and exclusive sovereignty of States over their air space. This principle which has been acknowledged in both common international law and in the domestic legislatures of most countries ... The principle of complete and exclusive sovereignty of each State over its air space makes flights of foreign planes over the territory of any State illegal without the State's consent.[101]

Tunisia explained that, because it was '[d]eeply attached to the well-established principles of international law, it is difficult for us to condone the violations of the air space of a sovereign State, whatever the reason for it may have been'.[102] Ceylon also argued that respect for state sovereignty was 'absolutely necessary for the preservation of peace among all nations' and that a state's territory 'cannot be invaded by any other State without its authority and permission'.[103]

The Snowden revelations are also important because they provoked a hostile reaction from various states within the international society, which invoked the language of international law to condemn the US's cyber espionage activities.[104] Chapters 3 and 4 of this monograph have already discussed these condemnations in the context of the rule of territorial sovereignty and diplomatic and consular law and there is little utility in repeating them again. Other states also denounced the US's actions as a violation of international law, although in doing so they failed to specify which international legal rules they regarded cyber espionage as violating. For example, the Foreign Ministry of Mexico condemned US espionage against the Mexican government and in particular the hacking of electronic devices belonging to the Mexican President Felipe Calderón as 'unacceptable, illegitimate and contrary to Mexican and international law'.[105] Even though Mexico's determination lacks legal precision, it nevertheless demonstrates that at a minimum Mexico regarded the US's cyber espionage activities as internationally wrongful.[106]

[100] 857th Meeting of the Security Council, UN Doc S/PV.857, 23 May 1960, para 72.

[101] 858th Meeting of the Security Council (n 51) paras 83–84.

[102] 859th Meeting of the Security Council, UN Doc S/PV.859, 25 May 1960, para 4.

[103] ibid para 51.

[104] 'The Edward Snowden leaks led to wide condemnation of mass surveillance and cyber espionage from victim states'; D Pun, 'Rethinking Espionage in the Modern Era' (2017) 18 *Chicago Journal of International Law* 353, 362.

[105] AJ Rubin, 'French Condemn Surveillance by N.S.A.', 21 October 2103, *New York Times*, www.nytimes.com/2013/10/22/world/europe/new-report-of-nsa-spying-angers-france.html.

[106] 'It is quite clear from the strong protests against transnational surveillance, as expressed both by individual states in Europe, South America and elsewhere, and by major intergovernmental bodies and fora such as the UN General Assembly, the Council of Europe, the European Parliament and Commission that *opinio juris*, if anything, is on the opposite side: that it is a principle of public international law, confirmed in international customary law, that transnational collection of data from a country without that country's consent, for either law enforcement or national security

Schmitt and Vihul correctly observe that the reactions of a number of states to the Snowden revelations were couched in political terms and thus their 'comments do not necessarily confirm their position on the legality of the [US's surveillance] programme'.[107] For example, France's claim that it 'cannot accept this kind of behaviour between partners and allies'[108] and Germany's statement that the US's conduct was 'completely unacceptable'[109] can be interpreted in a variety of ways, and do not unambiguously indicate that France and Germany considered the US's cyber espionage activities to be unlawful under international law.[110] This being said, an examination of the reaction of a number of other states to the Snowden leaks (Brazil, Indonesia, Mexico etc) does reveal 'references to international law violations [that] are unmistakeable'.[111]

Decisions of national courts can also give rise to expressions of *opinio juris* where the court endorses or rejects state practice on the basis of international law.[112] This is significant in the context of the current discussion because national courts have on a number of occasions concluded that espionage is unlawful under international law, at least with regard to the rule of territorial sovereignty.[113] The decision of the Federal Court of Canada in 2008 is particularly important because, not only did the Court determine that territorially intrusive forms of espionage are incompatible with international law, it went further and expressly rejected the proposition that the rule of territorial sovereignty embraces a customary espionage exception:

> The Service argues that the principles of international law at play in matters of national security are different and that the customary international practice as it relates to intelligence-gathering operations in a foreign state constitutes an overriding principle of international law that affords a basis on which to find that the Charter was intended to apply, and does apply, to security intelligence investigations outside Canada. I am not persuaded that in the national security context, the practice of 'intelligence-gathering operations' in foreign states is recognized as a 'customary practice' in international law. Again, no evidence or authority was adduced in support of this contention.[114]

purposes, is unlawful'; I Brown and D Korff, 'Foreign Surveillance: Law and Practice in a Global Digital Environment' (2014) 3 *European Human Rights Law Review* 243, 250.

[107] Schmitt and Vihul (n 38) 44.

[108] Quoted in 'Hollande: Bugging Allegations Threaten EU-US Trade Pact', 1 July 2013, *BBC News*, www.bbc.co.uk/news/world-us-canada-23125451.

[109] Quoted in 'Merkel Calls Obama about "US Spying on Her Phone"', 23 October 2013, *BBC News*, www.bbc.co.uk/news/world-us-canada-24647268.

[110] As Deeks explains, 'France, for instance, which has extensive surveillance capabilities, has used political, rather than legal, language to criticize U.S. surveillance'; A Deeks, 'The Increasing State Practice and Opinio Juris on Spying', 6 May 2015, *Lawfare*, www.lawfareblog.com/increasing-state-practice-and-opinio-juris-spying.

[111] Deeks (n 7) 644.

[112] '[State] practice is accompanied by *opinio juris*, as demonstrated by the positions taken by States *and the jurisprudence of a number of national courts* which have made clear that they considered that customary international law required immunity' (emphasis added); *Jurisdictional Immunities* (n 67) para 77.

[113] See references in chapter 3 at footnotes 27 and 28.

[114] *Re Canadian Security Intelligence Service Act* [2008] FC 301, [2008] 4 FCR 230, para 53.

A considerable number of states have therefore protested against the legality of political espionage under international law, determining that such conduct violates the rule of territorial sovereignty and diplomatic and consular law. This is significant because it strongly indicates that this activity has not attained customary international law status or, more specifically, that it does not benefit from customary exceptions to otherwise prohibitive primary rules of international law. In the the *Nuclear Weapons* advisory opinion, for example, the ICJ refused to find that customary international law prohibited the use of nuclear weapons because a large number of states had consistently voted against (or at least abstained from) General Assembly resolutions that declared the use of nuclear weapons unlawful.[115]

4.2. National Legislation

As we saw in section 3 of this chapter, a number of states have passed national legislation authorising their intelligence agencies to conduct espionage abroad. Although it is only a relatively small number of states that have adopted these laws, it is nevertheless a growing trend and it is therefore important to examine whether this type of state practice is coupled with the necessary *opinio juris* to contribute towards the development of customary international law.

National courts argue that, where national legislation is ambiguous, an interpretation must be preferred that is consistent with international law because it can be presumed that national legislatures must have intended to legislate compatibly with their international legal obligations.[116] Following on from this, scholars claim that where national legislatures (states) adopt legislation authorising foreign espionage, it can be presumed that they regard espionage as permissible under international law, that is, there is *opinio juris* in favour of the legality of this practice: 'given the fact that all states send spies to "clandestinely" collect information within other states, and that most states have passed domestic legislation establishing some form of legal authority for such clandestine activities, it would seem that there exists *opinio juris* on the practice of espionage'.[117] This line of argument is problematic for three reasons, however.

[115] '[T]he members of the international community are profoundly divided on the matter of whether non-recourse to nuclear weapons over the past 50 years constitutes the expression of an *opinio juris*. Under these circumstances the Court does not consider itself able to find that there is such an *opinio juris*'; *Nuclear Weapons* (n 15) para 67. See also *Texaco Overseas Petroleum et al v Libya* (1977) 53 *ILR* 389 (where the sole arbitrator rejected Libya's contention that several General Assembly declarations had crystalised as customary law on the basis that not all sections of the international society had supported them. In fact, all economically developed states had voted against the declarations or had abstained).

[116] 'English courts will presume that Parliament intended to legislate in accordance with its international obligations'; *Dietrich v R* (1992) 177 CLR 292, 306. See also *Minister for Immigration and Ethnic Affairs v Teoh* (1995) 183 CLR 273, 287.

[117] Lotrionte (n 5) 487–88.

First, the presumption that national legislatures intend to legislate compatibly with international law represents an interpretive device that national courts use to ensure that ambiguous legislation is interpreted consistently with the intentions of the legislature. This presumption is therefore a national law doctrine that aids statutory interpretation, rather than an international law doctrine that can be used to ascertain *opinio juris* for the purpose of customary international law formation.

Second, even if we assume that this presumption can, as a general matter, generate *opinio juris*, it is unlikely to furnish *opinio juris* in the context of customary exceptions to primary rules of international law. As the ICJ explained in the *Nicaragua* case, customary exceptions can only emerge where they are supported by clear and strong (as opposed to presumed and implied) expressions of *opinio juris*.

Third, this presumption can be rebutted where national legislatures recognise that the proposed legislation is incompatible with international law but decide to adopt it nevertheless. This is important in the context of espionage because there are examples of national legislatures enacting espionage legislation even though they accept that such conduct violates international law. For example, when the Senate Committee on Intelligence was discussing Section 102 of the FISA bill – which authorises US intelligence agencies to conduct electronic surveillance against diplomatic premises that are located on American soil – the Committee conceded that 'reasonable persons may harbour some doubt'[118] as to whether the activities permitted by Section 102 are compliant with diplomatic and consular law. To put the matter beyond any doubt, the Committee explained that the phrase 'notwithstanding any other law' had been inserted into Section 102 in order 'to make clear that, notwithstanding the Vienna Convention, the activities authorized by this bill may be conducted'.[119] In light of these statements, it cannot be presumed that the US legislature regarded this legislation as authorising conduct that is consistent with international law.

All in all, the use of national legislation to evidence *opinio juris* in support of the legality of political espionage is unconvincing and, ultimately, represents a flimsy basis upon which to justify the crystallisation of customary exceptions.

5. Conclusion

International legal scholars claim that acts of political cyber espionage that prima facie violate the rule of territorial sovereignty and diplomatic and consular law are

[118] Report, Mr. Boland, from the Permanent Select Committee on Intelligence, 95th Congress, 2d Session, House of Representatives, Report 95-1283, Part 1, Foreign Intelligence Surveillance Act of 1978, 8 June 1978, 70.

[119] ibid.

nonetheless permissible under customary international law. Whether states have carved out customary exceptions to these rules boils down to an assessment of whether this conduct is supported by an extensive pool of state practice accompanied by *opinio juris*.

Political espionage is 'part of the national security apparatus of every state'[120] and, indisputably, states frequently engage in this practice regardless of the legal prohibitions imposed by the rule of territorial sovereignty and diplomatic and consular law. To argue any differently would be astonishingly naïve and would deny the reality of international relations. Yet, the failure of states to publicly acknowledge responsibility for their espionage activities prevents the formation of state practice that is of sufficient quality to influence the content of customary international law. Moreover, even if we accept that there is extensive evidence of state practice in favour of these types of political espionage, the policy of silence that typically accompanies this conduct means that it is nevertheless bereft of the necessary *opinio juris*.

To conclude, 'there is little doctrinal support for a "customary" defense of peacetime espionage in international law'[121] and, as aptly observed by Wright, political espionage is best characterised as a 'consistently practised illegal activity'.[122]

[120] WC Banks, 'Cyber Espionage and Electronic Surveillance: Beyond the Media Coverage' (2017) 66 *Emory Law Journal* 513, 513.

[121] Forcese (n 84) 203.

[122] Q Wright, 'Espionage and the Doctrine of Non-Intervention in Internal Affairs' in Stanger (n 88) 3.

8

Cyber Espionage and the Doctrines of Self-Defence and Necessity

1. Introduction

States typically defend their espionage activities on the basis that they are necessary to protect their national security from the threats and dangers that proliferate within the world order. For example, after a US spy plane was shot down while in Soviet Union airspace in May 1960 the US Secretary of State justified this conduct on the grounds that:

> The Government of the United States would be derelict to its responsibility not only to the American people but to free peoples everywhere if it did not, in the absence of Soviet cooperation, take such measures as are possible unilaterally to lessen and to overcome this danger of surprise attack.[1]

Days later, US President Dwight Eisenhower similarly explained:

> No one wants another Pearl Harbour. This means that we must have knowledge of military forces and preparations around the world, especially those capable of massive surprise attack … [E]ver since the beginning of my administration I have issued directives to gather, in every feasible way, the information required to protect the United States and the free world against surprise attack and to enable them to make effective preparations for defense.[2]

In response to the Edward Snowden revelations, US President Barack Obama gave a lengthy speech outlining the nature and importance of the work carried out by the US intelligence community. In an interesting part of this speech, President Obama noted that the US would not engage in espionage 'unless there is a compelling national security purpose' to do so.[3]

State practice therefore indicates that '[t]he illegality of espionage … may be nullified by "necessity" or "self-defense" in borderline cases'.[4] With this in mind, this chapter examines the application of these doctrines to cyber espionage.

[1] Statement by Secretary of State Herter, 42 Department of State Bulletin, 23 May 1960, 816–17.
[2] Statement of President Dwight Eisenhower, 42 Department of State Bulletin, 11 May 1960, 851–52.
[3] *Remarks by the President on Review of Signals Intelligence*, 17 January 2014, www.obamawhitehouse.archives.gov/the-press-office/2014/01/17/remarks-president-review-signals-intelligence.
[4] I Delupis, 'Foreign Warships and Immunity for Espionage' (1984) 78 *AJIL* 53, 68.

Section 2 assesses the circumstances in which states can rely upon the doctrine of self-defence as contained in Article 51 of the United Nations (UN) Charter 1945 to justify acts of cyber espionage. Section 3 examines the criteria that must be met in order for states to invoke the customary international law doctrine of necessity to preclude responsibility for acts of cyber espionage that otherwise violate international law. Section 4 offers conclusions.

2. The Doctrine of Self-Defence

A steady stream of scholars has argued that the doctrine of self-defence as set forth in Article 51 UN Charter can be invoked to justify acts of political espionage. For example, Sulmasy and Yoo argue that 'intelligence collection can be viewed as a component of the right of self-defense recognized in [Article 51 of] the UN Charter'.[5] Lubin has also claimed that states possess a '*Jus Ad Explorationem*, or a right to spy',[6] which can be:

> read into the Charter Article 51 global security structure. In other words, to the extent that a specific intelligence gathering activity can be shown to serve either the short-term national security interest of a particular state, or the long-term goals of international stability and international peace and security, that operation would surely comply with the Charter, and indeed most operations do.[7]

Article 51 UN Charter is a primary rule of international law, which means that where the right to self-defence is established no violation of international law occurs.[8] Article 51 provides that '[n]othing in the present Charter shall impair the inherent right of individual or collective self-defence if an armed attack occurs'. At the outset, we must determine whether the doctrine of self-defence can be only invoked to justify unlawful uses of force as defined by Article 2(4)

[5] G Sulmasy and J Yoo, 'Counterintuitive: Intelligence Operations and International Law' (2007) 28 *Michigan Journal of International Law* 625, 636.

[6] A Lubin, 'Espionage as a Sovereign Right under International Law and its Limits' (2016) 24 *ILSA Quarterly* 22, 23. '[N]o one wants another invasion of Kuwait, another Khobar Towers, another World Trade Centre bombing, or a regional nuclear war between secret nuclear powers. To the extent intelligence collection makes it possible for the United States, or any other nation, to prevent such incidents, the use of international espionage as an instrument of self-defense seems justified'; RD Scott, 'Territorially Intrusive Intelligence Collection and International Law' (1999) 46 *Air Force Law Review* 217, 225–26 (citations omitted).

[7] Lubin (n 6) 26.

[8] Self-defence as contained in Article 51 UN Charter should not be confused with self-defence as reflected in Article 21 of the Articles on State Responsibility (ASR) 2001, which is a secondary rule of international law. Article 21 ASR precludes state responsibility for those violations of international law that occur as a result of or incidental to self-defence being exercised under Article 51 UN Charter but which cannot be justified as self-defence action. On the distinction between self-defence as a primary rule and self-defence as a secondary rule see N Tsagourias, 'Self-Defence against Non-State Actors: The Interaction between Self-Defence as a Primary Rule and Self-Defence as a Secondary Rule' (2016) 29 *Leiden Journal of International Law* 801.

UN Charter or, instead, whether self-defence is available more generally to justify internationally wrongful conduct that is non-forcible in nature.[9] This is a critical issue in the context of cyber espionage because it has been argued in chapter 3 of this monograph that, while such conduct is under certain circumstances internationally wrongful, it does not qualify as a use of force under Article 2(4) UN Charter.

In the *Wall* advisory opinion, Israel maintained before the International Court of Justice (ICJ) that the construction of a security wall to protect itself against terrorist attacks was a lawful act of self-defence under Article 51 UN Charter even though it did not amount to a use of force. Ultimately, the ICJ did not have to pronounce on whether Article 51 is available to forcible as well as non-forcible conduct because the Court rejected Israel's claim to self-defence on the basis that the violent acts to which it was subject were not attributable to a state and emanated from actors located within territory under its control. However, in her Separate Opinion, Judge Rosalyn Higgins explained that 'I remain unconvinced that non-forcible measures (such as the building of a wall) fall within self-defence under Article 51 of the UN Charter as that provision is normally understood'.[10] Similarly, two UN Special Rapporteurs on the law of state responsibility (Professors Robert Ago and James Crawford), as well as the International Law Commission's commentary to the Articles on State Responsibility 2001, concluded that Article 51 represents an exceptional right intrinsic to the use of force prohibition.[11]

It is generally the case that states invoke Article 51 UN Charter to justify forcible conduct. But if we subject Article 51 to a literal interpretation – as we are required to do by Article 31(1) of the Vienna Convention on the Law of Treaties 1969 – the wording of this provision does not limit the availability of self-defence to conduct amounting to a use of force. In fact, Article 51 encourages a broad reading of this provision given that it casts self-defence as an 'inherent right'. As Tams explains, Judge Higgins's interpretation 'seems to be based on an unduly restrictive reading of Art. 51. There is little indication in Art. 51 that measures of self-defence has to involve the use of force; where the defending state seeks to defend itself by measures not involving recourse to force (e.g., blockades), these will *a fortiori* be justified'.[12]

Self-defence is therefore available to justify cyber espionage. Whether the right to self-defence can be established hinges upon whether this conduct is in

[9] It is only where state conduct constitutes an internationally wrongful act that it requires justification on the basis of self-defence (and thus needs to satisfy the stringent criteria imposed by Article 51 UN Charter) because conduct that is not internationally wrongful is lawful per se.

[10] *Legal Consequences of the Construction of a Wall in the Occupied Palestinian Territory* (Advisory Opinion) [2004] ICJ Rep 136, para 35 (Separate Opinion of Judge Higgins).

[11] International Law Commission (ILC), *Eighth Report on State Responsibility by Robert Ago: Addendum*, UN Doc A/CN.4/318/Add.5-7 (1980) para 83; ILC, *Second Report on State Responsibility by James Crawford*, UN Doc A/CN.4/498 (1999) para 299; ILC, *Articles on Responsibility of States for Internationally Wrongful Acts, with Commentaries* (2001) Commentary to Article 21, para 1.

[12] CJ Tams, 'Light Treatment of a Complex Problem: The Law of Self-Defence in the *Wall* Case' (2005) 16 *EJIL* 963, 975 footnote 75.

response to 'armed attack', the defining element of the doctrine of self-defence. Even if an armed attack occurs, customary international law nevertheless requires that acts of cyber espionage in self-defence are necessary and proportionate in the circumstances.[13]

2.1. Armed Attack

Article 51 UN Charter does not stipulate the criteria for identifying when an armed attack occurs but in the *Nicaragua* case the ICJ explained that armed attacks are the most 'grave forms of the use of force' as defined by Article 2(4) UN Charter.[14] As we have seen in chapter 3, the conventional reading of Article 2(4) is that uses of force only include acts of violence that cause death or injury to people or damage to physical property. A use of force is grave where it produces physical damage that is of sufficient 'scale and effects' and in *Nicaragua* the ICJ gave the example of 'a mere frontier incident' as a use of force that is not of sufficient gravity to qualify as an armed attack.[15]

Can self-defence be invoked in relation to *anticipated* armed attacks? This is an important question in the context of the current discussion because states usually undertake cyber espionage in order to uncover threats to their national security before they materialise. Prior to the signing of the UN Charter, customary international law unambiguously contained a right to anticipatory self-defence. The key piece of state practice in this area is the often-cited *Caroline* incident of 1837, which revealed an acceptance among states that under customary international law self-defence can be invoked where the threat of an armed attack is 'instant, overwhelming, leaving no choice of means and no moment for deliberation'.[16]

Article 51 UN Charter preserves the right of states to act in self-defence when an armed attack 'occurs'. The grammatical construction of Article 51 therefore indicates that states do not have to wait for an armed attack to have *occurred* before they can act in self-defence.[17] To ensure consistency between customary

[13] *Legality of the Threat or Use of Nuclear Weapons* (Advisory Opinion) [1986] ICJ Rep 226, para 41 ('[T]he submission of the exercise of the right of self-defence to the conditions of necessity and proportionality is a rule of customary international law [which] applies equally to Article 51 of the Charter'). See also *Military and Paramilitary Activities in and against Nicaragua (Nicaragua v United States of America)*, Judgment (Merits) [1986] ICJ Rep 14, para 176.

[14] *Nicaragua* (n 13) para 191.

[15] ibid para 195. Similarly, the Eritrea–Ethiopia Claims Commission explained that '[l]ocalized border encounters between small infantry units, even those involving the loss of life, do not constitute an armed attack for purposes of the Charter'; *Eritrea–Ethiopia Claims Commission, Partial Award, Jus ad Bellum*, Ethiopia's Claims 1–8, The Hague, 19 December 2005, para 11. See generally Y Dinstein, *War Aggression and Self-Defence* (Cambridge, Cambridge University Press, 2017) 209–11.

[16] Letter from Secretary of State Daniel Webster dated 24 April 1841, in *Caroline Case*, 29 British and Foreign State Papers (1841) 1137–38.

[17] See C Focarelli, 'Self-Defence in Cyberspace' in N Tsagourias and R Buchan (eds), *Research Handbook on International Law and Cyberspace* (Cheltenham, Edward Elgar, 2015) 271.

international law (as reflected in the *Caroline* formula) and the UN Charter,[18] state practice has interpreted Article 51 as permitting self-defence in response to an imminent armed attack that is in the process of occurring even though its violent effects have yet to manifest.[19] Reflecting upon this state practice in the wake of the US-led military intervention in Iraq in 2003, the UN Secretary-General's *In Larger Freedom* report explained that 'imminent threats are fully covered in Article 51, which safeguards the inherent right of sovereign States to defend themselves against an armed attack. Lawyers have long recognized that this covers an imminent attack as well as one that has already happened.'[20] Thus, under Article 51 UN Charter, a threatened state is only permitted to engage in anticipatory self-defence in those narrow instances where 'the other side has committed itself to an armed attack in an ostensibly irrevocable way'.[21]

With regard to the present discussion, acts of political cyber espionage can be therefore justified on the basis of self-defence where they are designed to shed light on an armed attack that is imminently expected and which is likely to inflict grave violence.[22] However, self-defence cannot be invoked to justify acts of cyber espionage that are designed to uncover emerging threats.[23] Instead, non-imminent threats must be addressed by the UN collective security system rather than by states acting unilaterally in the name of self-defence.

In the contemporary era, cyber espionage is often utilised to counteract armed attacks carried out by non-state actors such as terrorist organisations. As we have seen, the ICJ adopts a narrow interpretation of Article 51 UN Charter, maintaining that the right of self-defence is only available 'in the case of armed attack by one State against another State',[24] that is, where the conduct constituting

[18] Customary international law continues to operate in parallel to Article 51 UN Charter: 'I do not agree that the terms or intent of Article 51 eliminate the right of self-defence under customary international law'; *Nicaragua* (n 13) para 173 (Dissenting Opinion of Judge Schwebel).

[19] For a discussion of this state practice see T Ruys, *'Armed Attack' and Article 51 of the UN Charter: Evolutions in Customary Law and Practice* (Cambridge, Cambridge University Press, 2010) chapter 4.

[20] Report of the Secretary-General, *In Larger Freedom: Towards Development, Security and Human Rights for All*, UN Doc A/59/2005, 21 March 2005, para 124.

[21] Dinstein (n 15) 233.

[22] Scott explains that 'the surreptitious collection of intelligence in the territory of other nations that present clear, articulable threats based on their past behavior, capabilities, and expressions of intent, may be justified as a practice essential to the right of self-defense'; Scott (n 6) 225.

[23] Wright therefore dismisses the US's contention that its use of spy planes against the Soviet Union during the 1950s and 1960s constituted lawful acts of self-defence on the basis that '[t]he danger apprehended by the United States flowed from an interpretation of Soviet policy and intent, not from an immediate threat of attack'; Q Wright, 'Espionage and the Doctrine of Non-Intervention in Internal Affairs' in RJ Stanger (ed), *Essays on Espionage and International Law* (Columbus, Ohio State University Press, 1962) 18. According to Forcese, 'spying in response to the proliferation of weapons of mass destruction and state-sponsored terrorism … is difficult to square with the doctrinal law of self-defense. It is not clear how spying in aid of self-defense is permissible where the right to self-defense is not yet triggered as a matter of international law by, among other things, a sufficiently imminent armed attack'; C Forcese, 'Spies Without Borders: International Law and Intelligence Collection' (2011) 5 *Journal of National Security Law and Policy* 179, 199 (citations omitted).

[24] *Wall* (n 10) para 139.

the armed attack is attributable to a state under the rules on state responsibility. The better view, however, is that self-defence can be invoked directly against the author of an armed attack regardless of whether its perpetrator is a state or non-state actor.[25] This approach most accurately reflects *lex lata* because it is in line with pre- and post-Charter state practice (and especially in relation to terrorist attacks)[26] and is also true to the wording of Article 51 UN Charter, which does not make the exercise of self-defence contingent upon the author of the armed attack being a state.[27] According to this interpretation of Article 51, what is required is that – from a factual perspective – an armed attack has occurred or is imminent.

2.2. Necessity

As already noted, self-defence action must meet the requirement of necessity to be lawful. The principle of necessity can be broken down into two constitutive elements. First, the necessity principle requires that conduct undertaken in the name of self-defence must be employed for 'strictly defensive objectives'[28] and not for punishment, revenge or law enforcement.[29] Second, the principle of necessity requires that self-defence action must be a last resort after all other peaceful measures have been exhausted or have been reasonably deemed to be futile and thus not worth pursuing.[30]

[25] D Bethlehem, 'Self-Defense Against an Imminent or Actual Armed Attack by Nonstate Actors' (2012) 106 *AJIL* 770. This was also the view of the majority of the *Tallinn Manual 2.0* Experts; MN Schmitt, *Tallinn Manual 2.0 on the International Law Applicable to Cyber Operations* (Cambridge, Cambridge University Press, 2017) 345.

[26] SC Res 1368 (12 September 2001); SC Res 1373 (28 September 2001).

[27] 'There is, with respect, nothing in the text of Article 51 that … stipulates that self-defence is available only when an armed attack is made by a State'; *Wall* (n 10) para 33 (Separate Opinion of Judge Higgins).

[28] *Eighth Report (Ago)* (n 11) para 83.

[29] 'If other objectives than self-defence may be detected (such as a change in a border, the appropriation of resources, the overthrow of a government, the destruction of infrastructure, the punishing of a State, etc.), the measure shall by definition no longer be a "defence" and shall no longer be "necessary". It will be at most a sort of punitive expedition akin to armed reprisals and by definition contrary to international law'; O Corten, *The Law Against War: The Prohibition on the Use of Force in Contemporary International Law* (Oxford, Hart Publishing, 2010) 484–85.

[30] 'The reason for stressing that action taken in self-defence must be *necessary* is that the State attacked … must not, in the particular circumstances, have had any means of halting the attack other than recourse to armed force. In other words, had it been able to achieve the same result by measures not involving the use of armed force, it would have no justification for adopting conduct which contravened the general prohibition against the use of armed force'; *Eighth Report (Ago)* (n 11) para 120. '[F]orce should not be considered necessary until peaceful measures have been found wanting or when they clearly would be futile'; O Schachter, 'The Right of States to Use Armed Force' (1984) 82 *Michigan Law Review* 1620, 1635.

The application of the principle of necessity to ongoing (which includes imminent) armed attacks is relatively straightforward. In these circumstances, state practice reveals that there is an 'almost irrebuttable presumption' that the riposte is defensive and that the victim state has no other choice than to act and attempt to suppress the attack.[31] Where an armed attack is ongoing, acts of cyber espionage benefit from this irrebuttable presumption and will be regarded as necessary.

Once an ongoing armed attack has been concluded but the victim state continues to take self-defence action (by committing cyber espionage, for example), the application of the necessity principle becomes 'more complicated'.[32] What is important is that we determine the timeframe within which self-defence can be permissibly exercised following an armed attack. One view is that if the threat of an armed attack is no longer imminent, the right to self-defence is extinguished because any reaction cannot be classified as defensive.[33] Such a strict reading of the necessity principle is not consistent with state practice which, recognising that it often takes time to attribute an attack to the responsible actor and to mount an effective response, allows victim states 'a leeway in time in which to initiate their defensive action'.[34] What is required, however, is 'a reasonable temporal proximity between the victim state's response and the armed attack itself'.[35]

Nonetheless, during this period the victim state is required to utilise peaceful measures to resolve the dispute before defensive options are employed or to at least contemplate their use and reasonably conclude that they will not be effective.[36] For example, states are expected to consider all available diplomatic options before

[31] D Akande and T Liefländer, 'Clarifying Necessity, Imminence, and Proportionality in the Law of Self-Defense' (2013) 107 *AJIL* 563, 564. 'The question of whether a state has available reasonable non-forcible measures is not, for example, of any practical relevance in situations where a state finds itself under direct physical armed attack, as it would be illogical to assume that there is any legal obligation upon it to attempt to negotiate or resort to, let alone exhaust, peaceful alternatives'; C Henderson, *The Use of Force and International Law* (Cambridge, Cambridge University Press, 2018) 230.

[32] O Schachter, 'The Lawful Resort to Unilateral Use of Force' (1985) 10 *Yale Journal of International Law* 291, 292. 'The element of time cannot be ignored. It is reasonable to require a victim of aggression, no longer faced with the emergency of an armed attack, to seek and exhaust all avenues of peaceful settlement'; ibid.

[33] 'When the act is accomplished, damage suffered, and the danger passed, then the incidents of self-defence cease'; *The Ralph* (1904) 39 US Court of Claims 204, 207. For a similar view see A Cassese, 'Terrorism is also Disrupting Some Crucial Legal Categories of International Law' (2001) 12 *EJIL* 993, 995–98.

[34] J Gardam, *Necessity, Proportionality and the Use of Force by States* (Cambridge, Cambridge University Press, 2004) 150.

[35] F Grimal and J Sundaram, 'Cyber Warfare and Autonomous Self-Defence' (2017) 4 *Journal on the Use of Force and International Law* 1, 14.

[36] In the *Oil Platforms* case, the ICJ concluded that even if Iran had committed an armed attack against the US, the US could not rely upon self-defence to justify its use of force because 'there is no evidence that the United States complained to Iran of the military activities of the platforms … which does not suggest that the targeting of the platforms was seen as a necessary act'; *Oil* Platforms *(Islamic Republic of Iran v United States of America)*, Judgment (Merits) [2003] ICJ Rep 161, para 76. See also *Nicaragua* (n 13) para 237.

engaging in self-defence action, such as liaising with regional and international organisations and exploring whether they can leverage their influence to help resolve the dispute peacefully.[37] As another example, where the armed attack was committed by a non-state actor, before the victim state can engage in self-defence action it must demonstrate that it is not possible to petition the state within which the non-state actor is located and request its assistance in addressing the threat. It is only where the host state is unable or unwilling to provide assistance that self-defence measures such as cyber espionage are deemed necessary.[38]

2.3. Proportionality

To be lawful, self-defence action must also comply with the principle of proportionality. This principle is often depicted as 'the essence of self-defence'[39] and it requires that any response is limited 'to what is reasonably necessary to promptly secure the permissible objectives of self-defence'.[40] It is thus crucial to ascertain the legitimate aims of self-defence because it is those aims that are used to determine whether the scope of the self-defence action is within permissible limits.

What constitute the legitimate aims of self-defence has polarised international legal scholars. On the one hand, there are those scholars who maintain that self-defence action can be only undertaken for the purpose of halting and repelling an actual or imminent armed attack.[41] Special Rapporteur Robert Ago was a prominent proponent of this view, concluding that '[t]he requirement of the *proportionality* of the action taken in self-defence, as we have said, concerns the relationship between that action and its purpose, namely – and this can never be repeated too often – that of halting and repelling the attack or even, in so far as preventive self-defence is recognized, of preventing it from occurring'.[42] This approach would mean that acts of cyber espionage must be limited to obtaining only that information which is necessary to enable the attack

[37] JA Green, 'The "*Rationale Temporis*" Elements of Self-Defence' (2015) 2 *Journal on the Use of Force and International Law* 97, 116.

[38] 'The inability or unwillingness of the territorial state to prevent the attacks originating from its territory is what makes the reaction in self-defence in the territory of that state necessary'; M Roscini, *Cyber Operations and the Use of Force in International Law* (Oxford, Oxford University Press, 2014) 85.

[39] I Brownlie, *International Law and the Use of Force by States* (Oxford, Clarendon Press, 1963) 279 footnote 2.

[40] MS McDougal and FP Feliciano, *The International Law of War: Transnational Coercion and World Public Order* (New Haven, New Haven Press, 1994) 242.

[41] Cannizzaro explains that self-defence action 'must necessarily be commensurate with the concrete need to repel the current attack, and not with the need to produce the level of security sought by the attacked state'; E Cannizzaro, 'Contextualising Proportionality: Jus ad Bellum and Jus in Bello in the Lebanese War' (2006) 88 *International Review of the Red Cross* 779, 785. See also A Cassese, *International Law* (Oxford, Oxford University Press, 2005) 355 and T Gazzini, *The Changing Rules on the Use of Force in International Law* (Manchester, Manchester University Press, 2005) 148.

[42] *Eighth Report (Ago)* (n 11) para 121.

to be resisted and repelled. On the other hand, there are those scholars who take a broader approach and argue that even if an armed attack has been completed or the threat of an imminent armed attack has passed, self-defence action can be still undertaken where there is 'a sound basis for believing that further attacks will be mounted'[43] or, in other words, to 'prevent any further reasonably foreseeable attacks'.[44]

A careful analysis of state practice reveals that states have embraced the latter, broader conception of what are the legitimate aims of self-defence.[45] This is important in relation to cyber espionage because it means that where a state was the victim of an armed attack or was subject to an imminent threat of an armed attack but the armed attack has ceased or the threat of an armed attack is no longer imminent, states can nevertheless continue to exercise their right to self-defence and collect information from actors that are reasonably believed to be planning and preparing future armed attacks.

Scholars argue that even if the aims of defensive action are permissible, such conduct is only proportionate providing that the damage it inflicts (upon the attacker, third party states, the wider civilian population, the environment etc) does not go beyond what is necessary to achieve self-defence. For these scholars, the principle of proportionality 'calls for a balance to be struck between the need to repel the attack and the harm that defensive military action is likely to result in for other values and interests at stake, such as values of a humanitarian nature'.[46] If this interpretation of the proportionality principle is correct, it has significant implications for the present discussion because, as the Snowden leaks revealed, states possess the technological capacity to collect massive amounts of confidential information but the technology they use is often incapable of effectively discriminating between legitimate suspects and innocent civilians. Even if the purpose of online surveillance is to target hostile actors that represent a threat to national security, if thousands and perhaps even millions of innocent civilians are incidentally caught up in the surveillance, such conduct must be regarded as disproportionate. According to this approach, acts of cyber espionage are only proportionate where they are targeted against suspects and, on balance, any collateral harm caused to civilians is acceptable given the need to protect national security and achieve self-defence.

[43] MN Schmitt, *Counter-Terrorism and the Use of Force in International Law* (George C Marshall, European Centre for Security Studies, 2003) 64.

[44] ibid 65. '[Self-defence action may be justified] when [a] State has good reason to expect a series of attacks from the same source and such retaliation serves a deterrent or protective action'; Schachter (n 30) 1638.

[45] See, for example, the justifications of the US and UK for their use of force against Afghanistan following the 9/11 attacks. Letter dated 7 October 2001 from the Permanent Representative of the USA to the UN Addressed to the President of the Security Council, UN Doc S/2001/946 (USA) and the Letter dated 7 October 2001 from the Chargé d'affaires a.i. of the Permanent Mission of the United Kingdom of Great Britain and Northern Ireland to the United Nations Addressed to the President of the Security Council, UN Doc S/2001/947 (UK).

[46] Cannizzaro (n 41) 784. For a similar view see Gardam (n 34) 162–86.

State practice does not support this interpretation of the principle of proportionality.[47] State practice demonstrates that whether the harm caused by self-defence action is permissible under international law is not regulated by the *jus ad bellum* principle of proportionality but is instead determined by other international law regimes, such as international human rights law and international humanitarian law. In the *ad bellum* context, the only restriction imposed by the principle of proportionality is that the victim state do no more than achieve the specific objective of defending itself. Thus, providing self-defence action is designed to halt and repel an armed attack or prevent reasonably foreseeable future attacks – that is, there is a 'rational connection'[48] between the riposte and securing the legitimate ends of self-defence – the principle of proportionality is satisfied. Whether a rational connection exists is invariably answered by the necessity criterion considered above because the gist of this principle is that there must be a temporal link between the armed attack and the response. If such a link is presumed (as is the case with ongoing attacks) or can be established (where there is a time delay between the armed attack and the reaction), the response is considered necessary but, if no temporal link exists, it will be regarded as retributive or punitive and thus unnecessary and unlawful. In practice, then, 'the proportionality and necessity criteria are truly two sides of the same coin'[49] and, as Kretzmer observes, the requirement that acts taken in self-defence are proportionate 'is not really proportionality at all, but purely a question of whether the force was necessary to achieve the legitimate ends of using force in self-defence'.[50]

3. The Doctrine of Necessity

Necessity is a secondary rule of international law insofar as it precludes state responsibility for violations of primary rules of international law in 'those exceptional cases where the only way a State can safeguard an essential interest threatened by a grave and imminent peril is, for the time being, not to perform some other international obligation of lesser weight or urgency'.[51] The doctrine of necessity therefore acts 'as a "safety valve", to relieve the inevitably untoward consequences of a concern for adhering at all costs to the letter of the law'.[52]

[47] For a discussion see Henderson (n 31) 237.
[48] D Kretzmer, 'The Inherent Right to Self-Defence and Proportionality in *Jus Ad Bellum*' (2013) 24 *EJIL* 235, 278.
[49] Ruys (n 19) 123.
[50] Kretzmer (n 48) 282.
[51] *Articles with Commentaries* (n 11) Commentary to Article 25, para 1.
[52] *Eighth Report (Ago)* (n 11) para 80.

Necessity is firmly established in customary international law and finds its contemporary articulation in Article 25 of the International Law Commission's Articles on State Responsibility (ASR) 2001:[53]

> 1. Necessity may not be invoked by a State as a ground for precluding the wrongfulness of an act not in conformity with an international obligation of that State unless the act:
> (a) is the only way for the State to safeguard an essential interest against a grave and imminent peril; and
> (b) does not seriously impair an essential interest of the State or States towards which the obligation exists, or of the international community as a whole.
>
> 2. In any case, necessity may not be invoked by a State as a ground for precluding wrongfulness if:
> (a) the international obligation in question excludes the possibility of invoking necessity; or
> (b) the State has contributed to the situation of necessity.

Given that necessity exculpates state responsibility for internationally wrongful conduct, this defence 'will only rarely be available to excuse non-performance of an obligation and … is subject to strict limitations to safeguard against possible abuse'.[54] Whether cyber espionage can be justified on the basis of necessity will now be considered.

3.1. Essential Interest

The defence of necessity is only available where an essential interest of the state is imperilled. The concept of essential state interest is 'capacious and protean'[55] and encompasses those interests that are of 'fundamental and great importance to the State concerned'.[56] Consequently, what is an essential state interest cannot be 'prejudged'[57] and must be assessed on a case-by-case basis. That being said, case law and state practice provide examples of state interests the protection of which have been regarded as essential.

[53] That Article 25 reflects customary international law has been affirmed on numerous occasions by international tribunals. See, for example, *Gabčíkovo-Nagymaros Project (Hungary v Slovakia)*, Judgment [1997] ICJ Rep 7, para 51 ('The Court considers, first of all, that the state of necessity is a ground recognized by customary international law') and *Wall* (n 10) para 140.

[54] *Articles with Commentaries* (n 11) Commentary to Article 25, para 2. 'If strict and demanding conditions are not required or are loosely applied, any State could invoke necessity to elude its international obligations. This would certainly be contrary to the stability and predictability of the law'; *CMS Gas Transmission Co v The Republic of Argentina*, ICSID Case No ARB/01/8, Award (12 May 2005) para 317.

[55] RD Sloane, 'On the Use and Abuse of Necessity in the Law of State Responsibility' (2012) 106 *AJIL* 447, 457.

[56] *Tallinn Manual 2.0* (n 25) 135.

[57] 'The extent to which a given interest is "essential" depends on all circumstances, and cannot be prejudged'; *Articles with Commentaries* (n 11) Commentary to Article 25, para 15.

An essential interest is undoubtedly implicated in those situations where 'the very existence of the State and its independence' is compromised.[58] Typically, threats to a state's continued survival emanate from actors that plan and prepare violent attacks against its territorial integrity or political independence.[59] Evidently, there is an overlap between the doctrines of self-defence and necessity insofar as where a state is subject to an actual or imminent threat of grave violence an armed attack occurs and, additionally, one of its essential interests is endangered. In such circumstances, the victim state is more likely to rely upon self-defence than necessity given that self-defence is a primary rule of international law whereas necessity is a secondary rule; said otherwise, self-defence justifies the riposte outright whereas necessity excuses state responsibility for an internationally wrongful act due to the exigencies of the situation.[60]

The utility of the doctrine of necessity is that it is available in a wider set of circumstances than the doctrine of self-defence. What amounts to an essential interest goes beyond the state's continued existence[61] and encompasses its 'political or economic survival, the continued functioning of its essential services, the maintenance of internal peace, the survival of a sector of its population, [and] the preservation of the environment of its territory or a part thereof, etc.'.[62] Most recently, in the *LG&E* case the Tribunal reaffirmed this broader understanding of what is an essential state interest:

> What qualifies as an 'essential' interest is not limited to those interests referring to the State's existence. As evidence demonstrates, economic, financial or those interests related to the protection of the State against any danger seriously compromising its internal or external situation, are also considered essential interests.[63]

[58] *Enron Creditors Recovery Group Corporation and Ponderosa Assets, LP v The Republic of Argentina*, ICSID Case No ARB/01/3, Award (22 May 2007) para 306.

[59] In fact, necessity grew out of state practice on the use of force and self-defence; see BC Rodick, *The Doctrine of Necessity in International Law* (New York, Columbia University Press, 1928).

[60] For a discussion of the distinction between justification and excuse in international law see F Paddeu, *Justification and Excuse in International Law: Concept and Theory of General Defences* (Cambridge, Cambridge University Press, 2018) chapter 1.

[61] Although note Sloane's observation that while theoretically a threat to any essential state interest can engage necessity, the reality is that '[t]ime and again, tribunals reject necessity because, as they observe, the threat to the invoking state does not threaten its very existence as a state'; Sloane (n 55) 460.

[62] *Eighth Report (Ago)* (n 11) para 2. Heathcote explains that what qualifies as 'an essential interest is not a fixed category … [but it] is not limited to safeguarding the very survival of the State itself. It includes, notably, the preservation of the natural environment or the ecological equilibrium, the economic survival of the State, and the maintenance of the food supply of the population'; S Heathcote, 'Circumstances Precluding Wrongfulness in the ILC Articles on State Responsibility: Necessity' in J Crawford, A Pellet and S Olleson (eds), *The Law of International Responsibility* (Oxford, Oxford University Press, 2010) 496 (citations omitted).

[63] *LG&E Energy Corp, LG&E Capital Corp, LG&E International Inc v The Republic of Argentina*, ICSID Case No. ARB/02/1, Decision on Liability (3 October 2006) para 251. 'In the Arbitral Tribunal's view, the term "essential interest" can encompass not only the existence and independence of a State itself, but also other subsidiary but nonetheless "essential" interests, such as the preservation of the State's broader social, economic and environmental stability, and its ability to provide for the

To date, tribunals have recognised the national economy,[64] the environment[65] and the 'health and wellbeing' of the population[66] as examples of essential state interests. This is significant because it opens up the possibility that acts of political cyber espionage that are designed to maintain national security can benefit from the defence of necessity as can acts of economic cyber espionage that are intended to protect the national economy.

3.2. A Grave and Imminent Peril

The doctrine of necessity requires that an essential state interest is in 'grave and imminent peril'. Whether a threat is grave depends upon its actual or expected impact upon the essential state interest. Put simply, the more 'severe' the threat is to an essential state interest, the more likely it is that the threat will qualify as grave.[67] To illustrate, cyber attacks against governmental networks and systems can endanger national security; but a cyber attack that forces offline computer networks and systems linked to national defence is far more likely to constitute a grave threat to national security than a cyber attack that temporarily disrupts a state's communications networks.[68] Similarly, a deep and prolonged economic recession represents a far more serious threat to a state's national economy than a temporary dip in economic performance.

Necessity is only available where the threat to an essential interest is imminent at the 'actual time' that the state takes recourse to internationally wrongful conduct.[69] Under what circumstances threats can be regarded as imminent was considered at length in the *Gabčíkovo-Nagymaros* case. In 1977 Czechoslovakia (as it then was) and Hungary signed a treaty that required joint investment by both states for the construction of two series of locks – one at *Gabčíkovo* in Czechoslovakia and the other at *Nagymaros* in Hungary – with the objective of producing hydroelectricity, improving navigation along the Danube and protecting the banks of the Danube against flooding. In 1989 Hungary announced that it was abandoning its participation in the construction of the locks, which the ICJ held to be a violation of its 1977 treaty obligations. In response, Hungary claimed

fundamental needs of the population'; *Impregilo SpA v The Republic of Argentina*, ICSID Case No ARB/07/17, Award (21 June 2011) para 346.

[64] *CMS* (n 54) paras 359–60; *LG&E* (n 63) paras 237–38.

[65] *Gabčíkovo-Nagymaros* (n 53) para 53.

[66] *Suez, Sociedad General de Aguas de Barcelona SA and Vivendi Universal SA v The Republic of Argentina*, ICSID Case No ARB/03/19, Decision on Liability (30 July 2010) para 260; *LG&E* (n 63) para 234.

[67] 'The Experts agreed that a peril is grave when the threat is especially severe. It involves interfering with an interest in a fundamental way, like destroying the interest or rendering it largely dysfunctional'; *Tallinn Manual 2.0* (n 25) 136.

[68] ibid 136–37.

[69] ILC Yearbook 1980, vol II, Part 2, 49.

that its responsibility for these violations was precluded on the basis of necessity, in particular that the construction of the locks would have a detrimental impact upon the surrounding environment.

The ICJ had 'no difficulty in acknowledging that the concerns expressed by Hungary for its natural environment in the region affected by the Gabčíkovo–Nagymaros Project related to an "essential interest" of that State'.[70] When determining whether the threat to this essential interest was imminent, the ICJ explained that 'a "peril" appearing in the long term might be held to be "imminent" as soon as it is established, at the relevant point in time, that the realization of that peril, however far off it might be, is not thereby any less certain and inevitable'.[71] This notwithstanding, the Court concluded that at the time that Hungary abandoned its participation in the construction of the locks, the threat that the locks would have represented to the environment had they been built was not 'sufficiently certain'[72] so as to be regarded as imminent. Instead, the Court held that the threatened harm was merely 'apprehended'.[73] With specific reference to the *Nagymaros* lock, the ICJ determined that the threat to the environment would only emerge where the lock operated under very specific conditions, namely, in peak-load time and continuously during high water. Yet, the ICJ found that 'the final rules of operation had not yet been determined … [and so] one would be bound to conclude that the peril was not "imminent" at the time at which Hungary suspended and then abandoned the works relating to the dam'.[74]

Whether a threat to an essential interest is imminent is fact-specific and depends upon the circumstances of each individual case. Yet, a threat to national security seems imminent where a state has been subject to a series of violent threats by another state and where the predacious state has taken demonstrable steps towards preparing its military for offensive action. Regardless of whether the doctrine of self-defence is available, the victim state may invoke necessity and engage in otherwise unlawful acts of political cyber espionage in order to identify when the attack will take place, what weapons will be used and what or who will be the target.

Similarly, envisage a scenario where a state is defaulting on its national debt, its banking sector is in disarray, the value of its currency is dropping rapidly and a number of large companies are on the brink of bankruptcy. These circumstances are likely to give rise to an imminent threat of economic collapse, thereby raising the possibility that the imperilled state can take recourse to economic cyber espionage in the name of necessity in order to avert or alleviate the crisis.

[70] *Gabčíkovo-Nagymaros* (n 53) para 53.
[71] ibid para 54.
[72] ibid para 56.
[73] ibid. The ILC also explains that '[i]t is not sufficient … that the peril is merely apprehended or contingent'; *Articles with Commentaries* (n 11) Commentary to Article 25, para 16.
[74] *Gabčíkovo-Nagymaros* (n 53) para 55.

3.3. No Other Means to Safeguard an Essential Interest

The plea of necessity is excluded if, as alternatives to the conduct that is in breach of international law, there are other lawful means reasonably available to a state to safeguard an essential interest from a grave and imminent peril, even if they are more costly or onerous.[75] In other words, states can only invoke necessity where, in order to protect an essential interest, there is no other choice than to act unlawfully.[76]

The 'no other means' requirement was considered extensively in the litigation against Argentina when, in the face of a severe economic crisis from 2001 to 2003, it violated various bilateral investment treaties by imposing higher than agreed tariffs on foreign investors. Argentina sought to excuse its unlawful conduct on the basis of necessity. In the *CMS* case, the Tribunal had to determine whether Argentina's conduct was the only way in which it could avail itself of the threat of economic collapse. The Tribunal found that prestigious economists legitimately disagreed over what policies were necessary to prevent economic catastrophe. From this, the Tribunal concluded that there were law-compliant policies reasonably available to Argentina to address the crisis and that Argentina should have exhausted these options before it adopted conduct that was not in conformity with its treaty obligations.[77] Thus, '[w]henever there is at least one other policy alternative, the effect of the *CMS* holding is to shut the door on necessity almost completely'.[78]

Interestingly, in the *LG&E* case the Tribunal arrived at a different conclusion, determining that Argentina's 'economic recovery package was the only means to respond to the crisis. Although there may have been a number of ways to draft the economic recovery plan, the evidence before the Tribunal demonstrates that an across-the-board response was necessary, and the tariffs on public utilities had to be addressed'.[79] However, the Tribunal adopted a very general approach to the

[75] 'The adoption by a State of conduct not in conformity with an international obligation towards another State must truly be the only means available to it for averting the extremely grave and imminent peril which it fears; in other words, it must be impossible for the peril to be averted by any other means, even one which is much more onerous but which can be adopted without a breach of international obligations'; *Eighth Report (Ago)* (n 11) para 14. 'The plea [of necessity] is excluded if there are other (otherwise lawful) means available, even if they may be more costly or less convenient'; *Articles with Commentaries* (n 11) Commentary to Article 25, para 15; *Gabčíkovo-Nagymaros* (n 53) para 55.

[76] For example, in the *Wall* advisory opinion the ICJ determined that Israel could not rely upon necessity to defend its construction of a security wall in violation of international law because it was 'not convinced that the construction of the wall along the route chosen was the only means to safeguard the interests of Israel against the peril which it has invoked as a justification for that construction'; *Wall* (n 10) para 140. Unhelpfully, the ICJ did not specify the other means available to Israel to avert the threat posed by terrorism.

[77] *CMS* (n 54) para 323. See MCH Thjoernelund, 'State Necessity as an Exemption from State Responsibility for Investments' (2009) 13 *Max Planck Yearbook of United Nations Law* 423, 426.

[78] M Waibel, 'Two Worlds of Necessity in ICSID Arbitration: *CMS* and *LG&E*' (2007) 20 *Leiden Journal of International Law* 637, 646.

[79] *LG&E* (n 63) para 257.

'only means' criterion. Rather than identifying the different measures that Argentina could have adopted to avert the crisis and explaining why they would have been ineffective (and thereby demonstrating that the unlawful measures undertaken by Argentina were the only available means to protect its essential interests), the Tribunal simply conceded that an 'across-the-board' recovery package was necessary. As Waibel observes, '[t]his approach of course pays very little heed to the "only way" criterion under customary international law'.[80]

Consider, for example, the situation where a state undertakes political cyber espionage against another state in order to respond to threats to its national security. Whether other means were reasonably available to the state to protect its national security than to engage in unlawful acts of espionage depends upon the circumstances prevailing at the time but general comments can be made. Most notably, where states fall into dispute, they are subject to a duty under international law to cooperate and to attempt to resolve that dispute peacefully.[81] Hence, it is only where all diplomatic efforts and legal channels have been exhausted, or are reasonably determined to be of no avail, that a state can invoke necessity and engage in unlawful conduct such as cyber espionage to confront a threat to its national security.

Where a state is faced with an economic crisis and, in response, it engages in unlawful acts of economic cyber espionage, it will have to demonstrate that other lawful measures would not have been sufficient to address the threat, such as adjusting its economic strategy, introducing austerity, restructuring its debt, securing loans etc. If necessity is only available where resort to unlawful conduct is genuinely inescapable, it will be a tall order for a state to satisfy a tribunal that the theft of trade secrets from foreign companies represented the *sole means* by which it could avert the threat to its economy.

3.4. Non-Contribution

A state is precluded from relying upon necessity if it has contributed to the onset of the crisis. Crucially, necessity is only unavailable in those circumstances where a state's contribution to the crisis is 'sufficiently substantial'.[82] In other words, contributory conduct that is 'incidental or peripheral' does not prevent a state from raising the defence of necessity.[83]

The issue of non-contribution was considered by those tribunals that had to determine whether Argentina could rely upon necessity to exonerate its responsibility for the violation of various bilateral investment treaties in the early 2000s.

[80] Waibel (n 78) 646.

[81] See A Peters, 'International Dispute Settlement: A Network of Cooperational Duties' (2003) 14 *EJIL* 1.

[82] *Articles with Commentaries* (n 11) Commentary to Article 25, para 20.

[83] ibid.

A number of the tribunals found that the policies adopted by Argentina during the 1990s contributed substantially to its economic crisis and that this contribution rendered the defence of necessity unavailable.[84] In particular, the *CMS* Tribunal concluded that Argentina's 'policies and their shortcomings significantly contributed to the crisis and the emergency and while exogenous factors did fuel additional difficulties they do not exempt the Respondent from its responsibility in the matter'.[85]

On a theoretical level, it may be possible to disentangle the endogenous and exogenous causes of a crisis. In practice, however, this task is likely to be extraordinarily difficult given that states inhabit a globalised world order where the root causes of crises cannot be neatly separated out into those that are domestic and those that are international.[86] Admittedly, it is only where a state *substantially* contributes to the onset of a crisis that necessity is unavailable, which makes it easier to determine whether, in and amongst the various factors contributing to the crisis, the state's actions preclude the invocation of the defence of necessity. Nonetheless, it is still very difficult to gauge whether a state contributed substantially to the emergence of a crisis. Consider the threat that states such as the US and the UK face from Islamic terrorism. Are these states precluded from relying upon the doctrine of necessity to justify acts of political cyber espionage because their policies towards Islamic states over the past two decades have substantially contributed to the emergence of this threat? Or, instead, is this type of extremism substantially attributable to a warped view of Islam espoused by terrorist groups, rendering the conduct of states such as the US and the UK marginal and peripheral? As a further example, consider the situation where a state is faced with an imminent threat of economic collapse and in order to avert this threat it engages in economic cyber espionage. Did the state substantially contribute to the onset of the crisis because of the laws and policies that it did or did not adopt? Or did external factors significantly dilute the state's responsibility, such as the laws and policies adopted by other states or international organisations or, more generally, a global economic slowdown? As Sloane notes, '[t]he complexity and sheer number of potentially relevant factors in such an analysis is daunting'.[87]

[84] *CMS* (n 54) para 329; *Enron* (n 58) paras 311–12; *Sempra Energy International v The Republic of Argentina*, ICSID Case No ARB/02/16, Award (28 September 2007) para 354. Although interestingly the *LG&E* Tribunal concluded that Argentina's policies had substantially contributed to the onset of the economic crisis; *LG&E* (n 63) para 256.

[85] *CMS* (n 54) para 329.

[86] Waibel (n 78) 642–43.

[87] Sloane (n 55) 489. '[S]imilar to what is the case in most crises of this kind [economic recession] the roots extend both ways and include a number of domestic as well as international dimensions. This is the unavoidable consequence of the operation of a global economy where domestic and international factors interact'; *CMS* (n 54) para 328. After asking what was the cause or causes of Argentina's economic crisis, the *Sempra* Tribunal explained that 'the truth seems to be somewhere in the middle, with both kinds of [endogenous and exogenous] factors having intervened. The mix has in fact come to be generally recognized by experts, officials and international agencies'; *Sempra* (n 84) para 353.

3.5. Balancing of Interests

Even if the above criteria are satisfied, Article 25 ASR precludes reliance upon necessity where a state engages in internationally wrongful conduct that seriously impairs an essential interest of the state(s) towards whom the international legal obligation is owed or of the international community as a whole.

Before we can consider whether unlawful conduct (such as cyber espionage) seriously impairs an essential interest, it is first necessary to identify *whose* essential interests must be taken into account. Article 25's reference to states is relatively straightforward but its use of the concept of the 'international community as a whole' is curious and the immediate question is: which actors does it comprise? Specifically, does it include all actors that are endowed with rights and responsibilities under international law, that is, international legal personality? If so, the international community encompasses not just states but also non-state actors such as international organisations and individuals. This is significant in the context of political cyber espionage that is directed against individuals because, as we saw in chapter 5, states are required to respect fundamental human rights under international human rights law and cyber espionage invariably violates the right to privacy. Depending upon various factors such as the nature and quantity of the information collected, interference with this fundamental human right can constitute a serious impairment of an essential interest of an individual.

I argue that the use of the concept of 'the international community as a whole' by Article 25 ASR does not require an assessment of the impact of the unlawful conduct upon individual members of the international community but, instead, upon the international community as a collective whole.[88] Generally speaking, international law imposes obligations upon states vis-a-vis each other. However, the ICJ has identified a limited category of international legal rules that impose obligations *erga omnes*. Obligations *erga omnes* describe those obligations that are intended to protect the basic values and common interests of all and which are therefore owed to the international community as a whole and which the international community as a whole has an interest in upholding.[89] By making reference to 'the international community as a whole', the objective of Article 25 is to ensure that specific interests of individual importance to a state do not take precedence over general interests of wider importance to the international community.[90] With this issue clarified, the question becomes which interests of the state and the international community as a whole can be regarded as essential.

[88] 'Article 25(1)(b) does not refer to the interests of individual members of this community but rather to those of the "international community as a whole"'; G Bücheler, *Proportionality in Investor-State Arbitration* (Oxford, Oxford University Press, 2015) 271.

[89] *Barcelona Traction, Light and Power Company, Limited (Belgium v Spain)*, Judgment [1970] ICJ Rep 3, para 33.

[90] R Boed, 'State Necessity as a Justification for Internationally Wrongful Conduct' (2000) 3 *Yale Human Rights and Development Journal* 1, 40.

What amounts to an essential state interest was discussed previously but it is worth reiterating that this concept is broad and includes the protection of national security, the national economy and the environment. One of the central arguments of this monograph is that where acts of political and economic cyber espionage penetrate computer networks and systems supported by cyber infrastructure physically located within the territory of another state, a violation of that state's territorial sovereignty occurs. Given that a violation of a state's territorial sovereignty represents a threat to national security, cyber espionage can be said to impair an essential interest of the victim state. Yet, not all threats to national security are the same; threats to national security exist on a continuum and can range from very serious to relatively minor.

Whether acts of political cyber espionage constitute a *serious* threat to the national security of the victim state (as Article 25 ASR requires) depends upon various factors such as the type and quantity of the information stolen and to whom that information belongs. Consider the situation where a state is subject to threats of violence by another state and it engages in political cyber espionage in order to better understand the nature of that threat. Where espionage results in the appropriation of highly sensitive information belonging to the opposing state – for example, its nuclear launch codes or information relating to how it will deploy its troops – this conduct is likely to seriously impair the opposing state's national security. However, there may be other types of information that the opposing state keeps confidential but the content of that information is relatively innocuous, such as perfunctory communications between junior civil servants. The appropriation of this type of information is more likely to cause the opposing state irritation, inconvenience and embarrassment rather than to seriously threaten its national security.

Also consider acts of political cyber espionage against an individual suspected of being involved in international terrorism. This conduct violates the territorial sovereignty of the host state but, given that the espionage is directed against an individual, the impact upon national security is likely to be nominal. Yet, if espionage is committed systematically against multiple individuals over a long period of time, the impact upon national security becomes more pronounced and in these circumstances it may be regarded as seriously impairing the host state's national security.

With regard to economic cyber espionage, while stealing trade secrets belonging to a foreign company adversely affects its financial security, the impact of this conduct upon the national economy of the host state varies depending upon the frequency and intensity of the espionage. One-off acts of economic cyber espionage that obtain information of limited significance to the victim company are unlikely to seriously threaten the host state's national economy but, in contrast, a sustained and coordinated campaign of economic cyber espionage that acquires access to highly sensitive information belonging to multiple companies is far more likely to represent a serious threat to the performance of the national economy.

What are the essential interests of the international community as a whole? As said previously, obligations *erga omnes* protect community interests. By their very definition, internationally wrongful acts that violate *erga omnes* obligations can be said to impair an essential interest of the international community as a whole. The critical question is which rules of international law have attained *erga omnes* status. This is contested and it is difficult to definitively list them. However, there are certain international legal rules that are widely accepted as imposing obligations *erga omnes*, such as the prohibition against genocide, slavery, aggression and racial discrimination.[91] Given the types of interests protected by *erga omnes* obligations, a violation of these types of international legal obligation will – *ipso facto* – be regarded as seriously impairing an essential interest of the international community as whole. Evidently, it is unlikely that acts of political and economic cyber espionage violate rules of an *erga omnes* nature.

A literal reading of Article 25(1)(b) ASR indicates that if unlawful conduct seriously impairs an essential interest of another state(s) or of the international community as a whole, reliance upon necessity is precluded. Yet, the reality is that the breaching state will have also established that it has an essential interest that is in grave and imminent peril. Rather than automatically preventing the breaching state from invoking necessity, tribunals have adopted a more pragmatic approach and have instead insisted that a 'balance [has] to be struck … between the interests of the respondent State and the individual interests of the State or States complaining of a breach'.[92] In other words, the defence of necessity boils down to a 'balancing test redolent of the choice-of-evils paradigm';[93] 'the point of emphasis is that the real or ultimate question raised by necessity turns out to be in large part about who, or which state or states, should bear the cost'.[94] Thus, for a breaching state to successfully raise a plea of necessity, the 'interest relied on must outweigh all other considerations, not merely from the point of view of the acting State but on a reasonable assessment of the competing interests, whether these are individual or collective'.[95]

But how do we go about balancing essential interests or, more specifically, what are the criteria that determine whose essential interests must be prioritised for protection? Sloane notes that given the heterogeneous nature of the international society states attribute different values to different interests,[96] rendering

[91] 'Such obligations derive, for example, in contemporary international law, from the outlawing of acts of aggression and of genocide, as also from the principles and rules concerning the basic rights of the human person, including protection from slavery and racial discrimination'; *Barcelona Traction* (n 89) para 34. See further *Wall* (n 10) paras 155–59.

[92] *Second Report (Crawford)* (n 11) para 292.

[93] Sloane (n 55) 487.

[94] ibid 506–07.

[95] *Articles with Commentaries* (n 11) Commentary to Article 25, para 17.

[96] 'In short, especially in the event of incommensurable social values or interests, one state's *safeguarded* essential interest will often be another's *seriously impaired* essential interest'; Sloane (n 55) 488.

this balancing exercise 'impracticable as it is abstruse'.[97] This being said, examples can be given to illustrate the application of this balancing test in the context of cyber espionage. For instance, where a state's national security is at threat of grave and imminent violence, acts of political cyber espionage are likely to be justifiable even though this conduct results in the collection of sensitive (and perhaps even top secret) information in violation of the territorial sovereignty of the opposing state. In contradistinction, where a state engages in economic cyber espionage in order to alleviate the effects of an economic crisis and in doing so targets companies within a state that is already experiencing profound economic difficulties, primacy is likely to be accorded to protecting the essential interests of the state that is the target of espionage and whose economy is already in dire straits.

4. Conclusion

States can rely upon the doctrines of self-defence and necessity to justify internationally wrongful conduct but, as this chapter has demonstrated, international law strictly limits their availability because to interpret them broadly would risk destabilising the international political and legal order.

Article 51 UN Charter can be invoked to justify acts of political cyber espionage where there is an actual or imminent threat of an armed attack. To be lawful, acts of cyber espionage taken in self-defence must be necessary and proportionate in the circumstances which, when taken together, essentially require that espionage operations must be designed to halt and repel the armed attack or to prevent further reasonably foreseeable attacks.

The defence of necessity precludes state responsibility for acts of political and economic cyber espionage not in conformity with international law where that conduct represents the sole means by which an essential interest of the state can be protected against a grave and imminent peril. Additionally, for the plea of necessity to be successful, the unlawful act of cyber espionage must not seriously impair an essential interest of the state(s) towards whom the obligation is owed or of the international community as a whole. In practice, necessity requires a difficult decision to be made: should the essential interest of the state invoking necessity be protected against a grave and imminent peril or, alternatively, should the essential interest of the state(s) towards whom the obligation is owed or of the international community as a whole be safeguarded from serious impairment? The facts of each case will determine whose essential interests must be prioritised for protection and whose must be sacrificed.

[97] ibid 488.

Conclusion

Cyber espionage describes the non-consensual use of computer operations to copy confidential information while it is stored in or transiting through cyberspace. Broadly speaking, states undertake cyber espionage in order to collect two different types of confidential information. Political cyber espionage is designed to enhance national security by acquiring confidential political and military information that is under the control of other state and non-state actors within the world order. Economic cyber espionage is intended to strengthen the national economy by obtaining trade secrets that are under the control of foreign companies. The objective of this monograph has been to examine the role of international law in regulating state-sponsored political and economic cyber espionage during times of peace.

A central claim of this monograph is that, except in narrowly defined circumstances, political and economic cyber espionage represent a threat to the maintenance of international peace and security. Political espionage constitutes a threat to international peace and security because it violates the principles of the sovereign equality of states and human dignity, which are foundational norms of the international society. Moreover, political espionage threatens international peace and security on the basis that, where states engage in this practice and violate the fundamental principles of the international society, this prevents the society from enjoying close and effective cooperation and from tackling common problems collaboratively.

With regard to economic espionage, I have argued that since the end of the Cold War states regard the maintenance of national security as being contingent upon a healthy and prosperous national economy. Acts of economic espionage inflict upon companies various direct and indirect costs, thereby jeopardising their financial success. Where national companies struggle financially, this has an adverse impact upon the national economy of the host state and thus upon its national security. Given that economic espionage threatens the maintenance of national security, this practice also threatens the maintenance of international peace and security.

Significantly, the threat that political and economic espionage represent to international peace and security is amplified in the cyber context. Because of the speed and ease with which malicious cyber operations can be mounted, and given the voluminous amounts of confidential information resident in cyberspace, political and economic cyber espionage has increased exponentially in recent years and is now a frequent occurrence within the international society. In order to counteract the threat to international peace and security posed by political and economic espionage – and in particular where these practices are cyber-enabled – I have argued that the international society must possess international legal rules that expressly and unambiguously prohibit such conduct.

With this conclusion in mind, the attention of this monograph turned to an assessment of whether international law applies to cyber espionage. International lawyers have long maintained 'there is something almost oxymoronic about addressing the legality of espionage under international law';[1] by extension, this argument holds that there is little interaction between international law and cyber-enabled espionage.[2] It is correct that international law does not regulate espionage per se and, in this sense, there is no such thing as an international law of espionage that can be adapted to apply to cyber espionage. But it is overly simplistic to conclude that international law 'has little to say about foreign surveillance'.[3] As Chesterman explained in 2006, espionage 'is less a lacuna in the legal order than it is the elephant in the room'.[4] If this is the case, the objective of this monograph has been to talk about the elephant in the room and, specifically, to identify the international legal rules that apply to cyber espionage and to scrutinise the extent to which they prohibit or otherwise constrain this practice.

My research has demonstrated that there is a 'patchwork of norms'[5] applicable to cyber espionage or, more specifically, to the conduct that underlies this practice. The rule of territorial sovereignty provides a potent source of international legal protection against cyber espionage. With reference to state practice, this monograph has argued that states extend their territorial sovereignty over those computer networks and systems supported by cyber infrastructure physically located within their territory, regardless of whether that cyber infrastructure is operated by a state organ or a private actor. Thus, acts of political and economic cyber espionage that intrude into these networks and systems in order to copy confidential information infringe the victim state's territorial sovereignty and are internationally wrongful.

Diplomatic and consular law also provides rules that regulate cyber espionage. Receiving states are subject to multiple and often overlapping obligations to respect the inviolability of the premises, property, documents, correspondence and means of transport of diplomatic missions and consular posts, thereby comprehensively prohibiting acts of political cyber espionage. Moreover, diplomatic missions and consular posts must comply with the laws in force within the receiving state. Diplomatic missions and consular posts are therefore precluded from engaging

[1] DB Silver, 'Intelligence and Counterintelligence' in JN Moore and RF Turner (eds), *National Security Law* (Durham, North Carolina, Carolina Academic Press, 2005) 965.

[2] In the context of cyber-enabled espionage, Khalil concludes that 'there are no significant international treaties or conventions in existence that establish principles regulating international intelligence activities. Customary international law simply fails to provide the international community with a set of rules governing espionage on foreign states and individuals'; C Khalil, 'Thinking Intelligently About Intelligence: A Model Global Framework Protecting Privacy' (2015) 47 *George Washington International Law Review* 919, 921–22 (citations omitted).

[3] A Deeks, 'An International Legal Framework for Surveillance' (2015) 55 *Virginia Journal of International Law* 291, 293.

[4] S Chesterman, 'The Spy Who Came in from the Cold War: Intelligence and International Law' (2006) 27 *Michigan Journal of International Law* 1071, 1072.

[5] ibid 1076.

in cyber espionage because this conduct runs into conflict with the national (and usually criminal) law of the receiving state and also international law more generally (such as the rule of territorial sovereignty).

International human rights law applies to cyber espionage. Human rights bodies require states to respect the human rights contained within the International Covenant on Civil and Political Rights (ICCPR) 1966 whenever they exercise their authority and control abroad and regardless of whether this authority and control is exercised online or offline. Moreover, while the European Court of Human Rights (ECtHR) has been less clear and less consistent in determining when a state's obligations contained within the European Convention on Human Rights (ECHR) 1950 apply extraterritorially, its post-*Banković* case law signals a willingness to adopt the model used under the ICCPR. *Ratione materiae*, cyber espionage constitutes a *prima facie* violation of the right to privacy. Privacy is not an absolute right, however, and its enjoyment can be permissibly restricted where, for instance, a state is able to demonstrate that the collection of confidential information is prescribed by law, pursuant to a legitimate societal aim and proportionate in the circumstances.

World Trade Organization (WTO) law provides protection against economic cyber espionage. Notably, Article 10*bis* of the Paris Convention 1967 requires members to assure to nationals (which includes legal persons such as companies) of other Paris Union members effective protection against acts of unfair competition. Undoubtedly, economic cyber espionage amounts to an act of unfair competition. Article 10*bis* therefore forbids members from engaging in economic cyber espionage against Paris Union nationals located within their territory and, given the construction of Article 10*bis*, against Paris Union nationals located abroad. Article 39.2 of the Agreement on Trade-Related Aspects of Intellectual Property Rights (TRIPS) 1994 is also useful in confronting economic cyber espionage insofar as it requires that members must provide nationals of other TRIPS members (including companies) with the possibility of preventing the acquisition, disclosure or use of confidential information within their control. While Article 39.2 does not directly prohibit members from engaging in economic cyber espionage, by requiring them to adopt laws and establish procedures that allow nationals of other TRIPS members to protect their trade secrets before national courts, Article 39.2 nevertheless renders an important contribution to the suppression of economic cyber espionage.

Within academic literature, the argument is made that, even if acts of political cyber espionage violate the rule of territorial sovereignty and the inviolability provisions of diplomatic and consular law, developments in customary international law have created exceptions to these prohibitive rules that nullify state responsibility for this otherwise unlawful conduct. While states are entitled to modify the scope of their international legal obligations by creating customary espionage exceptions, for these to form they must be supported by extensive state practice and *opinio juris*. However, espionage is largely committed in secret, and this monograph has claimed that secret state conduct cannot contribute towards the development of customary international law. Although there is compelling evidence that states routinely engage in espionage in violation of the rule of territorial sovereignty and diplomatic and consular law, it is nevertheless the case that such conduct is almost always unacknowledged by the responsible state. As such, it does not qualify as state practice and thus cannot give rise to customary exceptions. Moreover, even if we concede for the sake of argument that there is sufficient evidence of state practice of espionage, the policy of silence that surrounds this practice precludes the formation of the requisite *opinio juris* to support the existence of customary espionage exceptions.

The doctrines of self-defence and necessity can be invoked to justify acts of cyber espionage. Yet, to prevent their abuse, the availability of these doctrines is hedged with strict requirements. Self-defence can only be relied upon where there is an actual or imminent threat of an armed attack. Where a state engages in cyber espionage in order to counteract an armed attack, this conduct is only lawful where it is necessary to halt and repel the attack or to prevent further reasonably foreseeable attacks. With regard to the doctrine of necessity, this defence is only available in relation to acts of cyber espionage that are designed to mitigate a grave and imminent peril to an essential state interest. What is an essential state interest is defined broadly and includes threats to the continued existence of the state and to its national economy, thus opening up the possibility for necessity to exculpate state responsibility for acts of political and economic cyber espionage. For necessity to be available, acts of cyber espionage must represent the only available means for averting or mitigating the threat. Moreover, the state invoking necessity must not have substantially contributed to the crisis and its reaction to the threat (that is, to undertake cyber espionage) must not seriously impair the essential interests of those states to whom the legal obligation is owed or of the international community as a whole.

To return to the research question posed at the beginning of this monograph, does international law regulate political and economic cyber espionage? Certainly, the findings of this monograph have put to bed the idea that there is a *non-liquet* in international law when it comes to cyber espionage (and indeed espionage more generally). The contribution of this monograph has been to demonstrate that cyber espionage is actually subject to a vast array of international law – including general principles and specialised regimes – all of which play an important role in regulating this practice. However, while there is international law applicable to cyber espionage, this does not mean that there is an international law of espionage. But should there be?[6] After all, in other areas of international relations states have implemented *lex specialis* that directly and specifically regulates the subject matter in question, such as the law of the sea, international humanitarian law, international criminal law, international investment law etc.

[6] As Deeks notes, in recent years the absence of express rules on espionage 'has become stark and keenly felt'; Deeks (n 3) 293. Deeks goes on to explain that '[t]he Snowden revelations illustrate why the reasons for a *laissez-faire* approach to foreign surveillance are weakening. Not only are the reasons not to regulate becoming less persuasive, however; the reasons affirmatively to regulate foreign surveillance have strengthened'; ibid 319.

Historically, it was the secrecy that surrounded intelligence operations that prevented an international law of espionage from emerging. This is not surprising: if states refuse to acknowledge their espionage activities, this forecloses the possibility that an international law of espionage can form. Yet more recently, states have been much more prepared to talk about their intelligence activities,[7] with policymakers speaking openly and frankly about the important role that intelligence plays in their decision-making while also recognising the need for clear limitations upon when, how and against whom espionage is conducted.[8] In fact, a number of states have adopted laws that expressly regulate their foreign espionage activities. If states are now prepared to discuss their participation in espionage and acknowledge that espionage constitutes an integral feature of the cat and mouse game of international relations, this suggests 'that current conditions are ripe for states to employ international law to regulate foreign surveillance … [and that] states should seize this moment to regulate'.[9] This is my view. For me, states should proactively develop an international law of espionage – whether it be through the implementation of a treaty or incrementally through customary international law – that contains bespoke rules that effectively reconcile the competing interests implicated by different forms of espionage and which clearly delineate when and under what circumstances the collection of confidential information is acceptable. As Admiral Michael S Rogers explained to Congress during his confirmation proceedings for the positions of NSA Director and Commander of US Cyber Command:

> [T]he recent disclosures of a large portion of our intelligence and military operational history [by Edward Snowden] may provide us with opportunity to engage both the American public and our international partners in discussion of the … norms of accepted and unacceptable behaviour in cyberspace.[10]

[7] 'States historically were quite content to keep their views to themselves, but the Snowden leaks have evinced more explicit statements about their views of the relationship between international law and, in particular, foreign surveillance'; A Deeks, 'The Increasing State Practice and Opinio Juris on Spying', 6 May 2015, *Lawfare*, www.lawfareblog.com/increasing-state-practice-and-opinio-juris-spying. According to Kish, 'espionage has developed from isolated incidents to an established international function of States. Governments have publicly admitted the existence of their intelligence services and systematic espionage operations'; J Kish (D Turns ed), *International Law and Espionage* (The Hague, Martinus Nijhoff, 1995) xv.

[8] '[F]or our intelligence community to be effective over the long haul, we must maintain the trust of the American people, and people around the world'; President Barack Obama, *Remarks by the President on Review of Signals Intelligence*, 17 January 2014, www.obamawhitehouse.archives.gov/the-press-office/2014/01/17/remarks-president-review-signals-intelligence.

[9] Deeks (n 3) 294. For Demarest, '[t]he development of international legal principles regarding peacetime espionage has lagged behind changes in international intelligence gathering norms and practices'; GB Demarest, 'Espionage in International Law' (1996) 24 *Denver Journal of International Law and Policy* 321, 321.

[10] Advance Questions for Vice Admiral Michael S Rogers, USN: *Nominee for Commander, United States Cyber Command*, 11 March 2014, www.armed-services.senate.gov/imo/media/doc/Rogers_03-11-14.pdf. Similarly, in 2017 Legal Advisor to the US State Department Brian Egan explained that 'States should publicly state their views on how existing international law applies to State conduct in cyberspace' and that '[s]tating such views publicly will help give rise to more settled expectations of State behavior and thereby contribute to greater predictability and stability in cyberspace'; BJ Egan, 'International Law and Stability in Cyberspace' (2017) 35 *Berkeley Journal of International Law* 169, 172.

BIBLIOGRAPHY

Books

Beyleveld, D and Brownsword, R, *Human Dignity in Bioethics and Biolaw* (Oxford, Oxford University Press, 2001).

Blainey, G, *The Causes of War* (New York, Free Press, 1988).

Brenner, J, *America the Vulnerable: Inside the New Threat Matrix of Digital Espionage, Crime, and Warfare* (Penguin Press, 2011).

Brownlie, I, *International Law and the Use of Force by States* (Oxford, Clarendon Press, 1963).

Buchan, R, *International Law and the Construction of the Liberal Peace* (Oxford, Hart Publishing, 2013).

Bücheler, G, *Proportionality in Investor–State Arbitration* (Oxford, Oxford University Press, 2015).

Bull, H, *The Anarchical Society: A Study of Order in World Politics* (Basingstoke, Palgrave, 2002).

Buzan, B, *People, States and Fear: An Agenda for International Security Studies in the Post-Cold War Era* (Colchester, ECPR Press, 2007).

Cassese, A, *International Law in a Divided World* (Oxford, Clarendon Press, 1986).

Cassese, A, *International Law* (Oxford, Oxford University Press, 2005).

Cheng, B, *Studies in International Space Law* (Oxford, Clarendon Press, 1997).

Corten, O, *The Law Against War: The Prohibition on the Use of Force in Contemporary International Law* (Oxford, Hart Publishing, 2010).

Crawford, J, *Brownlie's Principles of Public International Law* (Oxford, Oxford University Press, 2012).

D'Amato, A, *The Concept of Custom in International Law* (Ithaca and London, Cornell University Press, 1971).

Danilenko, GM, *Law-Making in the International Community* (Dordrecht, Martinus Nijhoff, 1993).

De Carvalho, NP, *The TRIPS Regime of Antitrust and Undisclosed Information* (The Hague, The Netherlands, Kluwer Law International, 2008).

Denza, E, *Diplomatic Law: Commentary on the Vienna Convention on Diplomatic Relations* (Oxford, Oxford University Press, 2016).

Denza, E and Foakes, J (Sir Ivor Roberts ed), *Satow's Diplomatic Practice* (Oxford, Oxford University Press, 2017).

Dinstein, Y, *War, Aggression and Self-Defence* (Cambridge, Cambridge University Press, 2017).

Emberland, M, *The Human Rights of Companies: Exploring the Structure of ECHR Protection* (Oxford, Oxford University Press, 2006).

Footer, ME, Schmidt, J, White, ND and Davies-Bright, L (eds), *Security in International Law* (Oxford, Hart Publishing, 2016).

Frederking, B, *The United States and the Security Council: Collective Security Since the Cold War* (London, Routledge, 2007).

Gardam, J, *Necessity, Proportionality and the Use of Force by States* (Cambridge, Cambridge University Press, 2004).

Gazzini, T, *The Changing Rules on the Use of Force in International Law* (Manchester, Manchester University Press, 2005).

Gervais, D, *The TRIPS Agreement: Drafting History and Analysis* (London, Sweet and Maxwell, 1998).

Granick, JS, *American Spies: Modern Surveillance, Why You Should Care, and What To Do About It* (Cambridge, Cambridge University Press, 2017).

Grear, A, *Redirecting Human Rights: Facing the Challenge of Corporate Legal Humanity* (Basingstoke, Palgrave Macmillan, 2010).

Griffin, J, *On Human Rights* (Oxford, Oxford University Press, 2008).
Hart, HLA, *The Concept of Law* (Oxford, Oxford University Press, 1961).
Hastedt, G, *Espionage: A Reference Handbook* (Santa Barbara, California, ABC-CLIO, 2003).
Henderson, C, *The Use of Force and International Law* (Cambridge, Cambridge University Press, 2018).
Higgins, R, *Problems and Process: International Law and How We Use It* (Oxford, Clarendon Press, 1995).
Henckaerts, J-M and Doswald-Beck, L, *Customary International Humanitarian Law: Volume I: Rules* (Cambridge, Cambridge University Press, 2005).
Herman, M, *Intelligence Power in Peace and War* (Cambridge, Cambridge University Press, 1996).
Jennings, R and Watts, A, *Oppenheim's International Law: Volume 1, Peace* (London, New York, Longmans, Green & Co, 1996).
Johnson, LK, *Secret Agencies: US Intelligence in a Hostile World* (New York, Yale University Press, 1996).
Kennedy, M, *WTO Dispute Settlement and the TRIPS Agreement: Applying Intellectual Property Standards in a Trade Law Framework* (Cambridge, Cambridge University Press, 2016).
Kim, D-W, *Non-Violation in WTO Law: Theory and Practice* (New York, Oxford, Verlag Peter Lang, 2006).
Kish, J (Turns, D, ed), *International Law and Espionage* (The Hague, Martinus Nijhoff, 1995).
Kittichaisaree, K, *Public International Law and Cyberspace* (Cham, Springer, 2017).
Ladas, S, *Patents, Trademarks, and Related Rights: National and International Protection* (Cambridge, Harvard University Press, 1975).
Lepard, BD, *Customary International Law: A New Theory with Practical Applications* (Cambridge, Cambridge University Press, 2010).
McDougal, MS and Feliciano, FP, *Law and Minimum World Public Order* (New Haven, Yale University Press, 1961).
McDougal, MS and Feliciano, FP, *The International Law of War: Transnational Coercion and World Public Order* (New Haven, New Haven Press, 1994).
Milanovic, M, *Extraterritorial Application of Human Rights Treaties: Law, Principles, and Policy* (Oxford, Oxford University Press, 2013).
Morgenthau, HJ, *Politics Among Nations: The Struggle for Power and Peace* (New York, McGraw-Hill, 1985).
Nasheri, H, *Economic Espionage and Industrial Spying* (Cambridge, Cambridge University Press, 2005).
Oppenheim, L (Roxburgh, RF, ed), *International Law: A Treatise* (London, New York, Longmans, Green & Co, 1920).
Oppenheim, L (Lauterpacht, H, ed), *International Law: A Treatise* (London, New York, Longmans, Green & Co, 1955).
Paddeu, F, *Justification and Excuse in International Law: Concept and Theory of General Defences* (Cambridge, Cambridge University Press, 2018).
Reisman, WM, *Nullity and Revision: The Review and Enforcement of International Judgments and Awards* (New Haven, Yale University Press, 1971).
Richelson, JT, *America's Secret Eyes in Space: The U.S. Keyhole Spy Satellite Program* (New York, Harper & Row, 1975).
Riffel, C, *Protection Against Unfair Competition in the WTO TRIPS Agreement: The Scope and Prospects of Article 10bis of the Paris Convention for the Protection of Industrial Property* (Leiden, Brill, Martinus Nijhoff, 2016).
Rodick, BC, *The Doctrine of Necessity in International Law* (New York, Columbia University Press, 1928).
Roscini, M, *Cyber Operations and the Use of Force in International Law* (Oxford, Oxford University Press, 2014).
Ruys, T, *'Armed Attack' and Article 51 of the UN Charter: Evolutions in Customary Law and Practice* (Cambridge, Cambridge University Press, 2010).
Schachter, O, *International Law in Theory and Practice* (Dordrecht, Martinus Nijhoff, 1991).
Schmitt, MN, *Counter-Terrorism and the Use of Force in International Law* (George C Marshall, European Centre for Security Studies, 2003).

Schmitt, MN, *Tallinn Manual 2.0 on the International Law Applicable to Cyber Operations* (Cambridge, Cambridge University Press, 2017).
Shaw, M, *International Law* (Cambridge, Cambridge University Press, 2017).
Thirlway, HWA, *International Customary Law and Codification: An Examination of the Continuing Role of Custom in the Present Period of Codification of International Law* (Leiden, AW Sijthoff, 1972).
Tonkin, H, *State Control over Private Military and Security Companies in Armed Conflict* (Cambridge, Cambridge University Press, 2011).
Tzu, S (Clavell, J, ed), *The Art of War* (New York, Dell, 1983).
Villiger, ME, *Customary International Law and Treaties: A Manual on the Theory and Practice of the Interrelation of Sources* (The Hague, Kluwer International Law, 1997).
Waltz, KN, *Theory of International Politics* (London, McGraw-Hill, 1979).
Wight, M (Bull, H, ed), *Systems of States* (Leicester, Leicester University Press, 1977).
Wolfke, K, *Custom in Present International Law* (Wroclaw, Prace Wrocławskiego Towarzystwa Naukowego, 1964).

Articles

Abbott, KW, '"Trust But Verify": The Production of Information in Arms Control Treaties and Other International Agreements' (1993) 26 *Cornell International Law Journal* 1.
Akande, D and Liefländer, T, 'Clarifying Necessity, Imminence, and Proportionality in the Law of Self-Defense' (2013) 107 *American Journal of International Law* 563.
Argaman, S and Siboni, G, 'Commercial and Industrial Cyber Espionage in Israel' (2014) 6 *Military and Strategic Affairs* 43.
Baker, CD, 'Tolerance of International Espionage: A Functional Approach' (2003) 19 *American University International Law Review* 1091.
Bannelier-Christakis, K, 'Cyber Diligence: A Low-Intensity Due Diligence Principle for Low-Intensity Cyber Operations' (2014) 14 *Baltic Yearbook of International Law* 23.
Banks, WC, 'Cyber Espionage and Electronic Surveillance: Beyond Media Coverage' (2017) 66 *Emory Law Journal* 513.
Beaumont, JS, 'Self-Defence as a Justification for Disregarding Diplomatic Immunity' (1991) 29 *Canadian Yearbook of International Law* 391.
Bethlehem, D, 'The Secret Life of International Law' (2012) 1 *Cambridge Journal of International and Comparative Law* 23.
Bethlehem, D, 'Self-Defense Against an Imminent or Actual Armed Attack by Nonstate Actors' (2012) 106 *American Journal of International Law* 770.
Boed, R, 'State Necessity as a Justification for Internationally Wrongful Conduct' (2000) 3 *Yale Human Rights and Development Journal* 1.
Brenner, SW and Crescenzi, AC, 'State-Sponsored Crime: The Futility of the Economic Espionage Act' (2006) 28 *Houston Journal of International Law* 389.
Brown, G, 'Spying and Fighting in Cyberspace: What is Which?' (2016) 8 *Journal of National Security Law and Policy* 621.
Brown, I and Korff, D, 'Foreign Surveillance: Law and Practice in a Global Digital Environment' (2014) 3 *European Human Rights Law Review* 243.
Brown, G and Poellet, K, 'The Customary International Law of Cyberspace' (2012) 6 *Strategic Studies Quarterly* 126.
Buchan, R, 'Cyberspace, Non-State Actors and the Obligation to Prevent Transboundary Harm' (2016) 21 *Journal of Conflict and Security Law* 429.
Cannizzaro, E, 'Contextualising Proportionality: Jus ad Bellum and Jus in Bello in the Lebanese War' (2006) 88 *International Review of the Red Cross* 779.
Cassese, A, 'Terrorism is also Disrupting Some Crucial Legal Categories of International Law' (2001) 12 *European Journal of International Law* 993.
Chesterman, S, 'The Spy Who Came in from the Cold War: Intelligence and International Law' (2006) 27 *Michigan Journal of International Law* 1071.

Choi, W-M, 'Diplomatic and Consular Law in the Internet Age' (2006) 10 *Singapore Year Book of International Law* 117.

Colby, JE, 'The Developing Law on Gathering and Sharing Security Intelligence' (1974) 1 *Yale Journal of International Law* 49.

Danielson, MEA, 'Economic Espionage: A Framework for a Workable Solution' (2009) 10 *Minnesota Journal of Law, Science and Technology* 503.

Davies, A, 'The DSU Article 3.8 Presumption that an Infringement Constitutes a *Prima Facie* Case of Nullification or Impairment: When Does it Operate and Why?' (2010) 13 *Journal of International Economic Law* 181.

Deeks, A, 'An International Legal Framework for Surveillance' (2015) 55 *Virginia Journal of International Law* 291.

Deeks, A, 'Confronting and Adapting: Intelligence Agencies and International Law' (2016) 102 *Virginia Law Review* 599.

Delupis, I, 'Foreign Warships and Immunity for Espionage' (1984) 78 *American Journal of International Law* 53.

Demarest, GB, 'Espionage in International Law' (1996) 24 *Denver Journal of International Law and Policy* 321.

Dinstein, Y, 'The Interaction between Customary Law and Treaties' (2006) 322 *Recueil des Cours* 243.

Duquet, S and Wouters, J, 'Legal Duties of Diplomats Today: The Continuing Relevance of the Vienna Convention' (January 2015) Working Paper No 146, *Leuven Centre for Global Governance Studies* 1.

Duquet, S and Wouters, J, 'Diplomacy, Secrecy and the Law' (March 2015) Working Paper No 151, *Leuven Centre for Global Governance Studies* 1.

Edmondson, LS, 'Espionage in Transnational Law' (1972) 5 *Vanderbilt Journal of Transnational Law* 434.

Egan, BJ, 'International Law and Stability in Cyberspace' (2017) 35 *Berkeley Journal of International Law* 169.

Erdoğan, I, 'Economic Espionage as a New Form of War in the Post-Cold War Period' (2009) 2 *USAK Yearbook of International Politics and Law* 265.

Fidler, DP, 'Tinker, Tailor, Soldier, Duqu: Why Cyberespionage is More Dangerous Than You Think' (2012) 5 *International Journal of Critical Infrastructure Protection* 28.

Fidler, DP, 'Wither the Web?: International Law, Cybersecurity, and Critical Infrastructure Protection' (Fall 2015) *Georgetown Journal of International Affairs* 8.

Fitzmaurice, G, 'The Law and Procedures of the International Court of Justice, 1951–1954: General Principles and Sources of Law' (1953) 30 *British Yearbook of International Law* 1.

Fleck, D, 'Individual and State Responsibility for Intelligence Gathering' (2007) 28 *Michigan Journal of International Law* 687.

Forcese, C, 'Spies Without Borders: International Law and Intelligence Collection' (2011) 5 *Journal of National Security Law and Policy* 179.

Forcese, C, 'Intelligence Agencies and International Law' (2016) 102 *Virginia Law Review Online* 67.

Franzese, PW, 'Sovereignty in Cyberspace: Can it Exist?' (2009) 64 *Air Force Law Review* 1.

Fukuyama, F, 'The End of History' (1989) 16 *National Interest* 3.

Garcia-Mora, MR, 'Treason, Sedition and Espionage as Political Offenses under the Law of Extradition' (1964) 26 *University of Pittsburgh Law Review* 65.

Goldman, ZK and McCoy, D, 'Deterring Financially Motivated Cybercrime' (2016) 8 *Journal of National Security Law and Policy* 595.

Goldsmith, JL, 'Against Cyberanarchy' (1998) 65 *University of Chicago Law Review* 1199.

Green, JA, 'The "*Rationale Temporis*" Elements of Self-Defence' (2015) 2 *Journal on the Use of Force and International Law* 97.

Grimal, F and Sundaram, J, 'Cyber Warfare and Autonomous Self-Defence' (2017) 4 *Journal on the Use of Force and International Law* 1.

Halleck, HW, 'Military Espionage' (1911) 5 *American Journal of International Law* 590.

Handeyside, H, 'The *Lotus* Principle in ICJ Jurisprudence: Was the Ship Ever Afloat?' (2007) 29 *Michigan Journal of International Law* 71.

Hathaway, OA, Crootof, R, Levitz, P, Nix, H, Nowlan, A, Perdue, W and Spiegel, J, 'The Law of Cyber-Attack' (2012) 100 *California Law Review* 817.

Henkin, L, 'That "S" Word: Sovereignty, and Globalization, and Human Rights, Et Cetera' (1999) 68 *Fordham Law Review* 1.

Jamnejad, M and Wood, M, 'The Principle of Non-Intervention' (2009) 22 *Leiden Journal of International Law* 345.

Johnson, DR and Post, DG, 'Law and Borders: The Rise of Law in Cyberspace' (1996) 48 *Stanford Law Review* 1367.

Jupillat, N, 'From the Cuckoo's Egg to Global Surveillance: Cyber Espionage that Becomes Prohibited Intervention' (2017) 42 *North Carolina Journal of International Law and Commercial Regulation* 933.

Kearney, RD and Dalton, RE, 'The Treaty on Treaties' (1970) 64 *American Journal of International Law* 495.

Khalil, C, 'Thinking Intelligently About Intelligence: A Model Global Framework Protecting Privacy' (2015) 47 *George Washington International Law Review* 919.

Kilovaty, I, 'World Wide Web of Exploitations – the Case of Peacetime Cyber Espionage Operations under International Law: Towards a Contextual Approach' (2016) 18 *Columbia Science and Technology Law Review* 42.

Kilovaty, I, 'Doxfare: Politically Motivated Leaks and the Future of the Norm on Non-Intervention in the Era of Weaponized Information' (2017) 9 *Harvard National Security Journal* 146.

Kirchner, S, 'Beyond Privacy Rights: Crossborder Cyber Espionage and International Law' (2014) 31 *John Marshall Journal of Information Technology and Privacy Law* 369.

Kirgis, FL, 'Custom on a Sliding Scale' (1987) 81 *American Journal of International Law* 146.

Koh, HH, 'International Law in Cyberspace' (2012) 54 *Harvard International Law Journal Online* 1.

Koplow, DA, 'An Inference About Interference: A Surprising Application of Existing International Law to Inhibit Anti-Satellite Weapons' (2013–14) 35 *University of Pennsylvania Journal of International Law* 737.

Kozik, AL, 'The Concept of Sovereignty as a Foundation for Determining the Legality of the Conduct of States in Cyberspace' (2014) 14 *Baltic Yearbook of International Law* 93.

Kraska, J, 'Putting Your Head in the Tiger's Mouth: Submarine Espionage in Territorial Waters' (2015) 54 *Columbia Journal of Transnational Law* 164.

Kunz, JL, 'The Nature of Customary International Law' (1953) 47 *American Journal of International Law* 662.

Lin, HS, 'Offensive Cyber Operations and the Use of Force' (2010) 4 *Journal of National Security Law and Policy* 63.

Longobardo, M, '(New) Cyber Exploitation and (Old) International Humanitarian Law' (2017) 77 *Zeitschrift für Ausländisches öffentliches Recht und Völkerrecht* 809.

Lotrionte, C, 'Countering State-Sponsored Cyber Economic Espionage under International Law' (2015) 40 *North Carolina Journal of International Law and Commercial Regulation* 443.

Lubin, A, 'Espionage as a Sovereign Right under International Law and its Limits' (2016) 24 *ILSA Quarterly* 22.

Lubin, A, '"We Only Spy on Foreigners": The Myth of a Universal Right to Privacy and the Practice of Foreign Mass Surveillance' (2018) 18 *Chicago Journal of International Law* 502.

Malawer, SS, 'Chinese Economic Cyber Espionage: U.S. Litigation in the WTO and Other Diplomatic Remedies' (2015) 16 *Georgetown Journal of International Affairs* 158.

Mann, FA, 'The Doctrine of Jurisdiction in International Law' (1964) *Collected Courses of The Hague Academy of International Law* 1.

Margulies, P, 'The NSA in Global Perspective: Surveillance, Human Rights, and International Counterterrorism' (2014) 82 *Fordham Law Review* 2137.

McDougal, MS, Lasswell, HD and Reisman, WM, 'The Intelligence Function and World Public Order' (1973) 46 *Temple Law Quarterly* 365.

Meijers, H, 'How is International Law Made? – The Stages of Growth of International Law and the Use of its Customary Rules' (1978) 9 *Netherlands Yearbook of International Law* 3.

Melnitzky, A, 'Defending America against Chinese Cyber Espionage though the Use of Active Defenses' (2012) 20 *Cardozo Journal of International and Comparative Law* 537.
Michal, K, 'Business Counterintelligence and the Role of the U.S. Intelligence Community' (1994) 7 *International Journal of Intelligence and Counterintelligence* 413.
Milanovic, M, 'Al-Skeini and Al-Jedda in Strasbourg' (2012) 23 *European Journal of International Law* 121.
Milanovic, M, 'Human Rights Treaties and Foreign Surveillance: Privacy in the Digital Age' (2015) 56 *Harvard International Law Journal* 81.
Navarrete, I, 'L'Espionnage en Temps de Paix en Droit International Public' (2016) 53 *Canadian Yearbook of International Law* 1.
O'Hara, G, 'Cyber-Espionage: A Growing Threat to the American Economy' (2010) 19 *Commonlaw Conspectus* 241.
Orakhelashvili, A, 'Restrictive Interpretation of Human Rights Treaties in the Recent Jurisprudence of the European Court of Human Rights' (2003) 14 *European Journal of International Law* 529.
Parlett, K, 'The Individual and Structural Legal Change in the International System' (2012) 1 *Cambridge Journal of International and Comparative Law* 60.
Perina, AH, 'Black Holes and Open Secrets: The Impact of Covert Action on International Law' (2015) 53 *Columbia Journal of Transnational Law* 507.
Peters, A, 'International Dispute Settlement: A Network of Cooperational Duties' (2003) 14 *European Journal of International Law* 1.
Pisillo-Mazzeschi, R, 'The Due Diligence Rule and the Nature of International State Responsibility' (1993) 35 *German Yearbook of International Law* 9.
Pun, D, 'Rethinking Espionage in the Modern Era' (2017) 18 *Chicago Journal of International Law* 353.
Radsan, AJ, 'The Unresolved Equation of Espionage and International Law' (2007) 28 *Michigan Journal of International Law* 595.
Ratner, S, 'Introduction: State Intelligence Gathering and International Law' (2007) 28 *Michigan Journal of International Law* 539.
Reinbothe, J, and Howard, A, 'The State of Play in the Negotiations on TRIPS (GATT/Uruguay Round)' (1991) 13 *European Intellectual Property Review* 163.
Reisman, WM and Freedman, EE, 'The Plaintiff's Dilemma: Illegally Obtained Evidence and Admissibility in International Adjudication' (1982) 76 *American Journal of International Law* 737.
Richards, NM, 'The Dangers of Surveillance' (2013) 126 *Harvard Law Review* 1934.
Roberts, AE, 'Traditional and Modern Approaches to Customary International Law: A Reconciliation' (2001) 95 *American Journal of International Law* 757.
Schachter, O, 'The Right of States to Use Armed Force' (1984) 82 *Michigan Law Review* 1620.
Schachter, O, 'The Lawful Resort to Unilateral Use of Force' (1985) 10 *Yale Journal of International Law* 291.
Schmitt, MN and Vihul, L, 'Respect for Sovereignty in Cyberspace' (2017) 95 *Texas Law Review* 1639.
Scott, RD, 'Territorially Intrusive Intelligence Collection and International Law' (1999) 46 *Air Force Law Review* 217.
Scoville, H, 'Is Espionage Necessary for our Security?' (1976) 54 *Foreign Affairs* 482.
Severson, D, 'American Surveillance of Non-US Persons: Why New Privacy Protections Offer Only Cosmetic Change' (2015) 56 *Harvard International Law Journal* 465.
Seyersted, F, 'Diplomatic Freedom of Communication' (1970) 14 *Scandinavian Studies in Law* 193.
Siboni, G, and Kronenfield, S, 'Iran and Cyberspace Warfare' (2012) 4 *Military and Strategic Affairs* 77.
Siboni, G, and Israel, D, 'Cyberspace Espionage and its Effect on Commercial Considerations' (2015) 7 *Military and Strategic Affairs* 39.
Sikkink, K, 'Latin American Countries as Norm Protagonists of the Idea of International Human Rights' (2014) 20 *Global Governance* 389.
Simpson, G, 'Two Liberalisms' (2001) 12 *European Journal of International Law* 537.
Skillington, GL and Solovy, EM, 'The Protection of Test and Other Data Required by Article 39.3 of the TRIPS Agreement' (2003) 24 *Northwestern Journal of International Law and Business* 1.

Skinner, CP, 'An International Law Response to Economic Cyber Espionage' (2014) 46 *Connecticut Law Review* 1165.

Slaughter, A-M, 'International Law in a World of Liberal States' (1995) 6 *European Journal of International Law* 503.

Sloane, RD, 'On the Use and Abuse of Necessity in the Law of State Responsibility' (2012) 106 *American Journal of International Law* 447.

Smith, JH, 'Keynote Address: State Intelligence Gathering and International Law' (2007) 28 *Michigan Journal of International Law* 543.

Snyder, H and Crescenzi, A, 'Intellectual Capital and Economic Espionage: New Crimes and New Protections' (2009) 16 *Journal of Financial Crime* 245.

Soraghan, JR, 'Reconnaissance Satellites: Legal Characterization and Possible Utilization for Peacekeeping' (1964) 13 *McGill Law Journal* 458.

Strawbridge, J, 'The Big Bluff: Obama, Cyber Economic Espionage, and the Threat of WTO Litigation' (2016) 47 *Georgetown Journal of International Law* 833.

Sulmasy, G and Yoo, J, 'Counterintuitive: Intelligence Operations and International Law' (2007) 28 *Michigan Journal of International Law* 625.

Talmon, S, 'Determining Customary International Law: The ICJ's Methodology between Induction, Deduction and Assertion' (2015) 26 *European Journal of International Law* 417.

Tams, CJ, 'Light Treatment of a Complex Problem: The Law of Self-Defence in the *Wall* Case' (2005) 16 *European Journal of International Law* 963.

Tasioulas, J, 'In Defence of Relative Normativity: Communitarian Values and the Nicaragua Case' (1996) 16 *Oxford Journal of Legal Studies* 85.

Terry, PCR, '"Absolute Friends": United States Espionage Against Germany and Public International Law' (2015) 28 *Revue Quebecoise de Droit International* 173.

Tsagourias, N, 'Self-Defence against Non-State Actors: The Interaction Between Self-Defence as a Primary Rule and Self-Defence as a Secondary Rule' (2016) 29 *Leiden Journal of International Law* 801.

Van Schaack, B, 'The United States' Position on the Extraterritorial Application of Human Rights Obligations: Now is the Time for Change' (2014) 90 *International Law Studies* 20.

Värk, R, 'Diplomatic and Consular Privileges and Immunities in Case of Unfriendly Cyber Activities' (2014) 14 *Baltic Yearbook of International Law* 125.

Vidigal, G, 'Re-Assessing WTO Remedies: The Prospective and the Retrospective' (2013) 16 *Journal of International Economic Law* 505.

Von Heinegg, WH, 'Territorial Sovereignty and Neutrality in Cyberspace' (2013) 89 *International Law Studies* 123.

Wadlow, C, 'Regulatory Data Protection under TRIPS Article 39(3) and Article 10bis of the Paris Convention: Is There a Doctor in the House?' (2008) 4 *Intellectual Property Quarterly* 355.

Walsh, P and Miller, S, 'Rethinking "Five Eyes" Security Intelligence Collection Policies and Practice Post Snowden' (2016) 31 *Intelligence and National Security* 345.

Watts, S, 'Low-Intensity Cyber Operations and the Principle of Non-Intervention' (2014) 14 *Baltic Yearbook of International Law* 137.

Waxman, MC, 'Cyber-Attacks and the Use of Force: Back to the Future of Article 2(4)' (2011) 36 *Yale Journal of International Law* 421.

Wen, CJ, 'Secrecy, Standing, and Executive Order 12, 333' (2016) 89 *Southern California Law Review* 1203.

Wheeler, R, 'The Changing Composition of the Foreign Surveillance Court and What if Anything to do About it' (2014) 2 *Lawfare Research Paper Series* 1.

Williams, RD, '(Spy) Game Change: Cyber Networks, Intelligence Collection, and Covert Action' (2011) 79 *George Washington Law Review* 1162.

Witkow, BJ, 'A New "Spook" Immunity: How the CIA and American Business are Shielded from Liability for the Misappropriation of Trade Secrets' (2000) 14 *Emory International Law Review* 451.

Worster, WT, 'The Effect of Leaked Information on the Rules of International Law' (2013) 28 *American University International Law Review* 443.

Wortham, A, 'Should Cyber Exploitation Ever Constitute a Demonstration of Hostile Intend That May Violate UN Charter Provisions Prohibiting the Threat or Use of Force?' (2012) 64 *Federal Communications Law Journal* 643.

Chapters from Edited Collections

Anderson, R, Barton, C, Böhme, R, Clayton, R, van Eeten, MJG, Levi, M, Moore, T and Savage, S, 'Measuring the Cost of Cybercrime' in Böhme, R (ed), *The Economics of Information Security* and Privacy (Berlin and Heidelberg, Springer, 2013).

Bao, Y, 'The Protection of Public Safety and Human Life vs the Inviolability of Mission Premises' in Behrens, P (ed), *Diplomatic Law in a New Millennium* (Oxford, Oxford University Press, 2016).

Bronckers, M and van den Broek, N, 'Financial Compensation in the WTO: Improving Remedies in WTO Dispute Settlement' in Georgiev, D and van der Borght, K (eds), *Reform and Development of the WTO Dispute Settlement System* (London, Cameron May Ltd, 2006).

Brown, C, '"Really Existing Liberalism", Peaceful Democracies and International Order' in Fawn, R and Larkins, J (eds), *International Society after the Cold War: Anarchy and Order Reconsidered* (Basingstoke, Palgrave Macmillan 1996).

Buchan, R, 'Cyber Espionage and International Law' in Tsagourias, N and Buchan, R (eds), *Research Handbook on International Law and Cyberspace* (Cheltenham, Edward Elgar, 2015).

Buchan, R, 'The International Legal Regulation of State-Sponsored Cyber Espionage' in Osula, A-M, and Rõigas, H (eds), *International Cyber Norms: Legal, Policy & Industry Perspectives* (Tallinn, Estonia, CCDCOE, 2016).

Heathcote, S, 'Circumstances Precluding Wrongfulness in the ILC Articles on State Responsibility: Necessity' in Crawford, J, Pellet, A and Olleson, S (eds), *The Law of International Responsibility* (Oxford, Oxford University Press, 2010).

Falk, RA, 'Foreword' in Stanger, RJ (ed), *Essays on Espionage and International Law* (Columbus, Ohio State University Press, 1962).

Falk, RA, 'Space Espionage and World Order: A Consideration of the Samos-Midas Program' in Stanger, RJ (ed), *Essays on Espionage and International Law* (Columbus, Ohio State University Press, 1962).

Focarelli, C, 'Self-Defence in Cyberspace' in Tsagourias, N and Buchan, R (eds), *Research Handbook on International Law and Cyberspace* (Cheltenham, Edward Elgar, 2015).

Kastner, P and Mégret, F, 'International Legal Dimensions of Cybercrime' in Tsagourias, N and Buchan, R (eds), *Research Handbook on International Law and Cyberspace* (Cheltenham, Edward Elgar, 2015).

Labat, PG and Burke, N, 'The Protection of Diplomatic Correspondence in the Digital Age' in Behrens, P (ed), *Diplomatic Law in a New Millennium* (Oxford, Oxford University Press, 2016).

Milanovic, M, 'The Spatial Dimension: Treaties and Territory' in Tams, CJ, Tzanakopoulos, A and Zimmermann, A (eds), *Research Handbook on the Law of Treaties* (Cheltenham, Edward Elgar, 2016).

Milanovic, M, 'Jurisdiction and Responsibility: Trends in the Strasbourg Court' in van Aaken, A and Motoc, I (eds), *The ECHR and General International Law* (Oxford, Oxford University Press, 2018).

Moran, J and Walker, C, 'Intelligence Powers and Accountability in the UK' in Goldman, ZK and Rascoff, SJ (eds), *Global Intelligence Oversight: Governing Security in the Twenty-First Century* (New York, Oxford University Press, 2016).

Parks, WH, 'The International Law of Intelligence Collection' in Moore, JN, Tipson, FS and Turner, RF (eds), *National Security Law* (Durham, North Carolina, Carolina Academic Press, 1990).

Parks, WH, 'The International Law of Intelligence Collection' in Moore, JN and Turner, RF (eds), *National Security Law* (Durham, North Carolina, Carolina Academic Press, 1999).

Peter, M and Michaelis, M, 'The Law of Unfair Competition with Regards to Undisclosed Information' in Stoll, P-T, Busche, J and Arend, K (eds), *WTO: Trade-Related Aspects of Intellectual Property Rights* (Leiden and Boston, Martinus Nijhoff, 2009).

Peters, A, 'Privacy, *Rechtsstaatlichkeit*, and the Legal Limits on Extraterritorial Surveillance' in Miller, RA (ed), *Privacy and Power: A Transatlantic Dialogue in the Shadow of the NSA Affair* (Cambridge, Cambridge University Press, 2017).

Pirker, B, 'Territorial Sovereignty and Integrity and the Challenges of Cyberspace' in Ziolkowski, K (ed), *Peacetime Regime for State Activities in Cyberspace: International Law, International Relations and Diplomacy* (Tallinn, Estonia, CCDCOE, 2013).

Puig, JEF, 'Contemporary Developments Relating to the Inviolability of Mission Premises' in Behrens, P (ed), *Diplomatic Law in a New Millennium* (Oxford, Oxford University Press, 2016).

Randelzhofer, A, 'Article 2(4)' in Simma, B (ed), *The Charter of the United Nations: A Commentary* (Oxford, Oxford University Press, 2002).

Russell, RL, 'Achieving All-Source Fusion in the Intelligence Community' in LK Johnson (ed), *Handbook of Intelligence Studies* (London, Routledge, 2007).

Schmitt, MN, '"Attack" as a Term of Art in International Law: The Cyber Operations Context' in Czosseck, C, Ottis, R and Ziolkowski, Z (eds), *International Conference on Cyber Conflict* (Tallinn, Estonia, CCDCOE, 2012).

Schmitt, MN and Vihul, L, 'The Nature of International Law Cyber Norms' in Osula, A-M and Rõigas, H (eds), *International Cyber Norms: Legal, Policy and Industry Perspectives* (Tallinn, Estonia, CCDCOE, 2016).

Silver, DB, 'Intelligence and Counterintelligence' in Moore, JN and Turner, RF (eds), *National Security Law* (Durham, North Carolina Carolina Academic Press, 2005).

Stone, J, 'Legal Problems of Espionage in Conditions of Modern Conflict' in Stanger, RJ (ed), *Essays on Espionage and International Law* (Ohio, Ohio State University Press, 1962).

Veber, MT and Dine, MK 'Big Data and Economic Cyber Espionage: An International Law Perspective' in A Završnik (ed), *Big Data, Crime and Social Control* (London, Routledge, 2017).

Wickremasinghe, C, 'Immunities Enjoyed by Officials of States and International Organizations' in Evans, M (eds), *International Law* (Oxford, Oxford University Press, 2014).

Wrange, P, 'Intervention in National and Private Cyberspace and International Law' in Ebbesson, J, Jacobsson, Klamberg, M, Langlet, D and Wrange, P (eds), *International Law and Changing Perceptions of Security: Liber Amicorum Said Mahmoudi* (Leiden, Brill, Martinus Nijhoff, 2014).

Wright, Q, 'Espionage and the Doctrine of Non-Intervention in Internal Affairs' in Stanger, RJ (ed), *Essays on Espionage and International Law* (Columbus, Ohio State University Press, 1962).

Yoo, CS, 'Cyber Espionage or Cyberwar? International Law, Domestic Law, and Self-Protective Measures' in Ohlin, JD, Govern, K, and Finkelstein, C (eds), *Cyberwar: Law and Ethics for Virtual Conflicts* (Oxford, Oxford University Press, 2015).

Ziolkowski, K, 'Peacetime Cyber Espionage – New Tendencies in Public International Law' in Ziolkowski, K (ed), *Peacetime Regime for State Activities in Cyberspace: International Law, International Relations and Diplomacy* (Tallinn, Estonia, CCDCOE, 2013).

INDEX

www.ingramcontent.com/pod-product-compliance
Ingram Content Group UK Ltd.
Pitfield, Milton Keynes, MK11 3LW, UK
UKHW021238300926
15471UKWH00013B/585